The Derrida Dictionary

Also available from Continuum

The Sartre Dictionary, Gary Cox

Forthcoming
The Deleuze and Guattari Dictionary, Greg Lambert, Gary Genosko, Janell Watson and Eugene B. Young
The Gadamer Dictionary, Chris Lawn and Niall Keane
The Hegel Dictionary, Glenn Magee
The Heidegger Dictionary, Daniel O. Dahlstrom
The Husserl Dictionary, Dermot Moran and Joseph Cohen
The Kant Dictionary, Lucas Thorpe
The Marx Dictionary, Ian Fraser and Laurence Wilde
The Nietzsche Dictionary, Greg Moore
The Wittgenstein Dictionary, David Levy

The Derrida Dictionary

Simon Morgan Wortham

continuum

Continuum International Publishing Group
The Tower Building, 11 York Road, London SE1 7NX
80 Maiden Lane, Suite 704, New York NY 10038

www.continuumbooks.com

© Simon Morgan Wortham 2010

All rights reserved. No part of this publication may be reproduced or transmitted in any form or by any means, electronic or mechanical, including photocopying, recording, or any information storage or retrieval system, without prior permission in writing from the publishers.

British Library Cataloguing-in-Publication Data
A catalogue record for this book is available from the British Library.

ISBN: HB: 978-1-8470-6525-4
        PB: 978-1-8470-6526-1

Library of Congress Cataloguing-in-Publication Data
Wortham, Simon.
  The Derrida dictionary / Simon Morgan Wortham.
     p. cm.
  ISBN-13: 978-1-84706-525-4 (HB)
  ISBN-10: 1-84706-525-2 (HB)
  ISBN-13: 978-1-84706-526-1 (pbk.)
  ISBN-10: 1-84706-526-0 (pbk.)
  1. Derrida, Jacques – Dictionaries. I. Title.

B2430.D483Z95 2010
194 – dc22

2009052528

Designed and typeset by Kenneth Burnley and Caroline Waldron
Printed and bound in Great Britain by the MPG Books Group

Contents

Acknowledgements	vii
Introduction	1
The Derrida Dictionary	5
Bibliography	257

Acknowledgements

I want to thank those colleagues and friends who have generously taken time to read portions of the manuscript of this book. They include most especially Nicole Anderson, Derek Attridge, Robert Eaglestone, Heidi James, Martin McQuillan, J. Hillis Miller, Peter Nicholls, Nicholas Royle, Sean Gaston and Allison Weiner. I also want to acknowledge my indebtedness to some other key introductory writings on Derrida, in particular Geoffrey Bennington's 'Derridabase' in *Jacques Derrida*, Peggy Kamuf's invaluable introductions to the texts included in *A Derrida Reader: Between the Blinds* and Derek Attridge's commentaries in *Acts of Literature*. The wonderful work of other Derrida scholars and friends is so extensive and impressive to me that no acknowledgement could do it justice.

Introduction

While it does not claim to be absolutely encyclopaedic or comprehensive, this volume provides a grounding for those wishing to study Derrida's copious writings, arguments, terminology, influences, readings and ideas. The book aims to establish the clarity of Derrida's thinking, and to account for the complexity of his writings in both intellectual and stylistic terms. It includes many cross-referenced entries which seek to elucidate Derrida's thought (his manner of thinking as much as the conceptual resources he leaves behind); and in particular, it tries to give detailed and substantial accounts of the majority of his publications over a period of six decades. Derrida wrote prolifically and his output was vast. To my knowledge, there is currently no other resource in English that attempts such extensive coverage.

However, the notion that this book gives a *grounding* in 'Derrida' should be treated with considerable caution. As its reader will discover, that which *founds* or *institutes* always imposes itself, for Derrida, more or less violently, more or less unjustifiably, taking possession of its ground at the price of significant exclusions and contradictions. For Derrida, too, the metaphysical tradition which bases itself on the determination of being as presence is maintained on the strength of a repression of *différance* as the nevertheless groundless 'origin' which, in fact, constitutes that tradition's very possibility. For Derrida, then, one must carefully consider the limits and implications of establishing one's grounds. Similarly, if the reader (or, for that matter, the writer) of such a book hopes to determine a basis from which to *master* Derrida, it is important to recall that, for him, deconstruction entails the 'experience of the impossible' which, far from paralyzing all further thought or action, in fact gives the only possibility worthy of its name to responsibility, decision, invention, giving and forgiving, indeed the 'democracy to come'. For Derrida, then, the 'masterable-possible' or the 'I can' is less a prerequisite than a *limit* to that which deconstruction seeks to affirm in the name of the other and the future.

Admittedly, there are several texts, aside from those which currently remain untranslated or unpublished, that are not covered by this volume ('Biodegradables', 'Economimesis', 'Scribble (writing-power)', to mention just a few). And since Derrida's thought and critical practice permit no rigorous or stable distinction between major and minor works, such omissions are unjustifiable, perhaps unforgivable. Furthermore, it would be possible to rethink the key term entries to include others, and to rewrite 'otherwise' everything that appears under each heading. As Derrida might well have noted, this book could be entirely re-written from its margins and, in fact, ventures itself as nothing more than prefatory, the point of departure for just such a project.

In one sense, the aim of a dictionary is to present language as a whole, by capturing its more or less systematic relations and differences (however, dictionary-writers – a little like translators – are frequently forced to acknowledge the limits of the 'systematic' where language is concerned). Deconstructive language, writing and thinking, meanwhile, is sometimes presented as wilfully non-systematic, so that we might be tempted to imagine the simple hostility of deconstruction to dictionary-writing. Yet, far from turning its back on systematic thought, deconstruction tries to think the 'systemic' in the most rigorous way possible. One of Derrida's principal insights is that no system can ever be fully complete and self-sufficient. Instead, every system depends, basically, on non-systematizable elements which in fact produce and maintain the system's very possibility. For these reasons, a Derrida dictionary which acknowledges and indeed actively assumes its own limits and limitations is not necessarily an affront to deconstruction, although the task of such a 'work' should always be to inventively intensify an atmosphere in which the very ethos of the dictionary is rendered deconstructible, its supposedly encyclopaedic wholeness, coherence and integrity put in question between every cross-reference, amid the troubling necessity of each supplementing definition, indeed in every space or margin of the text. (Here we might ask: Is this introduction 'inside' or 'outside' the dictionary 'itself'? Is it a marginal inscription or an indispensable supplement? Does it supply the resources to embark upon and master the 'text' to come, is it the enabling condition of the 'work', or is it in fact funded by the body it seems to head, a 'body' which turns out to be just another introduction? See Derrida's account of Hegel's irreconcilable attitude to philosophical prefaces in the 'Outwork' to *Dissemination*, or his discussion

Introduction

of the parergon in *The Truth in Painting* . . .) It is for the reader to decide the extent to which the present dictionary is effective in terms of encouraging such inventive and questioning reading, reading from the margins.

As one in a series of philosophical dictionaries published by Continuum, the convention inherited by this volume demands minimal citation. Such a convention authorizes reference to Derrida's own *Circumfession*, a text which appears as a narrow horizontal band beneath Geoffrey Bennington's *Derridabase*. The latter, too, seeks to establish the conceptual coherence or consistency of Derrida's thought without recourse to quotations, as if his 'philosophy' could somehow be detached and represented outside the idiomatic specificity of certain sentences, phrases or texts. Bennington is, of course, immediately dubious about such a possibility, and indeed sets about the task with considerable irony. In Derrida's text, meanwhile, something like autobiography – 'circumfession' – proceeds by way of grafting together confession and circumcision (Derrida implies the latter to be at once a key feature of his own autobiography and a mark or incision in infancy that he could neither license nor resist). The grafting of confession and circumcision is, however, far from uncomplicated as an autobiographical gesture (autobiography as, literally, the self-inscription or self-marking of one's life). For circumcision cannot be confessed – an incisive mark received from the other, it violently cuts from and into memory. Nevertheless, Derrida's *Circumfession* registers, indeed affirms, the violence of the cut – for each mark is also a wounding incision in language – not only as it is performed by Bennington's cutting of Derrida's own words, but as it spurs writing itself. Whether or not this present volume 'cuts it' in these terms is, once more, for the reader to decide.

One last remark. Given the pressures of word length, and the sheer volume of the corpus at hand, I have chosen to devote as much space as possible to providing detailed accounts of the way in which Derrida treats certain problems and issues, how he reads particular philosophical or literary texts, and how he encounters an array of writers and thinkers. Since these confrontations are always singular and specific, I have not included extended descriptions of relevant philosophical and literary figures, which are in any case readily available in a number of locations, choosing instead to signpost those places in his writing where Derrida's relationship to each of them is at stake.

—A—

'A Certain Impossible Possibility of Saying the Event'   A late text by Derrida, published in English in 2007. See **actuvirtuality**, **event**.

'A Silkworm of One's Own (Points of View Stitched on the Other Veil)'   First published in English in 1996, and in French a year later. Here, Derrida addresses the metaphysical construal of truth in terms of revelation. In the **metaphysical** tradition, truth is precisely that which must be uncovered or disclosed. For metaphysics it is therefore effectively in the nature of truth that it should find itself veiled. The veil is not so much a simple impediment to the truth, then, as a principle trait where truth is concerned. As in **Spurs** (which includes subheadings such as 'veils', 'adornments', 'distances' and 'truths'), the question of **sexual difference** is here woven back into this thinking of truth as the veiling-unveiling of presence. (Indeed, as the essay's translator, Geoffrey Bennington, points out, 'voile' in the title could either be masculine (veil) or feminine (sail). In the manifold layers of such veils and sails one might find embroidered the whole history of sexual difference, indeed an 'other' history enfolded within this history.)

In 'A Silkworm of One's Own', Derrida reflects upon an eye operation which Hélène **Cixous** had recently undergone to address her extreme myopia. An account of this experience is to be found in 'Savoir', the text by Cixous alongside which 'A Silkworm' is published in **Veils**. Here, notwithstanding the obvious proximity of the verbs *savoir* (to know) and *voir* (to see), Cixous finds that somehow she must mourn the loss of her condition. Derrida had previously been ignorant of Cixous's myopia, he tells us, since it had been 'hidden' from him. The condition of her sight, whether before or after the 'corrective' procedure, is not itself simply visible or, for that matter, reliably knowable. (For instance, can we know what Cixous's 'improved' sight will mean for her writing and thinking?) Thus, the question of Cixous's eye surgery acquires a heightened degree of complexity in terms of the motif of a lifted veil. Indeed, as the translator's note tells us, the phrase '*points de vue*' that appears in the subtitle of Derrida's text not only translates as 'points of view', but also retains a slightly outdated sense of *pas* (not), which might even permit another translation as 'no view at all'.

This different possibility is therefore stitched on to the very motif of a 'point of view' as that which implies an open, seeing eye ('points' is also the term for a stitch). Here it might be recalled that in 'The Principle of Reason' (see **Right to Philosophy**), Derrida notes how, for **Aristotle**, an essential condition of the vision experienced by 'man' is the periodic lowering of the eyelid, a certain passage of blindness that permits sight itself. (See also **Memoirs of the Blind**.)

In 'A Silkworm of One's Own', however, Derrida seeks what he terms a 'verdict' without truth, a **writing** or **testimony** no longer so tightly entangled in the folds or unfolding of the veil. He therefore stitches or embroiders onto the veil an 'other' text, that of the **Jewish** prayer shawl called a tallith, which is itself woven into daily practices and rituals, and subject to the intricacies of religious rite and law. Yet this discourse of the tallith is as much woven into that of the veil as set alongside it – in the sense that, for Derrida, one cannot simply remove or lift the veil. To do so risks remaining within precisely the veil's own logic, indeed its **ontotheology**, with which one never finishes in seeking to tear the veil (not least since the ontotheological conception of 'truth' depends on a seemingly interminable interplay of the revealed and the re-veiled). For Derrida, however, the 'truth' of the tallith has as much to do with the **singularity** of its **event** before the **law**, as any revelation or un-veiling it gives us to think.

Acts of Literature   Published in English in 1992. Focusing on the question of **literature** in Derrida, this is an edited collection of writings including texts on Mallarmé, Kafka, Blanchot, Joyce, Ponge, Celan, Shakespeare and Rousseau, several of which are drawn from other well-known publications. The volume includes an interview with the editor Derek Attridge, entitled 'This Strange Institution Called Literature'. Here, Derrida reflects on the always **supplementary** relations of literature and **philosophy** (despite its classical commitment to thought over and above language, philosophy can no more extricate itself from the practice and movement of **writing** than the literary text can hope to free itself entirely of the residues of the philosophical tradition), and begins to put the question of **autobiography** on the borderlines between the two. Literature, however, is seen by Derrida as a relatively modern institution linked to the advent of a **law** which grants it the right, in principle, to say everything. But this very same 'law' of literature encourages excess and defiance of the law in a double sense: not only does the principle of literature's 'freedom' make possible political conflict between writers and dominant powers; but the very definition given to literature by law ('the right to say everything') tends to impede an authoritative demarcation or resettlement of the literary 'object'. In other words, the laws that govern the literary text remain difficult to determine or stabilize *by law*.

For these reasons, literature may well serve the **democracy to come**, which remains irreducible to – indeed, *the limit of* – any given political orientation, ideological programme or historical project. Derrida remarks on the irresponsibilization of the writer that issues from literature's legal institution and rights. While this may always encourage political conservatism or quietism (not only on the part of the writer, but also in terms of the image vested in literature by those who might wish to limit its powers), nonetheless literature's refusal to be held accountable in terms of an already given duty or **ethics** of writing might entail its greatest **responsibility**. When asked about the writers he has chosen to focus on, many of them treated in the texts that go to make up this volume, Derrida argues that each tends, in highly **singular** fashion, to put the question of literature by enacting critically the strange and paradoxical possibilities granted by its very law and institution. Thus, a literary **event** worthy of its name is powerful enough to put in question – and thus potentially to transform – the laws that make it possible. This very same capacity implies that such a literary text cannot be thought of as simply an example of a given generality, since it may instead displace or re-place the categorial 'whole' which we otherwise presume allots it. Thus, literary singularity is at once the unique event of an irreplaceable **signature**, **date** and inscription; and at the same time it is always given by way of a potent **iterability**, a transformative capacity for a **future** that remains, precisely, yet-to-be-determined. As Derrida puts it, literature makes a differential **mark**, different from itself within itself. It marks itself insistently, here and now, as a **promise** of the to-come.

The collection includes two pieces, 'Before the Law' and 'The Law of Genre', which deserve further comment in that they are less readily available elsewhere and contribute strongly to a sense of Derrida's thinking about literature. The first of these, taking its cue from **Kafka**'s short text of the same name, sets aside the essentialism that seems implicit in the question 'What is literature?', and turns instead to this problem of the 'law' that grants literature its peculiar 'laws'. Here, the institutional and juridical milieu which gives us literature in the modern sense calls for the limits of the literary work to be defined in terms of a number of attributes (authorship, title, the form and properties of the text, and so on), which each singular literary act nevertheless performs *critically*, or puts into question. Kafka's own text, as one that comes to be included in the larger body of writing known as *The Trial*, is thus revisited – in an essay by Derrida going by the same name ('Before the Law') – in order to analyze and, indeed, re-enact this complex interplay between the singular event of writing and the general settings in which it is read and repeated.

That the incipit of Kafka's story repeats the title (so that the parable comes with something like a double beginning), puts back into play the questions Derrida wants to ask about the always unstable origin and limit of the literary text, and its inherent or originary iterability. Promising neither an essential answer or reference point to the question 'What is literature?', nor a definitive exit from it, 'Before the Law' remains always . . . before the law. It does so, according to the plural and indeed equivocal possibilities that such a phrase itself carries. Thus the incipit ('Before the Law . . .') is before the title ('Before the Law') which is before it. The incipit comes before the law, just as a defendant faces a pre-eminent judge installed prior to their arrival. But the incipit also comes 'before', in the sense that the first line is also conceivably the inaugurating condition of a text – indeed, of an ultimately unmasterable series of **différantial** traces – which entitles the title to its (questionable) status. The always vexed question of whether *and in what sense* the title or the incipit comes 'before' is in other words also the question of what originates or institutes the literary text. (Here we might ask whether the title is, or is not, part of the literary work? Yes and no at once, since the title functions – however impossibly – as the enabling limit of the work, the very piece that gives the text its supposed 'wholeness' and yet the heading that must stand above or outside in order to unify and organize it.)

Such a question of literature's institution or inauguration therefore *remains* at stake the very **undecidability** or divisibility of this 'before', setting up a scene that is re-enacted throughout the mysterious face-to-face encounter which Kafka presents between the law's doorkeeper and the man from the country seeking admittance to the law. However, the law itself is never *presentable* as such. It is never made manifold, never ushered

actuvirtuality

in, and is itself nowhere to be faced. Instead, the odd and unsettling scene that we find in 'Before the Law' once more replays the enigmatic problem of the 'law' that it comes 'before'. This is a law (law *of* literature, in a multiple sense) that cannot extricate itself from – but which can only *appear* to transcend – the problems and issues of text and textuality which it doubtless thinks itself entitled to master by granting literature its very right.

'The Law of Genre', meanwhile, sees Derrida turn to **Blanchot**'s short fiction, *The Madness of the Day*. The idea of **genre** – not just in the literary sense, but in terms of genus, category and classification more generally – introduces questions of law, to the extent that it implies authoritative demarcation, institutionalizable differences, consistent and reliable principles of differentiation. However, as Derrida shows, the very mark of belonging to a 'genre' is not simply a feature of the genre itself. For instance, that which marks or **re-marks** a film as an example of the horror genre does not operate merely as a feature of that genre, but does something else too. Here, Derrida resorts to the terms employed by **speech act theory**: the relation of such a re-marking mark to the genre itself is a matter of *mention* and not merely of *use*. Thus, the mark which 'mentions', signals or re-marks the genre exceeds 'use' or participation in it, therefore going beyond the generic limits that in another way its very 'mentioning' serves to inscribe. This effect is constitutive and irreducible, 'the law of the law of genre' as Derrida puts it. Such a law calls upon genre to endure the very principle of contamination or impurity that nonetheless gives it its chance. Blanchot's text sees a narrative subject confronted by a law that is in a certain way double – one that appears as much in enigmatic, feminine silhouette, as in the guise of its more 'masculine' forms of enforcement. Indeed, it is the highly singular, inventive and perplexing nature of this text that renders it far less susceptible to traditional forms of interpretation which base their analysis on the conventions imputed to literary forms, or in other words, generic designations. Derrida seeks to preserve this powerful idiomaticity, resisting those forms of reading which might reduce or appropriate Blanchot's writing to a set of philosophical themes or propositions.

actuvirtuality   Another of Derrida's neologisms, the actual and the virtual endure a certain **graft** here. This term is allied to **artifactuality**, which recognizes the artificial constructedness of 'actuality' while refusing to boil down **events** – notably in their irreducible **singularity** – to a generalized realm of mere simulation or media-driven fictionalization today. (In a late text, **'A Certain Impossible Possibility of Saying the Event'**, Derrida therefore acknowledges the extent to which events may be produced or virtualized by what he calls 'today's information machines', but follows a somewhat different pathway than Baudrillard in forcefully drawing attention to the singularity of every **death** during the Gulf War, each a radically heterogeneous, asymmetrical event remaining irreducible to media appropriation and processing.) While, as Derrida observes, virtuality and actuality can no longer be opposed with any degree of philosophical rigour, the virtual must be considered an indispensable condition of the event that one must nevertheless continue to think of in terms of the actuality of **names**, **dates**, **signatures**, bodies, deaths, institutions and the 'here-now' that Derrida describes as the 'more-than-**present**' of today. In other words, the actuvirtual is nothing less than a product or facet of *différance* that Derrida sees not merely as a condition of literary or philosophical writing, but which structures the (deconstructible) 'present' itself.

To give an example. In 'Where a Teaching Body Begins and How It Ends' (see **Right to Philosophy**), Derrida describes the complex and conflictual matrix of powers and interests that structure the historico-ideologico-politico-institutional field of pedagogy, and which not only surround the École Normale, but shape more widely the history and question of national education and philosophical instruction in **France**. This non-self-identical matrix determines Derrida's function as an *agrégé-répétiteur* and thus establishes the relations of the teaching body (of both the professor and the faculty corps vis-à-vis the national body or bodies) to the classroom and its students. Thus Derrida confronts us with actual bodies, physical conditions, and the highly determined spacial configuration of a certain place. And yet, since this very same place of gathered bodies – in all its resonant significance – arises only on condition of certain effects of *différance*, there could never be a single teaching body (or, for that matter, a single body of teaching) so homogenous and self-identical as to reduce or neutralize within itself all the tensions and contradictions which in fact go to make it up. Such a body, to put it another way, could never be simply 'actual', or actualize all that forms and informs it. Thus, the teaching body is, precisely, constituted as **other** than itself, other than its identity as a supposedly transparent representation of the institutional-pedagogic and indeed socio-political corpus. So, while in its actual performance as a bodily manifestation it in fact virtualizes itself as just such a representation, the teaching body cannot but become haunted by a certain **spectrality** that inhabits the 'more-than-present' of this particular scene. It is in this sense that Derrida means the actuvirtual.

Adieu to Emmanuel Levinas   This volume contains two texts: 'Adieu' was delivered at **Levinas**'s funeral in 1995; while 'A Word of Welcome' was presented one year later to open a memorial conference on Levinas at the Sorbonne, organized under the auspices of the Collège International de Philosophie (of which Levinas was an early supporter). 'Adieu' commemorates Levinas's extraordinary influence in introducing to **France** the phenomenological tradition of **Husserl** and **Heidegger** during the 1930s and after, and in rethinking the legacy of **phenomenology** from a perspective that, for Derrida, alters the philosophical landscape for ever. Levinas is accredited with developing a thinking of **ethics** which also remains a profound reflection on **justice**, the state, Israel, and the politics of **memory** in our time. In the interests of just such a thinking, he is celebrated by Derrida as contributing in highly novel ways to the dialogue between the biblical and talmudic traditions, between the **Jewish** heritage and what we inherit from **Greek** and Roman origins and other Abrahamic monotheisms.

Derrida's funeral oration for Levinas aspires to dwell unabidingly at that point where language fails to provide a consoling and thus narcissistic return for the **mourning** survivor. In this, Derrida wishes to preserve a certain fidelity to Levinasian themes: in particular, to the thought of an ethical, **responsible** or 'just' relation to the **Other** as absolute alterity and anteriority. For Levinas, the relation to the Other, which is justice, calls for a thought of **death** that remains at odds with the existential-phenomenological tradition of Heidegger. For Heidegger, the relation to one's own death comes to define what is 'proper' to *Dasein* as its authentic condition of possibility. (In *Aporias*, Derrida questions this 'proper' possibility.) For Levinas, in contrast, the death of the Other is the first death. It is the death of the Other that individuates me in my responsibility for his mortality, thus entrusting to me my identity as a responsible 'I'. The relation to death which is first of all that of an absolute Other whom one cannot but *affirm*, reflects the theme of an *unconditional hospitality* for the stranger at an infinite distance. In 'A Word of Welcome', Derrida therefore dares to elevate hospitality as a principal Levinasian theme. However, just as a certain non-knowledge is the very element of a non-appropriative ('just') relation to the Other, so hospitality is distinctly opposed to thematization or formalization by Levinas. This Derrida well understands. As he acknowledges straight away, simply to say the word 'Welcome' risks appropriating a certain place of welcoming as one's own abode or element. Thus the welcomer – who is also, in another guise, the teacher – finds him or herself in danger of taking surreptitious precedence over the one to whom greeting is extended as, therefore, effectively an appropriative act. A fully self-possessed teaching or welcoming of this kind operates only within the existing field of what Derrida calls the 'masterable-possible', thereby annulling the very possibility of **invention**, **event** and **decision**, but also **friendship**, hospitality and **gift**. For Levinas, however, it is possible to rethink this logic of 'welcome' otherwise: hospitality is always that of the Other. Since it is the host who receives from his home the potential to be hospitable – which is itself a possibility granted only by that of the guest – it is therefore the guest himself who harbours or hosts the possibility of hospitality, a possibility which is extended to the host as, in effect, welcomed in his own abode. Thus the one who hosts is, in truth, hosted by the one he hosts. (This puts into question his freedom as traditionally construed – host and hostage remain inextricably linked at this very point where the subject of a 'masterable-possible' becomes subjected to a radical passivity beyond the classical distinction between the active and passive of a human subjectivity. One might note that the Levinasian reference to 'host' and 'hostage' or, in effect, 'host' *as* 'hostage', calls upon Derrida's attention in a number of places. For instance 'Pas d'hospitalité' in *Of Hospitality*.) According to this thinking, the home is not a place of property or possession any more than, for Derrida, the **archive** is merely a place of safe deposit for private or national treasures that one wishes to conserve but also display to visitors under specific conditions. Hospitality (of the Other) precedes property, place and possession (of the Self or Same), rather than the other way around. It is this thought of the (im-) possible conditions of 'welcome' and the 'home' that, in Derrida's reading of Levinas, gives rise to the possibility of another thought of the state, of national and international *law*, of the mutation of geo-political space, of refuge, asylum and so forth.

In this text on Levinas, Derrida explores the idea of a mediating 'third' – in effect, juridico-political regulation – as not only a violating dilution of the purity of a just relation to the Other, but also as a source of protection against the possible **violence** that may stem from an immediate ethics of the face-to-face. Turning to Levinas's complex notion that the political might be located 'beyond the State in the State', Derrida identifies in the unfulfilled and always fragile commitment associated with the eventful founding of a state (such as Israel in 1948) what may exceed its established hegemonic form: a **messianic** politics, associated in Levinas with a call for peace ('peace now') which, as Derrida observes, can neither be purely political – since by definition no pure politics could exist – nor for that matter purely apolitical. In Levinas's terms, this politics beyond politics, 'beyond the State in the State', draws us closer to the State of David than to that of Caesar or, in other words, to that of the Greco-Roman philosophico-political heritage, which is also inherited by Enlightenment thought. The latter itself remains a divided tradition, as Derrida points out, notably through a discussion of **Kant**'s notion of perpetual peace. Kant argues that perpetual peace as a juridico-political institution which is unavailable within the war-like state of nature might only be said to be achieved on condition of an absolute and indefinite cessation of the very possibility of war. Any remaining chance or risk of an outbreak of hostilities suggests merely a brokered peace, the politics of which are simply a continuation of war by other means. However, as Derrida notes, the necessarily fabricated or constructed nature of Kant's perpetual peace suggests a violent and impure institution. Highly attentive both to what distinguishes and relates them, Derrida contrasts Kant and Levinas: whereas Kant's idea of perpetual peace retains impurely in its very foundation traces of the violence it would seek decisively to overcome, for Levinas war is always made against (and thus made possible by) the face, which is what first of all welcomes. From this, Derrida concludes that the 'third' (juridico-political regulation as a means both to end and to continue by other means what we think of as war) is not just a simple interruption of a pure and just ethics of the face-to-face, a mere intrusion supervening in an extrinsic and secondary fashion. Instead, the 'third' is inextricable from the outset among the very conditions of possibility of ethics, justice and peace. Between Kant and Levinas, one must therefore **negotiate** with the non-negotiable 'in the State beyond the State' in the interests of a 'better' politics and law.

affirmation   Countering rumours of its supposed nihilism, destructiveness or negativism, Derrida consistently spoke of deconstruction as affirmative. Examples of deconstruction as affirmation abound throughout this volume, but see especially **yes, yes**.

Algeria   Derrida's place of birth and scene of his expulsion from school because of zealous implementation of the anti-semitic quotas called for by the Vichy government in France. Derrida often spoke of his 'nostalgeria'. See **Circumfession, hospitality, 'I Have a Taste for the Secret', Learning to Live Finally, Monolingualism of the Other, Negotiations, Points, The Other Heading**.

America and deconstruction   See **Memoires for Paul de Man**. For Derrida on America, see also **September 11**, 'Declarations of Independence' in **Negotiations**.

animal, animality   See **The Animal That Therefore I Am**. See also **Aporias, Of Spirit, Points, Politics of Friendship**, the '*Geschlecht*' essays in **Psyche, sovereignty**.

apocalypse   See the entry on **Psyche** for a discussion of apocalypse in 'No Apocalypse, Not Now' and 'Of an Apocalyptic Tone Recently Adopted in Philosophy'.

aporia   See **Aporias**, below, for an account of this term.

Aporias   Published in 1993. As Derrida observes here, **death** is often thought of as a border. In most cultures or contexts it is portrayed in terms of a voyage over the horizon to a beyond, or a passage across an ultimate threshold. And yet at the same time death is without border. This is not just in the sense that death itself could be said to traverse all the limits and separations that would divide one group, culture, context, tradition or, indeed, discipline from another. (As Derrida notes, all cultures have their own representations and understanding of death, and yet the very advent of culture is predicated on a relation to death – there may be no politics without **mourning**, he conjectures – which therefore crosses all boundaries.) Death has no border in the further sense that it is a word (like 'God') that will never in the end have designated a stable concept, an indubitable experience or a definite 'thing'. The referent or meaning of this noun cannot be definitively fixed or identified. Thus death overflows all the limits or delimitations that would in fact be needed to allow the crossing of a line, the passage across a threshold, an entry over the border. (Indeed, the question of **hospitality** treated by Derrida in several other texts therefore also arises here, again as an issue that we need to think of alongside questions of politics, the state and '**Europe**'.) Derrida thus links the thinking of death to the term '**aporia**'. For Derrida, this old **Greek** word suggests an absolutely impassable situation, one which cannot be resolved through rational analysis or dialectical thought. Neither can such a 'situation' be answered by a discourse that would be capable of taking the aporia as an 'object' of knowledge. In other words, the aporia is as much unsituatable as it is an identifiable 'situation'. Indeed, to situate or identify an aporia is to give a name to an experience that, by definition, cannot be 'properly' recognized or experienced *as such*. To put this another way, the aporia cannot be reduced to a mere *problem* that one might hope to project and thus solve. For Derrida, the paralysis seemingly imposed by an aporia is not just to be negatively marked. (Indeed, it is hard to think of an aporia inducing a static paralytic state, since it leaves an always restless, unresolved **remainder**.) Rather, aporias confront us with entirely undecided and indeed **undecidable** 'situations' that deeply interrupt and suspend all established programmes, norms, conventions, moralities, duties and expectations, precisely so as to open anew the possibility of **decision**, response and **responsibility**, perhaps even experience itself. To endure the '**impossibility**' of an aporia is thus to risk the chance of an 'other' possibility, an impossible possibility that is perhaps the only one worth its name. (An entirely 'possible' possibility would surely operate within an already existent field of 'potentials', and would thus open up no possibility beyond what may already be established, predicted or prescribed.)

The aporia as the unknowable-impassable therefore impinges without limit upon death, not only upon all the disciplinary inquiries that would make it their 'object' (in the various fields of biology, theology, psychology, anthropology, history, demography, and so forth), but also upon the existential analysis that **Heidegger** wants to portray as fundamentally prior to both the **metaphysical** construal of death and its disciplinary treatment, which he sees as typically responsible for presupposed concepts and premature criteriologies of death. For Heidegger, the authentic existence of *Dasein* (which as a being must be conceived in a prior way to the metaphysical conception of 'man', 'subject', 'self', 'soul' or 'consciousness') is properly to be thought in regard to death *as such*. It is death in its irreplaceable **singularity**, its non-substitutable 'mineness', which establishes what is 'proper' to *Dasein*. Here, as elsewhere in his writings, Derrida not only recalls **Levinas**'s misgivings about the 'mineness' of death in Heidegger. (For Levinas, it is the death of the **other** that is the first death, that which in fact individuates me as **responsible** mortal.) He also questions the basis on which Heidegger excludes the **animal** from this 'proper' death, or from the experience of death *as* death. As Derrida observes, Heidegger also distinguishes animals on the strength of their inability to speak: the animal is, for Heidegger, without language. Indeed, it is language that would seem to permit the identification of death *properly speaking*, or death *as such*. And yet, since no-one can ever properly testify to or credit death *as such* (for, impossibly, one would have to be dead to do so), this 'as such' falters at its critical moment, and with it the 'proper' (language) relation to death which forms the basis of a distinction that excludes the animal.

For Heidegger, death gives to *Dasein* its proper possibility as a being, yet it does so only in terms of a certain impossibility. For the condition of possibility of *Dasein* is, precisely, the very same death which it simply cannot assume or incorporate as an existent being. Death as the 'proper' possibility of *Dasein* cannot be a 'property' of its existence. *Dasein* thus grounds its possibility in terms of an impossibility that always awaits it, right from the beginning; an impossibility which it cannot properly master or resolve and which, remaining irreducible to its own existence and self-relation, cannot but be the 'improper' or inauthentic condition of *Dasein*'s proper possibility. The 'fundamentalist' claims of Heidegger's discourse, those which propose to go to the proper origin of the question, are therefore shown by Derrida to be unsound. Indeed, he concludes by resituating Heidegger's *Being and Time* in terms of a history dominated by the always deconstructible **ontotheologies** of the **religions** of the Book.

arche-writing   See **writing**. See also ***Of Grammatology***.

archive   See ***Archive Fever***. See also ***Cinders, Echographies of Television, Geneses, Genealogies, Genres and Genius, Paper Machine,*** **technicity**.

Archive Fever   First published in French in 1995. Here, Derrida notes that the history of **psychoanalysis** is not just a history of seminal events and discoveries found in archival records which may then be construed as an exterior deposit and secondary support. More fundamentally, archivization – which thereafter cannot be understood in any simplistic sense – *is* the very history of psychoanalysis. Psychoanalysis, as for instance **Freud**'s own work on dreams and obsessions amply demonstrates, is nothing less than a thinking of the **archive** which, however, struggles to detach itself securely from the (desired) object of its thought. Psychoanalysis, then, is irreducibly both archivo-analysis and archive fever.

In *Archive Fever*, it is the death drive that is found at, or as, the foundation of the Freudian archive. The death drive is the original discovery which prevents psychoanalysis from becoming, as Freud may worry, merely wasted paper and ink. Yet the death drive, as Derrida calls us to remember, itself encourages the destruction of **memory**, and indeed threatens to eradicate or efface the archive as monumental deposit. If the novelty of the death drive is therefore invoked by Freud as the principle reason for conserving the findings of psychoanalysis, then *a priori* the deposit works against itself, fails to support itself, feverishly inciting amnesia, incinerating what is consigned to archivable memory in a way that entirely flouts the economic principle of the archive as a reckonable accumulation founded stably on some exterior substrate.

Derrida thus reflects on the deconstructible concept of the archive. The archive takes place through a situation of domiciliation, putting under house arrest in a more or less permanent dwelling that which is archived. This typically marks an institutional pathway from the private to the public, but, as Derrida points out, not necessarily from the **secret** to the non-secret, since the archived text may – indeed, cannot but – always keep in reserve what in its attestation can never be reduced or exposed to mere evidence or proof. The archive is formed via acts of consignation through which residence is assigned and deposit made, but, while it is undoubtedly the aim of consignation to produce a coherent corpus in which each artefact or element translates itself in terms of a unified and ideal arrangement, this very same feature of the archive gives it a double economy. Every archive is at once conservative and institutive, wanting to reflect and defend the givenness of that which it inherits while engaging in highly artificial or unnatural processes and acts of selection and gathering in order to do so. Indeed, since it must make its own **law**, the archive is radically **inventive** or revolutionary as much as it is conservative.

For Derrida, the archivization of psychoanalysis (and one must register the double genitive here) is complexly shaped by **technologies** of communication and recording in Freud's time. Since archivization *is* in a sense the very history of psychoanalysis, these technologies cannot be thought to lie merely on the *outside* of psychoanalysis or come along afterwards. Rather, the technical conditions of archivization transact with in order to produce as much as record the **event** and advent of psychoanalysis. Thus, Derrida tells us, the entire terrain of the psychoanalytic archive, including its most profound contents and findings, would be unrecognizably transformed had Freud and his followers enjoyed access to the electronic media, devices and communications that characterize the era of computers, faxes and email.

Thus, writing technologies do not determine merely the conservational recording of psychoanalysis, but instead produce the very institution of its archivable event. This means that the event of psychoanalysis and the impression it leaves behind cannot be easily distinguished or stably separated: Derrida talks of the psychoanalytic 'impression', in the sense of the very pressure of printing, thought of in terms of a singular friction between printer and printed, between the event and its impression 'in print'. This pressure of the impression is at once unique in its occurrence, finding or making its trace in an irreplaceable instant of contact; and yet the implied synchronicity of the imprint, which might otherwise translate the archive's dream of a self-identical deposit and unified conservational arrangement, is itself disrupted at the origin, since the impression is always already divisible in its imminent repeatability. The impression, in other words, will have been possible only to the extent that its **iterability** haunts it from the beginning.

The **spectrality** which returns at the origin of this 'impression' leads Derrida not to reject its idea as merely a weak and fuzzy subconcept (as traditional or scholarly **philosophy** might well do), but instead to inscribe within it the very possibility of the **future**, and the very future of the concept of the archive. (In Derrida's thinking, the archive and the concept

artifactuality

of the archive do not find their origin or future in what is already or readily archivable.) For Derrida, therefore, archivization as itself archive-thinking is much less a matter of resorting to a past that we imagine to be already at our disposal. Instead of assuming an archivable, conservable concept of the archive, Derrida's thinking of the impression orients itself towards an **'other'** archive to which we might respond, as responsibly as possible, by remaining open to what begins by coming (back) from the future, the event *to come* of the archive.

Derrida therefore moves us away from the idea that an archive simply accommodates, monumentalizes, violates or amortizes the event. In *Archive Fever*, the question of the psychoanalytic archive is bound to a thinking of the psychoanalytic event to come, an event which already marks the entire landscape of our intellectual, disciplinary, historical and cultural archive, yet which will have transformed it, perhaps, in a still unanticipatable way. Thus, as *Archive Fever* turns its attention to an extended reading of Yosef Hayim Yerushalmi's *Freud's Moses: Judaism Terminable and Interminable*, the very event of Yerushalmi's book is viewed by Derrida in terms of a sudden and dramatic turn which threatens to unravel a painstaking work of scholarship fit for the archive itself. This comes at the point when Yerushalmi departs from the classical norms and conventions of scholarly writing in order to apostrophize inventively according to a complex **fiction** which hails Freud's spectre, only to register the futility of asking of it whether psychoanalysis might be called a **Jewish** science. This may never be knowable, Yerushalmi speculates, and would in any case depend on much future work, including **decisions** still to come concerning the very definition of 'Jewish' and 'science'. Thus, the relationship of such a 'science' to its own archive begins by coming from an unrecognizable future, especially due to (rather than just despite) its abundantly complicated history.

Aristotle (384BC–322BC) Greek philosopher. See, **'A Silkworm of One's Own'**, ***Margins of Philosophy***, ***Politics of Friendship***, ***Rogues***.

artifactuality Answering a question in an interview with *Passages* to mark the publication of *Specters of Marx* about whether he is in touch with actuality, Derrida first of all responds by acknowledging the extent to which his replies constitute an artifact, in other words, an artificial production of speech or writing determined by a host of protocols and conventions (always shot through with effects of **différance**) including those of academia, the media, and the so-called public and political sphere. And actuality is itself made, rather than given. It is always conditioned in its very production by institutions, hierarchies, economies, **technologies** and an array of interests and forces which one must try to recognize, not least since these very same forces frequently conspire to naturalize or impose a pre-critical sense of the actual. Thus an 'actuality effect' clings to what is in fact highly produced, and one can never go straight to the question of the 'actual', or gain direct access to its sphere, without taking patient consideration of these conditions of actuality according to another rhythm of thinking, one that necessarily differs in its very *time* from the simple urgency or directness frequently required of a supposedly effective engagement with 'actuality' itself. Yet such untimely thinking is, for Derrida, what may allow us to best confront not only actuality's '**present**' but the very possibility of its **future**.

Such thinking does not lead Derrida to insist too hastily on the idea of contemporary reality as simply a media fiction, or, put differently, to deny the possibility of the **event**. On the contrary, he reasserts **deconstruction**'s consistent **affirmation** of the **singular** as that which attends to the irreducible, and to what is irreducibly resistant to synthetic appropriation. This needs to be remembered all the while that one analyzes the synthetic productions which Derrida identifies with today's highly powerful information machines. The singular is much less an authentic essence, a unique 'real' or true origin which 'information' is unable to appropriate. It is far better described as a resistant after-effect found at the constituting limits of an artifactual synthetics that is itself produced by effects of **différance**. Nevertheless, the strange temporality of the singular – as, precisely, an untimeliness that resists the synthetic image of the 'present' or the 'actual' as urgently given – relates to the fact that the very possibility of artifactuality is itself conditioned from the outset by irreducible singularities, by the **trace**, by *différance*. Thus it is that the artifactuality associated with today's information machines cannot but (fail to) contain within itself an always *untimely* transformative **supplement** which opens up the possibility of the **democracy to come**. This way of thinking about *différance* offers a profound challenge to those who wish to associate the term simply with an equivocating apoliticism or an endlessly hesitant philosophizing.

See also **actuvirtuality**.

Austin, J. L. (1911–1960) British philosopher of language and speech act theorist. See **Margins of Philosophy**, **performativity**, **'Signature Event Context'**, **speech act theory**.

auto-affection See *Of Grammatology*, *On Touching*, *Speech and Phenomena*.

autobiography See *Acts of Literature*, *Circumfession*, *'Demeure'*, *Of Grammatology*, *The Animal That Therefore I Am*, *The Ear of the Other*.

autoimmunity See **democracy to come**, **demos**, **'Faith and Knowledge'**, *Resistances of Psychoanalysis*, *Rogues*, especially **September 11**, **university**.

— B —

Bataille, Georges (1897–1962) French writer and thinker. See especially *Politics of Friendship*, *Writing and Difference*.

being See *Margins of Philosophy*, **metaphysics of presence**.

Benjamin, Walter (1892–1940) German-Jewish literary critic, essayist, philosopher and translator. See especially **'Force of Law'**.

Benveniste, Émile (1902–1976) French structural linguist. See especially *Margins of Philosophy*.

Blanchot, Maurice (1907–2003) French writer and thinker. An immensely important figure for Derrida, not least in his thinking of literature.
See *Acts of Literature*, **'Demeure'**, **'Living On: Borderlines'**, **literature**, *Politics of Friendship*.

book   See *Dissemination, Paper Machine, Positions, Writing and Difference*.

— C —

Celan, Paul (1920–1970)   Poet of Jewish Romanian origin. Major poet of the German language in the post-war period. Celan is an important figure for Derrida in his thinking about **literature**, **testimony** or witnessing, survival, **singularity**, **iterability** and the **date**. See *Acts of Literature*, *Cinders*, literature, *Points*, 'Shibboleth', *Sovereignties in Question*.

Christianity/Christianization   See 'Faith and Knowledge', *Glas*, 'On Cosmopolitanism and Forgiveness', *Psyche*, *The Gift of Death*.

Cinders   Published in 1982. *Cinders* is occasioned by Derrida's concern to reread a phrase found in the acknowledgements to his own **Dissemination**, one he had written some fifteen years earlier: '*il y a là cendre*', 'cinders there are'. On the left-hand pages, in a text entitled 'Animadversions', Derrida tracks a succession of passages in earlier texts which seem to anticipate this phrase or suggest traces of it, citing in particular 'Plato's Pharmacy', **Glas** and **The Post Card**. On the right-hand side, meanwhile, we are given to read Derrida's philosophical prose poem, written as a polylogue of masculine and feminine voices (the number of which is not specified), spun around the motif of the cinder.

Derrida reflects on this work in an interview entitled 'There is No "One" Narcissism', originally prepared for French radio in 1986 (*Cinders* was itself made into a tape recording, with the play between **speech** and **writing** – thought of, perhaps, as a kind of *mal d'archive* or **archive fever** – becoming a key question in the prologue to the published text). Here, Derrida recalls how he came to return to this motif, becoming aware that it better named what he had sought to announce with words such as **trace**, writing or gramme. For Derrida, cinders or ashes gather themselves as a

Cinders

way of thinking about that which, while presenting or inscribing itself, erases itself completely. (As Derrida himself puts it, the cinder is 'a remainder without remainder', or 'something which is not'.) Put differently, the cinder at once participates in and renames the trace structure of 'writing', something which Derrida's texts attend to from the 1960s onwards. In exemplary fashion, the cinder thus names the absence of a positive identity and **proper name** for that which produces or makes possible every **presence**, every entity, every term or **being** (see also, for instance, **'Différance'**). Yet cinders is, too, just another among a chain of words running throughout Derrida's texts – trace, **supplement**, **remainder**, writing, dissemination, and so forth – which form an unmasterable 'series', since none of these terms take their measure against an ultimate origin or presence, the truth of Being. Thus, in one place in the text, Derrida remarks that the word 'cinder' is itself only a cinder of the cinder, an incinerated remnant ('cinder there is') of that which immolates (at) the origin.

For Derrida, then, the cinder – leaving nothing, finally, to reveal or unveil – names the absolute non-memory which burns at the origin of language. (In 'A Number of Yes', the first 'yes' as that which gives the very possibility of language, a 'yes' which all language therefore cannot but affirm, is nonetheless, like the gift, to be acknowledged – **'yes, yes'** – only at the expense of a certain repetitive return, a refabulation which also radically effaces, divides the origin destructively against itself, or against its metaphysical determination in terms of **presence**. Cinders would thus be a name for that which, precisely through its own **affirmation**, comes to destroy itself at the origin.) The cinder therefore becomes the motif for a radical destruction of **memory**, insofar as memory is itself construed in terms of the eventual unveiling and expression of truth. As Derrida notes in 'There is No "One" Narcissism', the cinder leaves in ashes every philosophy or psychology of consciousness, and even the psychoanalytic conception of the repressed unconscious which, for him, still cherishes the possibility of memory. In this interview, Derrida further reconsiders his allusions to a holocaustal destruction of memory (and thus perhaps of the very possibility of **testimony** and even of **mourning**), suggesting connections between *Cinders* and other of his texts on **Celan**, such as **'Shibboleth'**. However, Derrida also insists that the **(impossible)** experience of cinders reaffirms the gift-without-presence, giving itself over to an always hospitable non-keeping which interrupts every calculated relation or economic transaction, thus opening the very possibility of the relation to the **other**.

Ciph   French acronym for the International College of Philosophy, which Derrida helped to found in the early 1980s. See **Right to Philosophy I and II**, **university**.

Circumfession   Published in 1991. This text was first published in French alongside Geoffrey Bennington's *Derridabase*, under the general title *Jacques Derrida*. While Bennington's contribution, occupying the upper two-thirds of each page, seeks to elaborate the general system of Derrida's thought under a series of pertinent headings, *Circumfession* lurks beneath in shrunken typeface, divided by a dotted line, as if it were some kind of coupon, voucher, ticket, counterfoil or slip. (The suggestive possibilities of this perhaps feigned, yet always possible, detachability need to be reckoned with. So does the economic meaning or value of such 'slips' when one takes into account the economizing systematicity to which Bennington's text, looming above, aspires.) The book itself derives from a contract or wager whereby Bennington tasks himself with producing something like a Derrida database which, since it is to dispense with quotation entirely, proposes to establish the conceptual coherence and consistency of Derrida's thought beyond the idiomatic specificity of any particular sentences or phrasings. (Everything that remains to be said about this gesture on Bennington's part must be related also to this dictionary, which on the basis of its contract, its given protocols or genre, itself forgoes citation.) Derrida, meanwhile, aims to write a surprising, inventive, unanticipatable text which might elude the systematizing ambitions of *Derridabase*, ambitions that are doubtless forged with considerable irony and which Bennington calculates as in any case preprogrammed to fail.

Circumfession is undeniably written in the guise of an **autobiographical** work. It is divided into 59 periods or periphrases, one for each of Derrida's 59 years at the time the piece was composed. The text recounts the protracted decline of a **mother** named Georgette (Derrida's mother of the same name was to pass away near the end of 1991), and throughout gives names and details of relatives, various occurrences in childhood such as circumcision, wartime expulsion from school and loss of citizenship due to anti-semitic powers in **Algeria**, the premature death of two siblings (all of which cut into memory and leave it bereft), as well as other subsequent events which correspond to Derrida's own biography. Are we therefore in the midst of a volume divided neatly between, on the one (or upper) hand, the philosophical system of Derrida, lifted serenely from the body or corpus and, on the other, the life-writing of an empirical subject whose place is marginal or indeed excludable in that very same system? Elsewhere Derrida has observed that the classical philosophical gesture is to exclude the 'life' from the 'work' so as to preserve and protect the conceptual purity of thought from what might be considered the extraneous facticity of living itself. However, for Derrida this distinction between 'work' and 'life' must be rethought according to a more complex logic if one is to resist the metaphysical determination of **philosophy** in terms of the purity, **presence** or divinity of thought, and if one is to avoid construing a 'life' – like writing or the body in its classical sense – as merely a technical vehicle or material support, potentially corrupting inspired 'thought' at the very point it provides a conduit for the production of philosophical *oeuvres*. (Indeed, the irony of excluding precisely a *lived* life from the pure or *living* presence of 'thought' no doubt impels the rethinking that is called for here.) *Circumfession* as a coupon or counterfoil therefore vouches differently for the account of Bennington's (and for the division of 'life' and 'work') that it somewhat subversively countersigns. A (detachable?) part or example which is in a sense larger than the 'whole' it supports above itself, *Circumfession* at bottom *retains* itself so as to remain re-presentable as the vital 'slip' in a settling of accounts to come.

However, if what is idiomatic, biographical or autobiographical cannot so neatly be divided from the elaboration of philosophy's systematicity and integrity, nor can we be certain that *Circumfession* resists the abstract and ideal image of philosophy by confessing the simple 'truth' of a life. Fragments from **St Augustine**'s *Confessions* punctuate Derrida's own text, providing the occasion for us to recall his insight that **confession** construed simply as the revelation of 'what is' would remain superfluous before a God who already knows everything (as indeed *Circumfession* might become superfluous before 'G.' or Geoff who composes *Derridabase* as the transcendental or theologic programme for all of Derrida's writings, past, present or future). Thus 'truth' for Augustine is a truth that is *made*, and his contemplation of confession prompts Derrida to think of it as an act that acquires **performative** force and value, in that it transforms the condition of the subject and consequently the very 'meaning' of what is confessed. In the spirit of this radical inventiveness of 'truth', *Circumfession* testifies to the irreducible possibility of **fiction** as that which opens up the domain of what we would call **testimony**. Thus, instead of giving in to the fantasy of writing with the syringe rather than the pen, going straight to the vein, point or matter, simply letting or exposing what is 'there' beneath the skin, the text everywhere crosses confession with circum- words. Always somewhat circumspect in its apparently stark revelations (that Derrida has never stopped praying his whole life, that while writing the text he endured a sudden facial paralysis, that he recalls moments of childhood homosexuality, that he is perhaps the first philosopher willing to describe his penis), *Circumfession* circumscribes, circumvents, circles the circumference of a text that might otherwise be figured as a 'cut' (a circumcisable-exposable part). While the text reflects on the fact that Derrida has, in a sense, only ever written about circumcision (limit, **margin**, **mark**, exclusion, sacrifice, writing of or on the body, cutting/sowing in *Glas*), circumcision does not itself name the single, indivisible 'point' or 'truth' of Derrida. For, as its very text, *Circumfession* never quite circumpletes itself (to borrow Derrida's term), instead refiguring the circumcised or castrated part as a surround or ring relayed or passed into the open mouth, and from mouth to mouth (an open matrix, indeed), according to rites that in *Circumfession* are undecidably ancient, exotic-erotic and/or invented.

In many ways, this text concerns itself with what is taken away from us: Derrida's own words, cut from Bennington's *Derridabase*; the cut of circumcision, cut from **memory** itself; the inability of the dying, sightless mother to recognize her son and thus, in the present, to recollect or give him a name; the death of the mother that *Circumfession* itself 'takes' from her by anticipating the fact, too hastily seizing the last word, her last word (albeit in shrunken typeface which recalls the mother's own emaciation). In an important sense, we are all defined by what is taken from us. As Derrida once remarked in regard to *Circumfession*, an event such as birth – and, one might add, circumcision – heralds itself only in the **future**, as the unresolved **promise** of a past that was never witnessed or asked for by its recipient. Birth, circumcision, the name – in a sense, all of these are **impossible** to receive or acknowledge at precisely the point they are received. They constitute inheritance as **secret**, beyond acknowledgement or answer. (All of culture, Derrida suggests, institutes itself in this way, giving itself to those whose identity it grants by way of a sort of undercover breaking-and-entering, a theft at the origin of a **gift** which cannot be acknowledged in the present of its present.) Thus the **event** that remains to come, whether that of birth or circumcision, is *in its irresolvability* as multiple-repeatable as it is **singular**. Consequently, at one point Derrida feels compelled to say that it is (the threat of) circumcision that makes him write. While *Derridabase*, as a machine-like exposition of the system or programme that supposedly incorporates all of Derrida's thought, risks deadening the very possibility of a future (for 'Derrida' as both writer and writing), nonetheless the G. of *Derridabase*, rather like the sightless mother, will not have been able to see whatever survives – that which remains, indeed, as a sort of persistent and unprogrammable non-knowledge tied to the secret of circumcision that one inherits. As Derrida suggests, this unspoken or unspeakable secret – that which both cuts and binds – enters into the contract between Bennington (the hand from above which cuts) and Derrida (the one who continually inherits this incision from the future), as surely as it pervades the rite of circumcision itself. If Derrida himself writes with a sharpened tool so as to cut through the global-geologic domain laid out by Bennington, precisely in order to prevent the sedimentation of his thought in books that are destined to become better bound and less read, we might say nonetheless that a certain tissue continually reforms around the incision (just as it does in the Genet column of *Glas*), just as the mother's bedsores (*escarre*) reopen and scar anew, just as healing mouths open like wounds to envelop cut flesh.

Cixous, Hélène (b. 1937)   French-Algerian writer, poet, dramatist and thinker, friend of Derrida, called by him the greatest living writer in French. Published **Veils** with Derrida, and a book on him entitled *Portrait of Jacques Derrida as a Young Jewish Saint*. See **'A Silkworm of One's Own'**, **Geneses, Genealogies, Genres and Genius, H.C. for Life, That Is to Say . . .**

community   On a number of occasions, Derrida expresses his mistrust of this word, while engaging critically with its usage by a number of thinkers such as **Bataille, Blanchot** and **Nancy**. See **'I Have a Taste for the Secret'**, *On Touching*, *Politics of Friendship*.

Condillac, Étienne Bonnot de (1715–1780)   French philosopher, upon whom Derrida writes in **'Signature Event Context'** and also *The Archeology of the Frivolous*.

confession   In *Circumfession*, Derrida reflects on the insight that arises from **St Augustine**'s *Confessions*; namely, that confession construed simply as a statement of truth or the revelation of 'what is' would be wholly redundant before a God who already knows everything. Confession is therefore **performative** to the extent that, rather than merely stating something, it *does* something, producing an **event** which transforms the one that confesses as much as the status of what comes to be confessed. However, for Derrida, a performative that bases itself on the 'I can' or the 'masterable-possible' presupposes an already constituted power or capacity which remains at odds with what is eventful in a fundamental sense. Confession is therefore eventful only to the extent that its transformational enactment happens on condition of the **other**. See *Circumfession*, **event** and *Without Alibi* (in which Derrida reflects on the worldwideization of scenes of confession).

context   See **'Signature, Event, Context'**, **speech act theory**.

counter   In his later years Derrida noted the extent to which this term, and its family members, appears throughout his entire work, remarking on its always transforming repetition through and by means of a number of **graft**s: **countersignature**, which marks an original divisibility and **iterability** where one signs; contraband, a term for illicit goods smuggled across borders; *contretemps*, signalling anachrony and the inescapable structure of disjointed time as much as an unexpected or embarrassing mishap; *contrapartie* or counterpart, which introduces the question of exchange (for example the impossible **economy** of the **gift**) as much as indicating a pairing or opposition; *contre-exemple*, which implies an undismissable exception to the generality of a **law**; counter-institution, which names an effect of the deconstructibility of institutions of any kind, opening a distance or an angle between the institution and itself which indeed opens on to the possibility of an unprogrammable **future** and uncontained **other**. Both preposition and adverb, the word 'counter' and its French counterpart '*contre*' give, then, a sense of opposition, conflict, contrariety and contra-

de Man, Paul

diction, while also suggesting proximity, contact and the *vis-à-vis*. Counter, in other words, cultivates the formidable ambiguity of the word 'against', which can be found where one opposes most forcefully but also where one comes as close as can be. This 'with-against' structure of the *contre* proves significant and productive for deconstructive thought in many ways, for instance, in terms of Derrida's thinking of the impure diplomacy of **negotiation**; and indeed Derrida himself once remarked that what was at stake in all these words, as members of the *contre* family, was perhaps the most authentic relation of himself to himself – albeit an always divisible relation that must itself be thought in terms of the countersignature, the counterpart of 'me' to 'me', as well as in terms of *contretemps* and the counter-**example** one perhaps inevitably makes of oneself.

countersignature   See **counter, signature, 'Signature, Event, Context'**.

date   See especially **'Shibboleth'**.

de Man, Paul (1919–1983)   Belgian-born literary critic and theorist, member (with Derrida) of the so-called **Yale School**. The work of both on **Rousseau** established an early point of connection: the two first met in Baltimore at the famous 1966 Johns Hopkins conference on 'The Languages of Criticism and the Sciences of Man', an event which came to be seen as an important milestone in regard to Derrida's reputation and career. After de Man's death, the discovery of his wartime journalism prompted a scandal in which Derrida himself intervened, calling for patient and rigorous reading rather than hasty judgement. See **'Living On: Borderlines'**, ***Memoires for Paul de Man, Of Spirit, Psyche, The Work of Mourning, Without Alibi***.

death   See for instance ***Aporias, Archive Fever, Circumfession, Glas, H.C. for Life, That Is to Say . . ., 'I Have a Taste for the Secret', Learning to Live Finally, Specters of Marx, The Gift of Death, The Work of Mourning, Writing and Difference***.

decision, undecidability   To decide on the basis of the already decidable – that which equips us with the resources to decide, whether it be morality, duty, law or norm – is, for Derrida, less a decision in the strong sense than the discharging of a given obligation, the observance of an established convention, or the application of an existing knowledge. This leads to the paradox that a decision worthy of its name (if there is any) must take place in the midst of the undecidable. **Undecidability** – which might also be understood in terms of 'the experience of the **impossible**' – does not, then, merely paralyze decision, but instead gives it its very chance or possibility. We could say of the decision much that might be said of **justice** – its milieu is an absolute **responsibility** that must reinvent itself in **singular** fashion each time of asking, without complacent recourse to the already-possible possibilities that give us what may be considered 'decidable'. The decision is thus always urgent, in the sense that it may defer to nothing and no-one; and yet, since the decision's very conditions of possibility put it beyond what is *presently* decidable, one cannot count on the decision, or weigh its justness, in the present. One always decides too soon – every decision must intervene before all the evidence is to hand, something which we can never be sure of – and yet, to the extent that the decision cannot truly earn its name by mere recourse to the present, it also always endures a certain belatedness. Thus, one cannot reassure oneself of the decision by drawing on the conceptual apparatuses of **presence** (those which, historically, have established a somewhat virile and masterful atmosphere for the decision). Since any decision worthy of the name depends on the experience of undecidability rather than the given resources of the 'decidable', it is not of the order of the 'masterable-possible' or the 'I can'. Like responsibility, **invention, forgiveness, hospitality**, or **gift**, decision is in this sense always of the *other*. Such a challenging thought of decision is not cooked up by Derrida simply to stymie all practical decision-making or to delegitimize in advance any given decision. Rather, Derrida asks us to remember the **unconditionality** at the origin of the decision, in the interests of newly inventive and continually

deconstruction

pressing negotiations with decision-making in all its conditional forms (not least, in law, politics, and so on).

See also **Aporias**, **'Force of Law'**.

deconstruction   Where to begin, or end – if that were possible in the vicinity of this word? In 'Letter to a Japanese Friend', included in **Psyche**, Derrida discusses the problem of translating the term 'deconstruction'. The limits of translatability of the word raise questions of the stability of its meaning or definition across languages and idioms. Indeed, since deconstruction, as a 'good' if somewhat outdated French word, is also Derrida's inventive adaptation of Heidegger's German term *Destruktion*, the word is embroiled in translational issues from the very beginning. Deconstruction at once endures the limits of translatability – in other words, its various border-crossings are always marked by an untranslatable remainder – and yet it is always 'in' **translation**, calling for translation, without 'pure' origin. For Derrida, such problems do not merely affect the possibility of deconstruction's definition in a narrower sense, but they are always at stake in the very movement of deconstruction itself. There would be several ways to argue or demonstrate this. However, when we recall Derrida's suggestion that the secondarization of **writing** in relation to **speech** is constitutive of **metaphysics** itself, which prizes the spoken word as nothing other than the self-expression of living **presence**, it is hardly surprising that a deconstruction of the metaphysical tradition (that which determines **being** *as* presence) cannot but deeply question the possibility of a pure 'word' that is both totally beyond translation and never in need or demand of it. (For, surely, such a 'word' would be at once utterly impenetrable and completely transparent. For Derrida's deconstruction of the untranslatable 'word' and his thinking of translation's limits, see 'Des tours de Babel' in **Psyche** and also the entry, here, on **translation**.) Translation is not, therefore, a problem that deconstruction may overcome or dominate, but is instead one it must **affirm** and endure.

The French sense of the term implies formal, mechanical or architectural disassemblage. However, Derrida is quick to remind us that deconstruction does not restrict itself to the critical analysis of structures or systems. It does not limit its inquiry to the construction or the 'machine', or elaborate itself simply in these terms. Rather, the deconstructive thinking of **différance**, **trace**, **supplement**, **arche-writing**, etc., remains highly receptive to an asystematic reserve, a non-present remainder or heterogeneous **other** which exceeds all structures and systems even while making them possible. Deconstruction is not, therefore, as rumour would have it, negative, nihilistic or destructive, but instead it affirms an inappropriable difference, or the repressed other, as that which may yet come to transform whatever we inherit.

Alongside the question of translatability that engulfs as much as surrounds the word from the outset, the constitutive importance of this asystematic reserve for deconstruction means that it cannot be expressed in terms of a simple self-identity or, therefore, be taken as anything more than an improper term or 'nickname'. For similar reasons, deconstruction – precisely in its rigorous attention to the asystematic supplement of all systems, structures, or methodologies – is not to be confused with a plain *method* or *system* of inquiry. Nor may deconstruction be properly called a form of *analysis* or *critique*, since 'analysis' typically aims to uncover an essential ground, basis, or root, while 'critique' implies a standpoint of stable, critical distance from which the 'object' may be properly identified and evaluated as such. By way of its thinking of the supplement, trace, dissemination, *différance*, arche-writing, and so on, deconstruction everywhere puts in question both the unity and self-identity of a 'ground' and, relatedly, the possibility of a secure extraterritorial (subject) position. Thus, deconstruction isn't reducible to an *act* or to the manifestation of an independent intention, something that comes along from the outside and after the fact of the 'object' itself, since deconstruction puts a question mark against the very *grounds* of the subject and object alike. Deconstruction is already at work, then, in the play of *différance* which both constitutes and exceeds such 'grounds', operating indeed as or at the basis of every system, structure, form or identity. In seeking to affirm a radically heterogeneous and inappropriable other, deconstruction is, too, at the limits of **philosophy** (see ***Margins of Philosophy***, ***Positions***).

Deconstruction therefore puts at issue the third person present indicative and the predicative or propositional form of language (S *is* P) – another reason why the question of its own definition is also the question of definition in general.

For deconstruction as the 'experience of the **impossible**', see **'Force of Law'**, ***Negotiations***, ***Psyche***, **impossibility**. For the necessity of deconstruction's double gesture – interminable deconstruction of the existing

'Demeure: Fiction and Testimony'

field, on the one hand, and radically disruptive, deconstructive displacement of a given terrain, on the other; a strategic overturning of the hierarchies implicit in binary oppositions on the one hand, and a radical questioning of binary-oppositional thought on the other – see 'The Ends of Man' in *Margins of Philosophy*, *Positions* and *Writing and Difference*. For the undeconstructibility of **justice**, see **'Force of Law'**. See also the rest of this book.

'Demeure: Fiction and Testimony' This text responds to 'The Instant of My Death' by Maurice **Blanchot**, which it is published alongside of in English translation (2000). Blanchot's text recounts the recollections of a man who had narrowly escaped execution by a firing squad of Russian soldiers retreating through France during the last days of the Second World War. Derrida offers an extended reading of this work alongside his reflections on a letter sent to him by Blanchot a year earlier, which implies that the story is **autobiographical** and thus in some sense 'true'. This undertaking allows Derrida to make the point that, while **testimony** is conventionally expected to distinguish itself from what is merely **fictional**, the very structure of testimony implies the possibility of fiction itself, which is also that of simulation, dissimulation, perjury and **literature**.

The original occasion for this text was an event organized in 1995 by Michael Lisse under the title 'Passions of Literature'. Derrida traces the Latin origins of literature as a name and ties literature to a history of latinity which is itself far from simple, involving complicated migrations and translations. Nevertheless, this history is inextricably linked to that of Roman conceptions of **law**, citizenship, **religion**, church and state, or what Derrida terms **Christian** latinity.

Derrida explores the various meanings of 'passion' within this **Christianized** tradition. Tracing connections to the juridico-political theory of property and right, Derrida associates passion with liability, with **responsibility**, and with **confession**; but also with a suffering that cannot be mastered, with an archi-passivity before the **law** and the **other** that goes beyond the conventional distinction between passivity and activity insofar as it operates classically for human subjectivities, and with a martyrdom which, in the inimitable **singularity** of **death**, becomes allied to testimony as an unexampled making of truth on the part of an irreplaceable witness. Such testimony can only justify its name on the strength of its radical incommensurability with an informational or knowledge-based conception of truth. In its passion, testimony remains inassimilable to evidence, demonstration or proof. Its very possibility therefore goes hand-in-hand with that of perjury or lying, but also (therefore) with the possibility of fiction or, for that matter, literature. (Here, Derrida distinguishes between false and faulty witness. A contrary-to-fact statement, if unintentional, is flawed but not false testimony. The latter involves the deliberate intention to deceive, which nonetheless may never be discounted as a possibility from the confessional or **performative** making of truth beyond the realm of what is given as proveable in evidential terms: in other words, the **secret** or passion of testimony itself.) Finally, passion implies the endurance of a certain impurity, a lack of intrinsic property or essence; and thus in a number of ways passion entails suffering the fate of being unable to exist abidingly. Testimony remains irreducible to evidential proof, and thus at the always inventive point of attestation the making of truth keeps in reserve a certain indeterminable secret. The purity and reliability of witness or of autobiography is plagued by an undecidable co-possibility of truth and lies. Testimony remains structurally divided in the irreplaceable living instant which defines it by its own promise of repeatability. Literature has no essential form or character outside the function it is assigned as a right within modern democracies (the unconditional right to say everything), a right which it has no way of preserving or protecting within a stable or intrinsic abode of its own.

democracy to come Throughout his writings, Derrida continues to appeal to democracy. For instance, in his response to **September 11**, he insists that for all its flaws the **European** democratic tradition is preferable to the politics of fundamentalism (which are nonetheless complexly entwined with Western 'democratic' states), since for him the latter can have no **future**. However, here Derrida is not simply defending the given model of liberal democracy, which in a number of texts he puts into question. Rather, Derrida's notion of 'the democracy to come' appeals to classical understandings of the **demos**, as that which seeks to observe a double law of **unconditional** freedom and absolute equality. Derrida suggests that these ideals are not simply opposed to each other, but are themselves internally divided. For democratic thought, then, equality is not just the limit of freedom, but its very medium, just as in another sense

demos

equality comes to pass only on condition of a 'free' society. The double and divided **law** of the demos is, therefore, irreducible yet irreconcilable, demanding an ultimately irresolvable and thus always pressing **negotiation** between wholly non-negotiable and yet antagonistically inseparable values. In this sense, 'true' democracy is not achievable *as such*, and Derrida is frequently quick to distinguish his allusions to 'the democracy to come' from the notion of an ideal state or a utopian programme that could be projected along the horizon of a foreseeable future in which 'democracy' might at last attain full self-identity or self-presence. (Divided or ***différant*** at its very origin, democracy cannot render itself present, or render **presence** unto itself.) Rather, the **aporia** of the demos – the internecine or **auto-immune** struggle of equality and freedom – calls for unending vigilance, uncomplacent politics, highly **singular** engagement, and always inventive **decision**. Indeed, amid this enduring, vital struggle – one which cannot be resolved by recourse to constructed laws, customs or norms –we find the promise of the future itself. This is why Derrida suggests that it is democracy which, in precisely the *here-now*, grants the future its very possibility – including that of the meaning which democracy may itself yet acquire.

See also **On the Name, Politics of Friendship, Rogues, September 11**.

demos   In 'Autoimmunity', while dealing with the all-too-recent events of **September 11**, 2001, Derrida expresses his preference for the entirely flawed legacy and tradition of **European law** and its institutions over the violent strategies and discourse of fundamental Islamist terrorism. This is despite his own acknowledgement that the two are complexly inter-implicated rather than simply frontally opposed. Derrida's justification stems from his appeal to the **aporia** of the *demos*. At its classical root, the *demos* conjures and demands both the irreducible **singularity** of anyone, before any subject, citizen, state, or people, and also a fundamental equality which can only pertain in view of the law which itself defines citizenship. Thus, the *demos* confronts us with a differend or an unavoidable yet incommensurable encounter between what in human life is preserved in its incalculability (what remains 'free'), and what, at the same time, emerges on the strength of universal ratiocination or calculation according to a general law (that which establishes the measure of equality that vitally supplements freedom). Here, Derrida tells us, we find the impossible *there is* of the *demos*. This situation is impassable, and yet its impossible possibility in the here-now exposes us to what may arrive or happen; that is, to the **other** and the **event**. And, Derrida adds, to history, albeit a history we must think outside of simple causalities, teleological models or programmable expectations.

Descartes, René (1596–1650)   French philosopher, writer, mathematician and scientist. For Derrida's encounters with Descartes, see the first part of the second volume of **Right to Philosophy**, and his 'Cogito and the History of Madness' in **Writing and Difference** (where Descartes is important for Derrida's confrontation with **Foucault**).

destinerrance   A neologism of Derrida's which implies erring or wandering as always possible in embarking upon a certain destination. This may be linked to Derrida's thinking of the '**postal**' as that which rests on the constitutive possibility of non-arrival, the divisibility of the letter, or in other words an **iterability** or **dissemination** that does not guarantee full return. The word appears in a number of texts including those in the **The Post Card**, **Circumfession**, **The Other Heading**, 'Of an Apocalyptic Tone', and in 'No Apocalypse, Not Now', 'Telepathy' and 'My Chances/*Mes Chances*' in **Psyche**.

différance   See also Derrida's essay **'Différance'**, below. *Différance* is a famous neologism coined by Derrida to establish the limits of **phonocentrism**. *Différance* combines and develops a sense of differing and deferral implied by the French word '*différence*'. As homophones, however, the difference of these two terms cannot be captured by the spoken word. If *différance* means to say something (and we should question whether it 'means to say' anything at all, in the sense of an expressed intention), this cannot therefore become fully manifest in **speech**. Instead, *différance* unavoidably calls for a certain recourse to **writing**, in order to elaborate the difference (*différance*) at the origin of *différence*. Since the **metaphysics of presence** grants priority to speech as a means of full expression, *différance* thus marks the limit of logo-phonocentric thought.

For **Saussure**, the relation of the signifier to the signified is arbitrary and relational. Language is therefore construed by him as a system of differences. But, asks Derrida in his essay '*Différance*', what produces and

différance

maintains these differences? What gives possibility to the play of differing and deferring which allows signification to take place? To make such a force *signify* would be to include and present it as an element in the system which it supposedly renders possible. *Différance* is thus the non-signifying difference that traverses every **mark**, the unpresentable and unsystematizable remainder which at once constitutes and exceeds the mark's very possibility. (Derrida's **affirmation** of an originary *différance* answers those who would seek to reduce deconstruction to a mere linguisticism or crude textualism.)

While it makes conceptuality and nameability possible, *différance* cannot therefore be made to signify as a **proper name**, term or concept. If it is the play of *différance* that produces and maintains those systems of opposition (signifier/signified, speech/writing, presence/absence, nature/culture, etc.) which define the metaphysical tradition inherited by Saussure, *différance* is nonetheless not a master word, nor is it a stable heading. (Derrida frequently includes *différance* in an unmasterable chain or untitleable series that also includes the **trace**, the **supplement**, the remainder, writing, dissemination, **pharmakon**, **cinder**, and so on.) Nor is *différance* reducible to a positive – or, for that matter, a negative – term falling on one or other side of any given opposition. (Hence, *différance* is not to be construed either in terms of an original **presence** or a transcending absence. It cannot be thought to rise above the field of differences in which it is at play, any more than it might be 'properly' included within the signifying system that endeavours to reduce and contain *différance* or name it otherwise.) Since *différance* belongs properly to neither side of the opposition that it marks, Derrida is frequently given to correct the misperception that *différance* allows him merely to reverse the order of priority which puts speech before writing. Instead, *différance* calls us to rethink the relations of speech and writing in their classical sense, giving rise to an enlarged and transformed sense of writing which puts into question the metaphysics of presence.

Différance is a term that comes into play wherever Derrida reflects upon the deconstructible relations which both limit and maintain the **philosophy**, history, culture and politics of the Western tradition, a tradition constituted in terms of its metaphysical determination of **being** as presence.

See also **actuvirtuality**, **'*Différance*'**, ***Echographies of Television***, ***Positions***.

'Différance' This is the text of a 1968 lecture given to the Société française de philosophie. Derrida's neologism 'différance' demonstrates in wry fashion the limits of **speech** in attaining full and immediate self-presence or self-identity. Derrida's invented term alludes to the irreducibility of a movement both of spacing and temporalization (in *différance* both difference and deferral are at play) which in fact produces differences themselves, of the kind that **Saussure** wants to install at the heart of the arbitrary and relational identity of the sign for example. While such differences would seem to produce distinct or discernible forms (for instance, signs ripe for assured semiological analysis), the play of *différance* which engenders them obviously cannot be reduced to the stable determination of that which is 'different'; or, in other words, it cannot be unproblematically reduced to the range or field of differences which it originally makes possible. To illustrate this in other terms, the difference between two phonemes which permits them to remain operable as 'different' cannot itself be audibly expressed or positively articulated. (As Derrida suggests, Saussure indicated as much in acknowledging that language as a functioning system could never be reduced to the sum of linguistic utterances.) Each phoneme is therefore structured by that which it cannot simply include as present within its own 'identity' (intimating the fundamental impurity of so-called phonetic writing systems, as Derrida notes). *Différance* thus precedes and eludes full conceptuality since in setting up the possibility of differences or discernible distinctions it is what makes conceptuality, possible. Quite properly, one might dare to say, it lacks a **proper name**, functioning as it does to engender the very possibility of naming. And in French this difference between '*différence*' and '*différance*' cannot be heard, it must be written. Derrida's text thus obliges speech (for instance, that of the author delivering a lecture) to recite, refer or resort to **writing** in order to mark this difference at the origin of difference. While constituting its very possibility, *différance* disorders the stable functioning of the word, which in Saussurian terms involves the linkage of sound-image to concept. Put another way, the **undecidable** auditability of the 'a' of *différance* calls up the irreducible difference of writing that is, as Derrida puts it, secretly entombed within speech.

If *différance* endeavours to name – however impossibly – the play of forces which produce or maintain differences, if it somehow registers those intervals of spacing and temporalization that structure and sustain them, it cannot therefore be reduced to any of the classical oppositions which it precedes and makes possible. Thus it properly belongs neither to speech nor writing, subject nor object. It is neither simply active nor passive, sensible nor intelligible, nor can it be thought of adequately in terms of the distinction between present and absent. The classical or metaphysical construal of writing, one that deconstruction repeatedly calls into question, assumes ultimate reference to an absent presence, thus founding itself on this pair of opposing terms. In positing writing's referral to, or representation of, that which is originally and essentially existent, such a construal is, in Derrida's terms, **onto-theological**. Yet in naming the movement, play or force-field of spacing and temporalization which establishes the very medium of onto-theological categories and distinctions (presence/absence, plenitude/lack, sign/referent, apprearance/truth, body/spirit), *différance* remains beyond onto-theology and thus cannot acquire the status of a master term, a last or ultimate word. (In this sense, Derrida wants to distinguish *différance* from the ineffable God of a **negative theology**.) Instead, far from transcending the field of writing as its secret truth, *différance* always participates in a (*différantial*) chain that, for Derrida, includes the **trace, supplement, remainder**, writing, dissemination, and so on. As Derrida observes, this 'chain' would also include **Nietzsche**'s conception of '**force**' as a play of differences without original **presence** (there can be no force without the struggle between forces). It would recall effects of delay, detour and reserve in **Freud**, as well as the irreducible trace of the **other** in **Levinas**, the thinking of the difference between Being and beings in **Heidegger**, and so on. *Différance* is thus always the trace of these other traces. *Différance*, in other words, can no more properly transcend the field of differences it seems to name than it can be satisfactorily incorporated within their space. Instead, *différance* remains beyond the distinction between inclusion and exclusion that it makes possible. And since this thinking of *différance* displaces the possibility of a transcendent term outside of the general space of writing, a self-identical master word, original self-presence or ultimate truth, it denies us the stable vantage point from which to designate or comprehend this space as a fully systematic totality beyond the irreducible play of spacing.

Dissemination   This volume from 1972 includes three important texts, 'Plato's Pharmacy', 'The Double Session' and 'Dissemination', preceded by a preface, 'Outwork', which begins by informing the reader that: 'This (therefore) will not have been a book'. Less still, we are told, will *Dissemination* justifiably constitute a *collection* gathered together by some irreducible thematic coherence or simple logical consistency. Instead, by assuming the practice of **deconstruction** in all possible rigour and complexity, the writing found here serves to disorganize the always *instituted* unity of the **book** (both in its concept and its form); and, relatedly, works to disturb the supposed integrity of a philosophical discourse which always thinks itself possessed of the resources to control *as its own* the relation to an 'outside'. Thus, the movement of **différance** under way in these texts puts radically into question the process of dialectical synthesis by means of which **philosophy** classically hopes to incorporate, resolve, transcend and master *without remainder* all differences found at its margins or borders. Indeed, as Derrida points out, this very same aspiration on the part of philosophy to direct its own self-completion renders the preface, and the act of prefacing, ultimately inessential. Philosophy should have no lasting need of some preliminary or preparatory discourse. Rather, since philosophy itself names the transcendence of thought over language, concept over word, truth and **presence** over **writing** and difference, divine seed over worldly husk, a philosophy worthy of its name must be characterized by an ability either to digest and incorporate or overcome, delegitimate and thus relegate from its domain all that is merely *prefatory*. Yet since the metaphysical tradition, from Plato to Hegel to Husserl and beyond, seems bound to configure the arrival of philosophical truth in terms of a process of overcoming philosophy's 'outside' or its '**other**' – a procedure upon which philosophy in all its purity finally depends – such activity must be thought of as a moment that borders on philosophy without being philosophy 'proper'. Since this moment cannot ultimately be the moment of philosophy itself, and yet cannot be excluded from the process of philosophy's self-completion, typically it is driven into philosophical prefaces where it can be badged as an inessential outwork (a merely empirical stage or formal device) and yet where it functions, unavoidably, as the inextricable **supplement** of philosophy. (Indeed, if it is true that what philosophy names is no more nor less than the endeavour to appropriate its 'own' outside, as Derrida observes at the outset of ***Margins of Philosophy***, then philosophy will have been nothing other than the preface it always wanted to go beyond.) Through close attention to **Hegel** in particular, Derrida charts philosophy's always highly entangled and ultimately deconstructible attempts to master and resolve the problem of the preface as supplement. Indeed, it is notable that such attempts by philosophy (which could only ever construe themselves as 'on the way to' philosophy) typically occur in, and thus depend on, prefaces. Thus, as originary supplement the 'prefatory' disseminates itself on or across all borders, undoing the very possibility of a purely philosophical representation of the text (or divine 'Book') of metaphysics.

This, too, is the relation of 'Outwork' to *Dissemination* as that which '(therefore) will not have been a book'. 'Outwork' (indeed, the 'prefatory' in general) is thus something like the **pharmakon** treated in 'Plato's Pharmacy': at once medicine and poison, a supplement that may be both remedial and toxic, a 'good' and 'bad' drug at once. 'Plato's Pharmacy' closely reads the *Phaedrus*. Here, we find **Socrates** on a rare excursion beyond Athens's walls. Or rather, more tellingly, he travels to the city's borders, limits or margins. There, in the company of Phaedrus, Socrates discusses a written speech by the sophist Lysias. The manuscript of the work is concealed under Phaedrus's cloak. This furtively kept resource is a dangerous supplement. Phaedrus has not learnt the speech by rote, since he desires instead to convince Socrates of his ability to reconstitute and weigh its reasoning without recourse to mechanical memorization. However, the precedence of living philosophical '**speech**' over 'writing' to which this gesture aspires threatens to unravel in the concealing folds of Phaedrus's garment, and indeed in the very text of *Phaedrus* itself. (Even writing in its possibly 'good' sense as an aid to living **memory** always risks the 'bad' possibility of encouraging mechanical reference to written inscriptions, and thus a sort of forgetfulness bordering on somnambulance, so that this potentially remedial distinction between 'good' and 'bad' would remain susceptible to the very logic of the *pharmakon*. 'Good' writing, indeed, could only inscribe itself by borrowing from the resources of its 'bad' sibling. Thus, Plato's impossible *dream*, as Derrida calls it, of a memory without supplement – that is, without sign – itself demonstrates the feebleness of this distinction between 'bad' and 'good' writing. For Derrida, Plato's is a sleeper's dream, one not awake to the abyssal grounds of its vision.)

As Socrates would have it, then, the written text of the sophist Lysias may be represented as a drug which has lured him, the philosopher of

logos, from the Athenian polis. If there is to be staged a trial of writing, however, this proceeds not directly but through the consideration of a myth. (Since the condemnation of writing's impurity and inferiority in relation to true living knowledge might be thought of as a founding gesture of philosophy, this recourse to mythic retelling acquires an ironic significance, as for that matter does the use of the **metaphor** which links the book to the drug. Indeed, by failing to question more generally the use of myth and metaphor which powerfully assists its arguments, philosophy falls into the very trap of unthinking repetition which establishes the grounds for its own condemnation of writing. Thus the *pharmakon* seeps or leaks across the border: myth and metaphor are, like the *pharmakon*, both supplementing aid and self-administered poison, indeed, sleep-inducing drug. Yet they are also that which allows speech, even of the Socratic variety, to become a heady concoction. Whence the significance of Socrates's death by drinking poisonous hemlock.)

At the banks of the river Ilisus, Phaedrus retells the tale of Orithyia, brought to the water's edge by Pharmacia, only to be carried off by Boreas. Pharmacia, as Derrida observes, is also the common noun which signifies the administering of the *pharmakon*. Thus, Pharmacia as a figure of virginal purity and healthful promise also brings death. As undecidably both life-giving remedy and deathly poison, the *pharmakon* affiliated with her name is not to be considered a simple substance or essence, but is instead characterized by an untranslatable self-difference at its origin. Thus, it cannot be reduced to a philosophical proposition or concept, but instead works its remedy/poison in the folds of philosophy's garments, indeed in the very lining of philosophy's self-enfoldedness. For Derrida, it is this untranslatability or ambivalence of the *pharmakon* that is wrestled with throughout the *Phaedrus*. For to progress the dialogue in the context of the question of the written text of the sophist, Socrates retells the Egyptian myth of Theuth, who presents the god-king Thamus with the **gift** of writing. Thamus, here the father figure of living speech, the one who upholds *logos* with his very presence, receives this gift most warily as itself a *pharmakon*. (Writing, for Thamus, is merely a technical and auxiliary means of representation, a lifeless husk or monument in relation to living speech, a bastard son outside the family 'proper'.) However, the familial metaphor which establishes the paternity and thus the power of logos is itself a dangerous supplement, for it implies that the power of speech as a pure expression of living presence emanating from a god-king who is without, above or beyond writing is itself deeply dependent on the family metaphor in which it is enfolded. A metaphor, indeed, enfolded in a myth – (difference) found at the paternal origin of Western logos. Difference – call it *pharmakon*, supplement, trace, *différance*, writing – which therefore produces the entire text of metaphysics; or which concocts the 'pharmaceuticals' of the Western tradition in the deep recesses of a backroom or background that Derrida is tempted to call a pharmacy. This 'pharmacy' – which, despite its best efforts, Plato's *Phaedrus* cannot dominate, master or control – is also something like a theatrical scene in which the brewing of potions vies with a staging of the errant festivities of life-death; the spirit, the seed, the semen and the drug, overspilling themselves into the other.

The two remaining texts in the volume take their cue from the work of individual authors. 'Dissemination' offers an extended reading of Philippe Sollers's *Numbers*. The textual and typographical complexity of Derrida's essay, along with his continued experimentation with citational practice, once more puts the question of writing, and of **literature**, to the field of concepts which give rise to a thematic interpretation of texts. Here, in particular, Sollers's putting into play of certain numerical, algebraic or arithmetical figures – as sources of enumeration – provides the occasion for a striking deconstructive performance on Derrida's part. 'The Double Session', meanwhile, opens with a single page on which **Mallarmé**'s short prose work *Mimique* appears inset into a passage excerpted from **Plato**'s *Philebus*. This interposition inaugurates anew the encounter between a **metaphysics** of 'truth' of the Platonic stripe, and the issue of the poetic, with which Platonism classically deals by way of censure or exclusion. In particular, Derrida's reading locates in *Mimique* the question of mimesis. In its traditional concept, of course, mimesis has helped to order philosophy's typically pejorative attitude to poetry, literature or the arts. Here, mimesis is always understood ontologically, in terms of reference to a more original presence, being, reality or truth. However, in the process of conjuring up a mime drama, Mallarmé's *Mimique* for Derrida does nothing other than *mime* the discourse of mimesis exemplified by the text from *Philebus*, to the point where it fabricates a simulated version which powerfully resists assimilation to the concept of mimesis proposed by Platonic doctrine (for the mime mimes nothing but the mimetic itself, and thus refers itself to no imitated 'truth' or presence), while at the same time pointing to the fragility of the very distinction between mimesis and (its) mimicry. The two are, in other words, held apart by the most slender of veils: one scene of writing inscribed within the (folds of the) other. Indeed, Derrida shows how Plato's conception of mimesis itself operates on the basis of a certain non-self-identicality. Mimesis, in its Platonic sense, is marked by an internal division between that which conceals 'truth' with its false likeness, and that which unveils, reveals, refers to, relifts and relieves 'truth' itself. Thus, the very concept of mimesis in Plato duplicates or repeats itself – *writes* itself – in an ambivalent and always supplementary way.

For Derrida, Mallarmé's text itself gives us a name for the slender veil as an always deconstructible separation: the **hymen**. Such a hymen not only divides and connects at once Plato and Mallarmé, as exemplary names for the age-old confrontation between philosophy and the arts more generally, but asks for its deconstructibility to be read back into the entire field of conceptual distinctions on which mimetic discourse is classically founded: those that determine our understanding of the relationship between the original and the copy, the signified and the signifier, the referent and the sign, literature and truth. Thus, perhaps like the folds of Phaedrus's cloak, the hymen envelops what it partitions (hence it 'joins' the 'series' without any 'proper' or master term: *différance*, trace, supplement, *pharmakon*, etc.) 'The Double Session' is itself divided into two adjoining parts, the second of which enfolds beyond *Mimique* the more general text of Mallarmé within this deconstructive thinking, reading or writing of the hymen. Here, Derrida shows how, by remaining irreducible to thematic interpretation and commentary (that which, in the last instance, hopes to unveil 'meaning'), Mallarmé's writing retains its deconstructive power.

For **dissemination**, see also **graft**.

— E —

Echographies of Television   This volume includes the text of a filmed interview with Bernard Stiegler, conducted on 22 December 1993. Derrida begins by asserting his right of inspection over the images and text prior to publication, not because he suffers from an illusory sense of some possible control which may ultimately be imposed on his part, but because this very principle – rather like that of an **unconditional hospitality** in relation to its conditional version – clarifies the task of analyzing and transforming the conditions of image production and media presentation today. This interview explores the question of the rise of new media, tele-technologies and **technicity**, on a number of fronts. The discussion investigates the extent to which these technologies may transform the history, politics and accessibility of national archives – which also raises the question of citizenship, rights, the nation, the state and the politics of cultural **memory** in a certain situation of transition. (For Derrida, one inherits in the **archive** not a preconstituted stock or store, but precisely a responsibility to the **future**, a chance and injunction to testify to the possibility of inheritance itself, which must therefore be inventive rather than conservative, calling for unexampled decision rather than mere preservation. These questions of inheritance, archive, and indeed the changing legacy of print culture are variously addressed in 'The Principle of Reason', **Archive Fever**, **Paper Machine** and **Geneses, Genealogies, Genres and Genius**.) The concepts, practices and ideals associated with a certain heritage of the 'national' are not alone affected by the development of tele-technologies since, as Derrida suggests, the much-needed transformation of international **law** may be brought about through developing newly modified concepts of the city, nation or state amid changing socio-economico-technological conditions. Derrida and Stiegler examine the questionable notion of broadcasting 'live' or in 'real time' (the 'live' and the 'real' are always already conditioned by tele- or technical effects), while also exploring the specific impact such ideas and assumptions may have on contemporary human perception and experience, let alone ideology and politics. The question is raised of whether or not a protectionist stance on the part of France against worldwide market forces (the so-called cultural exception) works in the interests of less mediocre cultural productions and, for that matter, democracy, free expression and a worthwhile public sphere. Derrida is reluctant to decide between the cultural exception and the market (a national policy of protectionism will hardly defeat **global** capital, for instance), preferring instead a less simple negotiation among the always-divided borders that not only separate France from the United States, say, but which also disrupt the supposed self-identity of each territory or concept (whether that of the nation or of the market). The question of television and tele-technologies is also linked to a **democracy to come** that is not reducible to established concepts of citizenship, territory or state-domination, but which instead finds its opportunity, perhaps, in a more dislocated topolitics (in this interview, Derrida admits some sympathy with the adage that totalitarianism cannot long survive beyond a certain development of the telephone network), albeit one that can equip itself to address the tormented desire for the 'at home' which gives rise to resurgent nationalisms and fundamentalisms of all sorts. Disputing the idea of a technological **community** as implying too great a degree of homogeneity, Derrida asks instead how technology is *shared*, allowing this usage to resonate with the work of Jean-Luc **Nancy**. This sharing, insofar as television is concerned, combines antagonistically the experience of near global distance with an intrusive kind of intimacy in the home, an **exappropriating** proximity to the other within-without oneself. Television is also the experience of a 'presentification' which nonetheless seems infinitely repeatable. The allied topics of film, photography and the spectrality of a living-dead, singular-repeatable image are addressed near the end of the interview (Derrida also talks of his viewing preferences, which include the religious programmes televised in France on a Sunday morning), and indeed the question of the **spectre** leads back towards Derrida's book on a Marx still to come (***Specters of Marx***). It is also in this volume that Derrida evokes the Rodney King trial in Los Angeles in 1991–92 in order both to distinguish **testimony** from the informational order of knowledge associated with evidence (the videotape of King's beating was accepted as evidence but not testimony, which had to be given by the film-maker himself), and to reflect on the inextricable relation of testimony – as always given, on a promise, in the living present – to a discourse, language or grammaticality which permits testimony's repeatability and thus disturbs its purity in regard to the technical domain. (Alongside this argument we can put another: the film or photograph may seem to improve the chances of reliable authentification, but at the same time constitute technical fabrications which therefore risk increasing a certain margin of doubt.) Furthermore, for Derrida, while an authentic reality prior to the 'technical' remains an entirely dubious notion, the 'technical' itself is not simply reducible to an object or instrument of knowledge. The origin of technology cannot be technical any more than the foundation of law might itself be considered legal or lawful, or any more than the origin of reason may be justifiably located in reason itself, so that the technological derives from an alterity which puts into question an essence or self-identity which may be objectified and thus instrumentalized.

Echographies of Television also includes part of an interview with the journal *Passages* in the same year, published under the title 'Artifactualities'. Since 'actuality' – particular insofar as it conveys a precritical sense of the 'actual' – is always conditioned in its very production by a variety of institutions, hierarchies, technologies and economies, and in general by a complex network of forces, including the state as well as national and transnational powers, an 'actuality effect' derives from what is, in actuality, very highly produced. Derrida's neologism thus includes a sense of both the artificial and the artefact as irreducible supplements of the actual. 'Actuality' in its always singular production (that is to say, one which happens each time of asking, as it were), is therefore cross-cut by effects of **différance** which call for patient thought beyond the ruse of an immediate '**present**'. The thinking of **actifactuality** therefore calls for another neologism on Derrida's part, that of **actuvirtuality**, which allows Derrida to think the complex yet inextricable relation of the virtual to the 'here-now'.

Undertaken to mark the publication of **Specters of Marx**, in this interview Derrida rethinks the possibility of the event and indeed the potential transformation of the 'political' in the face of contemporary 'actifactualities'. He reasserts deconstruction's persistent **affirmation** of the **singular** as that which in its *différance* remains irreducibly resistant to synthetic appropriation within the field of production. For Derrida, artifactuality as precisely an effect of *différance* harbours a transformative **supplement** which cannot be wholly recuperated by the information machines of today. A certain inheritance of the Enlightenment in the name of the democracy to come perhaps dwells in a future whose possibility will never have been totally dominated by these machines.

Edmund Husserl's Origin of Geometry: An Introduction   Published in 1962. See **Speech and Phenomena**.

ethics   See **Adieu, Glas, On The Name**, responsibility, **The Gift of Death, Without Alibi**.

Europe, European   See example, *Learning to Live Finally*, *Monolingualism of the Other*, *September 11*, *Specters of Marx*, *The Gift of Death*, *The Other Heading*.

event   For Derrida, an event worthy of the name must be radically **singular**, irruptive, unanticipatable and, in a certain way, beyond apprehension. An event must uncontainably overflow its own '**context**' and representation. In recounting an event, let alone attributing its meaning or significance, one must draw upon discursive and other resources that are available within an existing field. Yet to earn its name, for Derrida, the event must go beyond the realms of an already-possible possibility. (In these terms, Derrida frequently reflects on the event – if there is any – of **decision**, **invention**, **hospitality**, of the **gift**, of **forgiveness**, and so forth.) The event in its absolute singularity is thus resistant to cognitive description, critical objectification, interpretative reduction and, for that matter, 'theoretical' elaboration.

In a late text on '**A Certain Impossible Possibility of Saying the Event'**, Derrida notes the tension between this thinking of the inappropriable surprise of the event, and the extent to which today's 'information machines' produce as much as record the events with which they deal. (Recently, for instance, a Brazilian TV presenter was charged with ordering killings, then alerting his station's TV crews to ensure they were first on the scene. Such charges imply that his show was in fact behind the crimes that it reported. However, this specific example hardly does justice to the complexity of media 'productions' of events on a worldwide scale, upon which Derrida begins to reflect in his response to **September 11**. In this later essay, meanwhile, Derrida notes that such media 'productions' are all the more powerfully effective for passing themselves off as mere reporting.)

In his thinking of the event, Derrida nonetheless insists upon that which remains irreducible to media appropriation, for instance each and every single death in warfare. The absolutely inassimilable remainder of such happenings (those *différantial*, un-presentable traces which, in a sense, make them eventful) must be continually recalled, or at any rate impossibly endured, every time we seek to participate or intervene in debates about so-called 'major' events. In this sense, Derrida's arguments simply do not fit the narrative of those opponents of deconstruction who wish to associate it with some sort of glib 'postmodern' relativism or textualism. (See also, here, other entries on **technicity**, **artifactuality** and **actuvirtuality**.)

In 'A Certain Impossible Possibility of Saying the Event', Derrida reflects once more on the impossible event of invention, decision, hospitality and forgiveness. For him, **confession** is also an event to the extent that it goes beyond a mere statement of 'truth' or 'fact' (**St Augustine** asks why he must confess when God already knows everything), serving instead as a **performative** act which *transforms* both what is confessed and the one who confesses. However, a performative that bases itself on the 'I can' or the 'masterable-possible' assumes an already-given power or capacity which remains at odds with the event. Confession is eventful only to the extent that its transformative performance happens on condition of the **other**. The gift – if there is any – would be an event, too, to the extent that it would overflow any economy of exchangeable values, going beyond that which may be reckoned with or reckoned up, accounted for or acknowledged.

However, while we began by remarking the event's radical singularity, one must also note that for deconstruction the event is never simply 'pure', uncontaminated, or self-sufficient. Such thinking would re-tie the event to a logic of **presence**. For Derrida, the event in its irreplaceable uniqueness nonetheless marks itself only through the possibility of **re-marking**. Thus, for him, the event is iterable as much as it is singular all the way down. **Iterability** constitutes as much as it divides the event.

See also, for instance, ***Psyche***, **September 11**.

example A powerfully deciphering thinking of the logic of the example, and of the exemplarity of the example, can be found almost everywhere that Derrida engages with questions about identity, history and politics: of a nation, **France**, for example; of a continent, **Europe**, for example; of an institution, the **university**, for example; or of a discipline, **philosophy**, for example. In each of these instances, the example functions in a highly determined yet fundamentally double, equivocal fashion. On the one hand, the example gives itself as an unexceptional selection, a 'one-among-others', in order to align with and reaffirm a general or universal concept or category of which it is, precisely, a particular case. On the other, we must also ask about the very exemplarity of the example – what commends it as an example. Precisely the selection of the example implies a teleological privilege or priority determining its exemplarity. Any example truly worth its name is always in some sense the *good* example. France, Europe, the university, or philosophy all function as examples, then, in order to affirm the powerful claim of a universality that they bear within themselves. At the same time, however, the exemplarity of these examples has to do with the idea that they serve as privileged models without which the universal concept (and, indeed, the discourse of universality) would struggle to get going. Thus, for example, it is possible to show that the notion of the discipline (in both its history and its concept) is thought from the perspective of philosophy itself. Without France, we would not have the concept or history of the nation that we do. Western man is not just one example of humankind, but in many ways (about which we should be tirelessly vigilant) powerfully determines our concept of humanity. To go further, Europe can never be thought of as merely an example of a continent, since the very logic and discourse of the example exemplifies Europe itself. The example, the part, therefore turns out to be larger than the whole which supposedly allots its identity as one of a given series. In the process, of course, this situation – the very same one that grants exemplarity – disrupts the telos of the example, jeopardizing precisely the mastery or **sovereignty** of the universal claim that gives the example its prized exemplarity. Put another way, the exemplary example is without example. However, while this analysis of the example's workings encourages the utmost vigilance about the politics of universalizing claims or concepts, which perhaps inevitably exemplify themselves in very particular ways, Derrida is not just interested in remarking the deconstructibility of forms of identity which are typically determined or attributed by dint of examples that turn out to be exemplars. Instead, in inheriting its legacy – which is also that of Europe, the Enlightenment, and so forth – the exemplary or unexampled example opens on to the other of itself, gives itself in its **singularity** to the possibility of the **other**. The example without example makes possible the **event**, calling for **decision** and **responsibility**.

exappropriation Within the movement of appropriation – of taking possession or putting into 'place', of the return or coming to **presence**, of the constitution of the 'proper' and the marking of that which belongs – there is the irreducible possibility of depropriation, dislocation, **différance**, **supplementation**, **destinerrance**, **iterability**, **re-marking**, the **other**.

Thus, for instance, exappropriation enters into the structure of the **signature** and the **proper name,** but also **hospitality, invention, decision, confession**, and so forth.

— **F** —

'Faith and Knowledge: The Two Sources of "Religion" at the Limits of Reason Alone'   This text, which can be found in *Acts of Religion*, was prepared for a round-table event held at Capri in 1995. Asked by Giovanni Vattimo to devise some preliminary remarks, Derrida begins by reframing the 'question of religion' by thinking in terms of language(s) and nation(s). Furthermore, he follows a path which leads out from **Kant**'s *Religion Within the Limits of Reason Alone*, in which two types of **religion** are identified. While 'cult' religions base themselves more passively on prayer and desire ('faith'), 'moral' religion demands action in the interests of the good conduct of life ('knowledge'). In 'moral' religion, the emphasis shifts away from the historical revelation of God, and towards the harnessing of the will to moral ends. Thus, practical reason and knowledge are apparently preferred to dogmatic faith. For Kant, Christianity is the single historical example of 'moral' religion. And its effect is to conceive of and encourage moral conduct that is independent of God's revelation, presence, or indeed existence. Thus Christianity as 'moral' religion may be thought to announce the very death of God. Judaism and Islam, meanwhile, may be considered the last two monotheisms which rebel against the secularizing **Christianization** of the world. Meanwhile, within the realms of Western philosophy, **Nietzsche** and **Heidegger** are seen to question and resist the yoking together of religion and morality in the Christian tradition. In his critique of religion, **Marx**, too, is seen to complexly address the Kantian legacy, founding his critical analysis on a certain rationality that in fact belongs to the paradigm of 'moral' religion itself. In fact, Heideggerian thought is also seen by Derrida to proceed somewhat on the basis of this double bind.

Derrida takes his address as the occasion to speculate on what is to be found at the origin of this double origin of religion. In particular, he speaks of a **messianicity** without messianism, one older than all religions and all messiahs – a messianicity which opens itself, for better or worse, to the wholly **other** and to an unanticipatable and radically interruptive **future**, without first establishing for itself a horizon of expectation or grounding itself in a prophetic discourse. (One might link this messianicity to the 'yes' or '**yes, yes**' as both originary affirmation and promise, treated in texts such as 'A Number of Yes' and 'Ulysses Gramophone: Hear Say Yes in Joyce'.) Such messianicity belongs properly to none of the Abrahamic religions yet marks each of them in particular ways. The desire for **justice** rather than simply the **law** stems from this messianicity. Indeed, this basic relationship between the 'messianic' and the 'just' puts in question traditional distinctions between mysticism and reason, pre- and post-Enlightenment. Moreover, like any institution, a 'religion' founds itself on foundations that are unfounded prior to its advent or instituting instant. This is something that Derrida explains at greater length in **'Force of Law'**. Here, the law is seen to be founded neither 'lawfully' nor 'unlawfully' (for legality and illegality are possible only once the law is founded). The law thus institutes itself by means of what is in some way 'other' than itself. Likewise, the institution of Christianity as a 'moral' religion cannot be thought of in purely rational terms. The origin of this 'moral' religion of 'reason' or 'knowledge' precedes and exceeds both reason and knowledge. In similar vein, Derrida unravels the supposed distinction between the realms of religion and technology. Since they are indelibly marked by the structure of the promise, all professions of faith imply a repeatability from their very origin, and thus install a **technics** and a technical possibility, say of language (although not only of language), from the very beginning. Thus Derrida wants to analyze the ways in which religions today employ, as much as deride, technology.

Derrida links his thinking of the messianic without messianism to a discussion of **khôra**, referring us to the texts found in ***On the Name***. Khôra as that which spaces, and which thus gives place itself, is here 'located' at or as an always unpresentable, unmasterable 'origin'; a quasi-origin (like ***différance***) then, which may also be the site of intersection between the Abrahamic religions and the politico-onto-theology of the **Greek** tradition. By seeking to demonstrate the interimplication of 'faith' and 'knowledge' as two sources of 'religion' both within Christianity and at its frontiers with other faiths, Derrida asks – against the backdrop of a media-fuelled discourse on 'the return to religion' – that we rethink the distinction between fundamentalists and those who wage war on fundamentalism. This involves a rethinking of Christianity which as 'moral' religion inflicts a double (indeed, **auto-immunitary**) **violence** both upon itself and others, by violently repressing its own mystical foundations while waging war on God from the very beginning.

family   See *Dissemination*, *Glas*, *Politics of Friendship*, *Psyche*, **sexual difference**.

fiction   See *Circumfession*, *'Demeure'*, literature, *Memoires for Paul de Man*, performativity, *'Signature Event Context'*, testimony, *Without Alibi*.

force   See *'Force of Law'*. For force and form see 'Force and Signification' in *Writing and Difference*.

'Force of Law: The "Mystical Foundation of Authority"'
Found in *Acts of Religion*. The first part of this text was presented at the Cardozo Law School in 1989 for a colloquium organized by Drucilla Cornell, providing the opportunity for Derrida to address not only philosophers and literary scholars, but also representatives of what has become known as 'critical legal studies', a movement at its height in the 1980s that was influenced by perspectives in critical and post-structuralist theory. Critical legal studies wants to analyze the extent to which **law** is made and practised according to relationships of politics and power, with the express aim of actively intervening in this politics.

Derrida begins his lecture by recalling that Kant himself understood force and enforceability as essential to the very concept of law (or, more precisely, law as the exercise of **justice**) rather than as a secondary phenomenon occurring merely at the point where law is applied or upheld. However, Derrida wishes to distinguish somewhat between justice and law.

Law cannot ground itself lawfully. The law in general cannot rationally assert its own legal basis, since that which produces or originates the law must by definition pre-exist both the 'lawful' and the 'unlawful'. Thus, one can neither say that law is wholly legitimate nor, for that matter, simply illegitimate. In fact, the latter proposition would seem only to reinforce an implied ideal of 'legitimacy' (which may therefore be reasserted only as a political strategy or expediency, not as a rational ground). Rather, law is simply forceful or violent at its origin, in that it establishes – or, rather, *constructs* – its authority in circumstances where some prior authorization cannot justly be claimed. Put another way, the law's foundations are, precisely, *unfounded*. For Derrida, this is what may be detected in Pascal's reference to 'the mystical foundation of authority'.

Here, then, **deconstruction** has to confront a significant complication. For while such law is *de*constructible through and through, it cannot therefore be rationally challenged from a perspective that would assert the law's 'illegitimacy', at least not without the risk of repeating the very same gesture that founds such law in the first place: namely, the mystification of force as 'authoritative' or 'legitimate'. In other words, deconstruction cannot simply 'oppose' itself to law as unfounded in its very founding, if by such 'opposition' is meant a wholly differentiated standpoint with its own firm foundation. Thus, in acknowledging the inherent force of law (including that of its own), deconstruction does not try to effect law's 'illegitimation' or delegitimation. Instead, Derrida seeks to contrast law with justice.

However 'just' laws may appear to be, one obeys them on the strength of their supposed authority. Law calls us to comply with an already constructed context, an 'authoritative' setting, a prescribed rule, a predetermined machinery, an established order or programme, a settled contract, a given set of rights, and so forth. To act lawfully may seem to be the result of a responsible **decision**, but since in so doing we merely apply a given rule, the law *as* law calls for no decision or **responsibility** worthy of its name. Even where justice is apparently enshrined in law, the possibility of the 'just' decision radically wanes where law upholds or enforces itself. In dutifully observing the law, the most active and vigilant responsibility to 'justice' is threatened. Derrida wants to think of justice in this way, then, in order to wrest it somewhat from a law that is always *in* **force**, and thus constitutive of particular forces and interests.

How does justice differ from law? In contrast to the law – which, *as* law, always prescribes – one cannot predetermine or prejudge justice. One cannot calculate it in advance. Indeed, one can account for it after the fact only to the extent that it remakes (itself as) law, at which point the instant of justice – if there is any – has passed, having been incorporated into law itself. In these terms, justice is, precisely, unrepresentable and, thus, never fully or 'justly' **present**.

Put differently, one cannot 'count' on justice. There is no justice without the decision, yet no decision can be assuredly just. Each decision must be radically interruptive, intervening in an immediate and urgent fashion, without having the limitless knowledge that might truly justify it. (Indeed, full knowledge might also ruin the 'just' decision, since a wholly informed judgement would presumably provide itself with all the reassurances one expects from mere dutifulness, or irresponsibilizing 'law').

If one cannot 'count' on justice, this also means that it cannot be thematized or objectified as such. Justice cannot be construed or constructed from the standpoint of a self-same knowledge or a stable and reliable practice. In contrast to the legal basis that is in force in allowing one to say 'I am lawful', one may never be sure whether 'I am just' is indeed justly said. For justice does not itself give us the means to know this. Justice will never shelter us from responsibility and decision in the way law may do. Thus, it may be that (for deconstruction) the continual appeal to justice, precisely as it goes unanswered, prompts anew the very possibility of the 'just'.

'Unrepresentable' and 'incalculable' justice thus gives rise to **aporias**, or to the experience of the **impossible**. Indeed, Derrida argues that there is no justice without the ordeal or call of impossibility. To remain within an already possible possibility is to remain in some sense within the 'law', which paradoxically allows no real possibility worthy of its name. Radical possibility is thus what is promised by the impossibility of justice.

Justice and law are heterogeneous, and yet as Derrida acknowledges they are interimplicated and must be negotiated as such. For if force without justice is plainly unacceptable, and if law must by definition enforce itself *generally* at the price of countless singular injustices, nevertheless justice cannot be rendered without force of law. Justice must, in a very deep sense, turn away from the law. However, in so doing it must give itself this very law beyond the law, and to be worthy of its name must result in decisions which inevitably reinterpret, reinvent and reinstitute the law. Yet the 'just' decision, if there is any, must be carefully understood. If there is no justice without decision, equally there is no decision worth its name that is simply of the order of the masterable-possible, or the 'I can' (thus, of a subject or a 'self'). For such a 'decision' would remain too closely tied to the already possible possibility which we might call 'law'. Justice and decision, then, must be thought of in terms of the **other** to come. Before all calculation, symmetry, or economical exchange, justice must come from the other, and be owed to the other.

Whereas law is constructed and is therefore deconstructible, for Derrida such justice is unconstructable and thus undeconstructible. This is also a way to affirm its indestructibility. Yet **unconditional** justice calls on us to rethink and reinvent the conditional forms of the law. Its very incalculability demands calculation or **negotiation**. Deconstruction thus intervenes between undeconstructible justice and the deconstructibility of law in the interests of just such a negotiation, and for a **future** still to come.

The second part of the essay was distributed at the Cardozo Law School colloquium and then presented at an event held in 1990 at UCLA on 'Nazism and the "Final Solution": Probing the Limits of Representation'. This section deals with Walter **Benjamin**'s 'Critique of Violence' (*Zur Kritik der Gewalt*). As Derrida points out in the first part of his text, *Gewalt* translates not merely as **violence** but also legitimate power. In Benjamin's very title, then, we are confronted with an inextricable connection between institutional authority, notably in its legal or state form, and violence itself. Derrida argues that Benjamin's text emerges within a Judaic tradition that makes a distinction between mythical violence, which stems from a **Greek** legacy devoted to preserving the law, and divine (Jewish) violence, which seeks the law's destruction. For Derrida, however, we must acknowledge upon reading Benjamin's text that institutional 'violence' – as that which preserves the law – serves also to *repeat* the instituting violence that founds the law. In Derrida's terms, the violence inscribed at the origin of law is at once **singular** and **iterable**. Its very repeatability is, indeed, an essential part of the singular event of founding, which, far from being purely self-contained and unique, institutes or *posits* according to the structure of the **promise**, or the 'to come'. Thus, the two sorts of violence (mythical and divine) are more complexly intertwined than they may appear at first glance. Indeed, via Benjamin, Derrida shows how the right to strike, notably as it occasions the possibility of a general strike, exposes the extent to which violence re-erupts within the law: the state legally sanctions the right to strike as effectively a violence against (the violence of) the state; yet effectively sanctions, too, its right to react violently against the perceived excesses of a general strike. Indeed, paradoxically, the strike may be deemed revolutionary – and thus worthy of 'legitimate' violent suppression – precisely to the extent that it aims to found a new law. But only this new law in its apparent 'legitimacy' will retrospectively authorize or justify the revolution. Thus the whole history of the law is nothing other than the story of ceaseless violence, of an interminable play of forces, inscribed in or on the law itself. Reading Benjamin, Derrida reflects on the police as an unlocatable or '**spectral**' presence, inhabiting the border between the two types of violence he seeks to analyze. The police are responsible for law enforcement but, more and more, they undertake to *force* the law. For Derrida, the police increasingly arrogate the right to force the law (i.e., to interpret, determine or remake it), frequently just where they claim to be engaged in enforcing it. Indeed, this may be a structural feature of the police as a modern phenomenon: the police progressively corrupt from within the very law that in fact projects its intertwined forms of violence precisely via the forces of the police.

Derrida reads Benjamin's essay in terms of the interwar critique of bourgeois liberal democracy, its parliamentary form and law, indeed its representative politics and representational (or principally instrumental) language. Yet this critique crops up not only in Marxist or leftist thought but also, of course, in the politics of the far right and in fascist and totalitarian language and rhetoric. In Benjamin's essay, and perhaps in this critique more generally, liberal democracy is scorned for its refusal to acknowledge its own founding violence and thus its violent foundations. Liberal democracy may thus be seen as a hypocritical compromise. Derrida, however, worries that Benjamin's evocation of a divine violence that might annihilate existing, hypocritical law is too 'messianico-Marxist' and 'archeo-eschatological', indeed that it draws near to a holocaustal form of thinking which, of course, gave rise to the discourse and history of the very 'worst'. As he had done in 'Interpretations at War: Kant, the German, the Jew', Derrida seeks to analyze the Judeo-German 'psyche', postulating densely interwoven links between German 'Jewish' and 'non-Jewish' thinkers (if such a distinction were possible): Cohen, Buber, Rosenweig, Scholem, Adorno, Arendt, **Husserl**, **Heidegger**, Schmitt and Benjamin. He particularly wants to distinguish deconstructive negotiation and affirmation from Benjaminian and Heideggerian forms of 'destruction'.

forgiveness   For Derrida, to forgive only what is deemed forgivable amounts to following a pre-established morality, duty or norm, and thus constitutes a largely prescribed response determined by an already existent field of possibility. While in many cases such forgiveness is doubtless preferable to its opposite, for Derrida the deeper paradox of forgiveness is that, to be truly worthy of the name, forgiveness must not be content with forgiving the forgivable, but must instead test itself against the unforgivable, venturing itself against that which cannot be forgiven. The '**impossible**' or the **aporetic** thus establishes the fundamental setting for forgiveness in the stronger sense. And yet, because it is only when forgiveness is confronted with the unforgivable that it has the chance to truly earn its name, the unforgivable establishes not only the *limit* but precisely the *condition of possibility* of forgiving.

Forgiveness worthy of the name must therefore be absolutely **singular**, radically **inventive** and strongly asymmetrical or aeconomical in relation to given morality, good conscience, or dischargeable obligation. It cannot be reduced to a meaning or knowledge that might be stably reproduced or deployed in advance by an **ethics**, **law**, culture, or **philosophy**. Nor can it ever finally resolve, achieve or **present** itself *as such*, in the sense that a concluded forgiveness would always have transformed the unforgiveable into the forgiveable, at which point forgiveness would not culminate in itself but in fact begin to disappear from view. In its fundamental sense, therefore, forgiveness is not of the order of the 'masterable-possible' or the outcome of an indivisibly **sovereign** intentionality. Instead, like **responsibility**, forgiveness remains tied to the **secret**, the other, the non-present remainder.

In thinking of forgiveness in this way, Derrida is not seeking simply to paralyze every practical act of forgiving. Nor, in some poorly calculated manner, does he aim to delegitimize in advance all expressions of forgiveness by holding up an unrealizable ideal. Rather, since Derrida sees the Western religious and cultural heritage as inextricably divided between the **unconditional** and conditional senses of forgiveness, he seeks to remind conditioned forgiveness (which typically manifests itself as an expression of mastery or sovereignty) of the unconditionality that abides at its always divided origin. For Derrida, singular – and, thus, ultimately unjustifiable and unforgivable – **negotiations** must always take place between unconditional forgiveness on the one hand (which, as Derrida recognizes, must express itself in conditional forms if it is not to remain mere piety), and conditional forgiveness on the other (which cannot claim anything of its name without reference to the unconditional sense of forgiving).

See also **'On Cosmopolitanism and Forgiveness'**.

'Fors'   See *The Work of Mourning*.

Foucault, Michel (1926–1984)   French philosopher and cultural historian. For Derrida and Foucault, see especially 'Cogito and the History of Madness' in *Writing and Difference*, and his essay on Foucault in *Resistances of Psychoanalysis*. See also *The Work of Mourning*.

France/French   See for instance *Echographies of Television, Learning to Live Finally, Margins of Philosophy, Memoires for Paul de Man, Monolingualism of the Other, Paper Machine, Right to Philosophy, Without Alibi*.

Freud, Sigmund (1856–1939)   Founder of psychoanalysis. For Derrida on Freud, see for instance *Archive Fever*, **'Différance'**, *Psyche, Resistances of Psychoanalysis, The Post Card, Writing and Difference*. See also **psychoanalysis** and 'phallogocentrism' in **logocentrism**. See also **technicity**, *The Ear of the Other, The Work of Mourning*.

friendship   See *Memoires for Paul de Man, On the Name, Politics of Friendship*, **promise**, *The Work of Mourning*.

Fukuyama, Francis (b. 1952)   American philosopher and political economist. See *Specters of Marx*.

future   Despite rumours to the contrary, **deconstruction** seeks not simply to dwell upon, deride or dismantle the past, whether that of a philosophical tradition, literary canon or cultural heritage. Instead, deconstruction endeavours to **affirm** that which *remains* to be inherited, that which may yet come for a **future** still to be determined. Derrida's thinking of **différance**, **trace**, **supplement**, **arche-writing**, etc., insists upon a non-present remainder that traverses every **mark**, constituting the chance of each text, every term, value or identity, indeed every possibility. Since this *différance* is irreducible to (although also constitutive of) **presence**, it overflows what may be deemed 'present', in the 'present'. Thus, in precisely the 'here-now', deconstruction opens itself to traces of the **'other'** still to arrive. One name for such an 'other' is '**the democracy to come**', which in *Politics of Friendship* begins perhaps to arise on the hither side of the fraternal model of politics that we inherit. (The democracy to come, however, is irreducibly non-self-identical. It is divided at its origin between the incalculable demands of freedom and equality. Thus 'democracy' cannot be projected in terms of an eventual full presence. Nevertheless, to the extent that this internal division constantly puts the question of democracy before us, the always futural dimension of democracy in fact spurs and renews democratic thinking and engagement in the 'here-now'.) In exposing itself to 'the experience of the **impossible**' (**forgiveness** of the unforgivable, welcome of the unwelcomable, uninventable **invention, decision** at the point of radical undecidability, and so on), deconstruction calls on us to rethink possibility itself, beyond the domain of what is already possible and thus, in a sense, no longer possible in fundamental terms. Once more, then, Derrida's work places great emphasis on the future – an unpredictable, unprogrammable future – as that which deconstruction seeks to affirm. Moreover, the **singularity** of each literary **event** so prized by Derrida (the singularity, that is, of an exceptional inscription, signed irreplaceably on an unrepeatable date) is possible only on the strength of the text's possible ***re-marking***: that is, by way of an **iterability** which transforms as it repeats. Thus, each singular 'text' awaits the **signature** and event of a reading to come, one that *will have been dated* in just the same way as the 'original' it is given to read.

For the psychoanalytic archive as that which remains to come, see ***Archive Fever***. For the futural remains of Marxism, see ***Specters of Marx***. For invention and the future, see ***Psyche***. For friendship, memory, mourning, the promise and the future, see ***Memoires for Paul de Man***, ***Politics of Friendship***, ***The Work of Mourning***. See also the **democracy to come**, in conjunction with ***Politics of Friendship***.

— G —

Geneses, Genealogies, Genres and Genius In May 2003, Derrida spoke at the Bibliothèque nationale de France (BNF) in celebration of Hélène **Cixous**'s donation to the library of an archive of letters, notebooks and dream journals. This volume, originally published the same year, contains the text of this event.

Just as any **testimony** worth its name must maintain its **secret** at precisely the point it is weighed as reliable attestation, keeping in reserve that which is radically heterogenous in relation to 'evidence' or 'proof', so for Derrida this encrypted writing by Cixous smuggles in as contraband precisely what is unavowable, even as it is being avowed in Derrida's own text. The library is thus radically altered through the encryption of this address constituted by the Cixous **archive** as unavowable-avowed, hence as the unreadable-readable or as an unsaveable-saving. Speaking thus – and yet speaking secretly – beyond its own depositing, storage or potential immobilization, Derrida tells us that the Cixous archive inhabits the theatricalized space of the psyche, engaging and disturbing the **other** so that its scenography (its unsaveable-saving) becomes that of the unconscious. Cixous's texts engage the **memory** and pervade the dreams of the true guardian of the archive, who, not unlike the faithful guardian alluded to by Derrida in 'The Principle of Reason' (see **Right to Philosophy**), must double-keep what they do not have and what is not yet. This is nothing other than the possibility of the 'to come', since to keep without a certain double keeping, to merely defend, conserve, encircle or enclose, is to risk the greatest infidelity, just as those who blindly assert the principle of **reason** badly negotiate a tautological circle or barrier on the one side (reason's basis or justification is . . . reason) and what is abyssal on the other (if reason cannot ground itself in reason without risking irrationalism or question-begging, what is its foundation?).

The faithful guardian must therefore observe a certain strategic rhythm, something like a 'blink', neither maintaining a hard-eyed watch over reason's transparent good sense, nor falling into blind dogmatism, but opening and closing the eye in (viewless) view of a certain barrier and a certain abyss. Such a double keeping demands of the faithful guardian that he or she gather in a certain way of non-gathering, a gathering of what cannot be gathered, a winking eye cast over what cannot be brought to light. And since the Cixous archive addresses the library's 'unconscious' as much as its double-keeping guardian (who must avow the unavowable, keep beyond keeping), its **gift** implies a certain transformation of the BNF itself, intruding on or prizing open that metonymic series of which Derrida speaks in **Paper Machine** – thesis, book, library, institution, law, statute, state deposit, nation state – in order to expose and commit the Library to the '**unconditional**', beyond or in spite of the 'national'. This is the donation's dangerous, incomprehensible, unmasterable gift, a powerless-powerful other in (excessive) relation to the forms of **sovereignty** encrypted within that metonymic series to which *Paper Machine* alludes. Elsewhere, Derrida might be tempted to risk the name of **literature** in regard to such a gift.

Derrida insists that the Cixous corpus, as imagined thus, therefore remains inestimably vaster than the library that is supposed to contain it. This strange relation between the part and the whole, spoken of at length by Derrida elsewhere, exposes the BNF not only to its supposed 'outside' or to new and unfinishable forms of international interdisciplinary research, but to the 'unconditional' beyond sovereignty or state, an unconditional exteriority which resides at the heart of the archive.

The extensive problematic of the archive into which we are thrown by *Geneses, Genealogies, Genres and Genius* (the subtitle of which is 'The Secrets of the Archive') also reintroduces the question of computerization and electronic media, one that Derrida tackles with great rigour in **Archive Fever** and *Paper Machine*. Will the **technological** innovations associated with Derrida's own generation keep the archive endlessly open while causing paper to get burnt up by something like a death drive? As Derrida observes, Cixous always writes by hand, using a pencil or pen rather than a machine or machine-tool such as a typewriter or a word processor. This, for Derrida, is exceptional today, and of vital significance for the question of the archive: what, for example, might be the relation between a hand-writing and a dream-writing?

This text includes an extended reading of Cixous's *Manhattan*.

On Derrida and Cixous, see also Derrida's **H.C. for Life, That Is to Say . . .** Here, their relationship comes down to a question of 'taking sides' between life and **death**. While Derrida admits to being drawn to death's side, he nonetheless strongly affirms Cixous's siding with 'life'. Since such

gift 63

'siding' remains an act of faith, however, one stakes one's very life on such an **affirmation**, so that death's irreducible possibility remains a condition of 'life' long before the end, indeed from the very beginning. Death is encrypted within life, and once more the question of crypts within the Cixous archive is brought to bear.

genre   See 'The Law of Genre' in *Acts of Literature*.

Genet, Jean (1910–1986)   French writer and, in later life, political activist. See ***Glas***, ***Negotiations***.

German(ness)   See especially ***Of Spirit***, ***Psyche***.

Geschlecht   See ***Psyche***.

gift   For Derrida, a thinking of the gift, notably in its relationship to concepts and practices of economy and exchange, remains a significant task for **deconstruction**. In the Western tradition, **religion**, **metaphysics** and culture conspire to elevate the gift as an ideal expression of a **sovereign** power, whether that of God, king, master or state; and indeed a thinking of the connections between sovereignty and gift remains indispensable at or as a thinking of origins. (We might note the near unavoidable recourse to an economic language in the earliest description of these relations here; a language to which, for Derrida, the gift remains fundamentally resistant, however embroiled it may become.) Gift economies – the specific cultural, ideological and political formations that draw centrally on a concept and practice of giving rather than on the idea of a planned or market economy – arise in a number of historical contexts, and arguably every economy, even the most market-driven, displays some sort of agonized debt to or ambivalent concern with the gift as a nevertheless **impossible** and unreclaimable point of origin. Of vital importance to a historico-philosophical thought of the gift is the legacy of a **Christian** notion of the unrepayable giving of God's loving (self-) sacrifice (although the intersection of Christianity with other religious traditions of gift-giving calls for careful analysis), producing an irredeemable debt that for **Nietzsche** creates an historical culture of *ressentiment*. One might also think, in terms of an array of historical models and legacies, of the significance of patronage and favour for Renaissance kingship and early modern aristocratic culture, the politics of public charity in the nineteenth century, and the practice of humanitarian aid today, all of which intersect complexly with the emergence of those conditions which give rise to a capitalist economic system in its various stages of development.

In ***Given Time*** (which also reflects on Baudelaire's short tale, *Counterfeit Money*), Derrida dwells on Marcel **Mauss**'s *The Gift* as a seminal analysis of gift-giving in archaic societies. While it is the very concept of the gift in Mauss which moves social thought from bare economic rationality towards a consideration of the symbolicity of this rationality within the context of 'total social fact' (a transition which itself makes possible the interdisciplinary field of the contemporary humanities, and which also helps explain the critical *interest* taken in the gift by an array of notable thinkers and writers including **Levi-Strauss**, **Bataille** and Baudrillard), Derrida suggests that Mauss in fact speaks of anything but the gift, both when he locates the gift's essential meaning in terms of exchange rituals that establish collective relations within a generalized economy, and indeed when he gives an *account* of the gift in his work according to the very same logic or rationality of exchange: *The Gift* for the gift.

Put another way, the conditions of possibility of the gift require careful thought, particularly since, as Derrida notes, these conditions are also those of the gift's impossibility. For a gift to be reciprocated, as is generally customary and often furtively required, implies the gift's re-entry into the economic domain. Nothing is truly given, it is only that something is exchanged (albeit frequently in polite and veiled fashion). Moreover, if in this situation the gift places the other in debt, it may be less a sign of benevolence than an aggressive, self-serving act, giving nothing other than poison and thus coming close to what Derrida terms the ***pharmakon***. Even to merely acknowledge an unrequited gift, for example through a simple expression of gratitude, gives back something in return, in the form of the acknowledgement itself; while to understand oneself as giving often permits or encourages the donor to receive something from *themselves* in return, whether in the form of self-congratulation or the allaying of guilt. Obligation, indebtedness, repayment and return thus seem to pervade and annul at every turn the possibility of giving and receiving the gift, and for that matter the giving and receiving of an account of the gift within the economies of academic discourse, culture and community, which cannot but take *interest*, pay *credit* or extract critical *value* in regard to any such (exchangeable) account. The gift thus only ever exists or gives itself in the context of the conditions of exchange in which it can no longer give at all. As such it cannot attain **presence** in the present, nor hope for all debts to be settled in relation to the impossible **event** of itself in a pre-archaic past, nor bet on some full restitution to itself in a utopian future.

The gift is thus **singular**, and singularly **other**, in that it keeps in reserve or as remainder something that cannot be reduced to any economy of what might be considered accountably exchangeable, reckonably shareable or calculable presently or in time. Derrida's thinking of the gift therefore confronts us once more with the limitations or deconstructibility of the **metaphysics of presence**, not least in conjunction with the potential for an analysis *otherwise* of the legacies and futures of economic thought, practice and rationality, which all too often display or betray an agonized relationship to the gift. Yet equally (although this 'equally' misleadingly implies economic balance), the gift remains part of the **affirmative** dimensions of Derrida's thought, allied to the pre-critical **'yes'** which one must powerlessly say to language prior to approaching it as an object of knowledge or critique, and thus of economic exchange or of the 'masterable-possible'. Moreover, if to do the 'possible' in a customary sense is for Derrida simply to operate within the established structure of the field in order to realize what is in a sense already prescribed by it (i.e., at the more fundamental level, no possibility at all), then the gift's impossibility – like that of the impossibility of **invention, forgiveness** or **hospitality** – may, paradoxically, open on to the only possibility worth its name, a possibility which gives up on mastery as far as possible in the interests of another **future** with which one cannot so easily economize.

Given Time: 1. Counterfeit Money Published in French in 1991. See **gift**.

Glas Published in 1974. The bicolumnar structure of this text divides each page of *Glas* between, on the left-hand side, a sustained piece of **Hegel** scholarship concentrating principally on the *Philosophy of Right* and the *Phenomenology of Spirit* and, on the right, an investigation of the texts of Jean **Genet**. The linearity of each column, however, is disturbed by proliferal introductions of parenthetical remarks or citations from other sources in marginal windows pervading the main body of text (a formal device known as the judas). Furthermore, the absence of a conventional beginning or ending to each column necessarily thwarts any idea of the self-containment of either 'text', while the striking nature of their juxtaposition, intensified by the extraordinary layout, unusual design and typographical complexity of the book, prompts irresistible sideways glances, uncontainable border crossings and unanticipatable intertextual effects which define and (de)constitute the book's very architecture.

In Hegel's *Philosophy of Right*, the **family** plays a central part in the syllogistic reasoning that connects marriage, education, property, capital and civil society. The unification of the family through marriage and child-rearing finds its external embodiment in the synthesis of the civil sphere, education and capital. Indeed, the production of free (educated and property-holding) individuals through child-rearing within bourgeois society itself brokers the transition from family to civil life, and thus leads to the constitution of the state. The family therefore acquires pivotal importance in the whole system of Hegel's philosophy of right, notably in its relationship to his thinking of politics, **ethics** and society. Yet it is not only that the family repeats intact the entire dialectical system, but also that it renders that system problematic. For Hegel, the fundamental meaning of family is filiation, which (at the exclusion of material, natural and **animal** realms) itself defines **Spirit**. In the **Christian** faith (that is, through the incarnation of Christ) the family ties between father and son connect infinite to finite Spirit, God to man. The human family itself embodies the story of a divine filiation which incarnates itself in the figure of Christ. For Hegel, Christianity inaugurates true filiation at the point it overcomes and replaces the Old Testament rights and duties prized by **Judaism** with an ethical paradigm of love and freedom. In this (Greco-Christian) story of filial reproduction, the Jew is excluded as irredeemable within the movement of dialectic synthesis which filiation itself seems to name. The **mother**, too, is largely reduced to a material conduit who remains extrinsic to the dialectical process to be found in the story of filiation. (Here, Hegel does not stray far from Aristotelian biology which interprets **sexual difference** according to the familiar oppositions between spirit/matter, active/passive, and so on.) Only the father's image finds divinity in the filiation of infinite and finite Spirit (God and man) – Christ's (and man's) mother is merely 'actual'. The fact that the mother cannot be fully included within the divinely filiated

graft In *Dissemination*, Derrida famously observes that 'to write means to graft'. For Derrida, **writing** (in both its 'ordinary' guise and in the enlarged or 'general' sense developed by **deconstruction**) is always a matter of the graft. All writing involves a cutting, a marking, an incision in language (one that doesn't simply come from 'within' language as some kind of self-contained organism). But such incision or inscription is always accompanied by **différance**, **trace**, **supplement** (an irreducible addition at the origin) which enters in as a condition of writing's very production or, rather, its disseminal structure. Cutting is thus also splicing (together). To write is to graft in that one always cuts and splices, *plus d'un*, between texts (that is, as Derrida puts it in *Dissemination*, without the 'body proper'; thus, **dissemination** as always pluralizing 'germination' without 'first insemination'). 'The graft' is a term that appears, for instance, in Derrida's reading of the **Joycean** text. Grafting is at once affirmed as irreducible by deconstruction and adopted as a strategy in order to heighten the deconstructibility at work in each 'text' we may be given to read.

See also **actuvirtuality, counter, 'Living On: Borderlines', logocentrism, 'Signature Event Context'**.

Greek See *Adieu, Aporias*, 'Faith and Knowledge', 'Force of Law', *Glas*, logocentrism, *Margins of Philosophy, On Cosmopolitanism and Forgiveness, Paper Machine, Politics of Friendship, Psyche, Writing and Difference*.

Greph French acronym for the Research Group on the Teaching of Philosophy (Group de Recherches sur L'Enseignment Philosophique) founded in 1975 to resist proposed government reforms which threatened to restrict the place of philosophy in French national education. Derrida had a strong hand in the formation of this group. See ***Negotiations, Right to Philosophy*, university**.

— H —

H. C. for Life, That Is to Say . . . First presented at a conference on Cixous at Cerisy-la-Salle in 1998. See **Geneses, Genealogies, Genres and Genius**.

Hegel, Georg Wilhelm Friedrich (1770–1831) German philosopher. For Derrida's major engagements with this thinker, see in particular **Margins of Philosophy** and the Hegel column of **Glas**. See also **Positions**. On Hegel and philosophy/philosophical prefaces, see **Dissemination**. On Hegelianism and the discourse of the end of history, see **Specters of Marx**. (See also **The Other Heading** for European history and dialectics.) For the deconstructibility of Hegelian ethics, see **The Gift of Death**.

For Bataille and Hegelianism, see Derrida's essay in **Writing and Difference**. For Hegel and **sexual difference**, see the interview 'Choreographies' in **The Ear of the Other**. For Hegel and de Man, see **Memoires for Paul de Man**. See also 'The Age of Hegel' in **Right to Philosophy**.

Heidegger, Martin (1889–1986) German philosopher. Derrida returns to Heidegger, and thus suggests his significance, in a large number of texts. However, Derrida is frequently careful to distinguish his own thinking from Heidegger's. While it certainly does not exhaust the possible approaches to Heidegger, the disputed question of the relationship between Heideggerian philosophy and Heidegger's own connection with Nazism is not overlooked by Derrida.

For Heidegger, Dasein and **death**, see **Aporias**, and also **Learning to Live Finally**, **The Gift of Death**.

For Heideggerian *destruktion*, see **deconstruction** (see also **'Force of Law'** for Heidegger, **Benjamin** and **messianicity**).

For the difference between Being and beings, see **différance**.

On Heidegger and humanism, see 'The Ends of Man' in **Margins of Philosophy**.

On Heidegger and the **animal**, see **The Animal That Therefore I Am**.

On Heidgger and **metaphysics**, see **Positions**. (See also 'White Mythology' in *Margins* for Heidegger and **metaphor**; and in this connection, too, 'The Retrait of Metaphor' in **Psyche**.)

hospitality 71

For Heidegger, **religion**, morality and **Christianity**, see **'Faith and Knowledge'**.

For Heidegger and the untimely, see **'I Have a Taste for the Secret'**; and, on punctuality, **Speech and Phenomena**.

For Heidegger and representation, see 'Envoi' in **Psyche**. In **Psyche**, too, see the **Geschlecht** series of essays, which treat a whole series of interconnected issues in, or via, Heidegger (sex, race, stock, generation, gender, **family**, lineage, species, **sexual difference**, philosophical nationality, **Germanness**, **technology**, the hand, the **gift**, etc.). (See also, here, the entry on **technicity**.)

For other references to Heidegger, see **Right to Philosophy**, **The Ear of the Other**, **The Other Heading**, and especially **Writing and Difference**.

On Heidegger, 'spirit' and **Nazism**, see **Of Spirit**. For the question of Heidegger's relation to National Socialism, see also 'Heidegger, the Philosophers' Hell', 'How to Concede, with Reasons?' and 'Eating Well' in **Points** (which also includes a further text on Heidegger, 'Istrice 2'). (See **Points**, too, for the affair surrounding a poor-quality translation of Derrida's 'Heidegger, the Philosophers' Hell', played out in *The New York Review of Books*.)

On *Being and Time*, see 'Ousia and Grammē' in **Margins of Philosophy**. On 'The Origin of the Work of Art', see **The Truth in Painting**.

For **Levinas** and Heidegger, see **Adieu**, **The Gift of Death**. For Heidegger and **de Man**, see **Memoires for Paul de Man**. For Heidegger and **Nancy**, see **On Touching**.

hospitality In 'A Word of Welcome', an address written to commemorate Emmanuel **Levinas** (see **Adieu**), Derrida acknowledges that to offer welcome – as he seems to do at the beginning of his speech – inevitably suggests that the welcomer is abidingly at home, or in their element. To welcome is therefore not only a matter of giving room to, or making space for, the other; it also allows the welcomer to, in effect, police the threshold, to commandeer the site of welcoming for themselves, and thus to establish precedence over the other to whom the welcome is extended. In the process, the **other** is effectively appropriated precisely in terms of this scene of welcoming, with all the relations of hierarchy, power and control that it implies. Given in the name of hospitality, such a welcome is therefore not truly worthy of the name of hospitality. However, as Derrida goes on to explain, Levinas wants to think the 'welcome' in a different way. For Levinas, the very possibility of hospitality comes from the guest, without whom one could not be hospitable. Indeed, to go further, the possibility of the host, and therefore of the 'at-home' itself, derives from none other than this guest. In this sense, the one who hosts is, in effect, hosted by the one whom he hosts. If hospitality finds its very condition of possibility in the other, and indeed if it diminishes wherever hospitality is confined to the order of the 'masterable-possible', then for Levinas 'host' and 'hostage' become inextricable, less as a form of wilful disempowerment of the welcomer on Levinas's part (for such would surely make of Levinas just another 'host'), than through the advent of a radical passivity that goes beyond the classical distinction between an active and passive subject.

As Derrida frequently reminds us, to welcome the welcomable guest is, like forgiving the forgivable, simply to follow a code or a norm. It is to realize an already existent, already 'possible' possibility. By turning hospitality back into something that is 'masterable-possible', such a welcoming fails to live up to hospitality's name. One must therefore seek to keep open the possibility of hospitality in its **unconditional** form, as an opening to the wholly other, the unwelcomable guest, the absolutely unanticipatable *arrivant*. Indeed, as Derrida argues in his essay **'On Cosmopolitanism'** (which, written during the 1990s, discusses asylum-seeking in the context of the historical form of the *polis*), the unconditional principle of hospitality must be continually rearticulated on the stage of international relations and politics, in order to moderate and perhaps transform existing forms of **sovereignty**, right and **law**. Nonetheless, if unconditional hospitality is not to remain simply an abstract ideal, it must **negotiate** (perhaps hospitably, although only in the complex sense this term now acquires) with the conditional forms that hospitality must inevitably take, seeking to modify them in the interests of the **democracy to come**.

Hospitality is at issue across a number of Derrida's texts. In **'I Have a Taste for the Secret'**, for instance, Derrida describes the inhospitable environment of his childhood, both in terms of the anti-semitism that lead to his expulsion from school in **Algeria** and his feelings of outsiderdom in relation to the Algerian **Jewish** community at that time. Such inhospitality, he suggests, may have influenced his sense of not-belonging as a matter of ethico-political responsibility to the other. Similarly, in **Monolingualism of**

the Other, Derrida reflects not only upon Algeria's 'hosting' of the Jews during the nineteenth and twentieth centuries (in unparalleled fashion, citizenship was withdrawn from them as a group during the Second World War), but also upon the complex ways in which the **French** language *hosts* him.

See also ***Adieu to Emmanuel Levinas***, **'I Have a Taste for the Secret'**, ***Monolingualism of the Other***, ***Negotiations***, ***Of Hospitality***, ***On Cosmopolitanism and Forgiveness***.

Husserl, Edmund (1859–1938)   German philosopher and founding phenomenologist. An extremely important figure for Derrida, especially in his earlier career. For Derrida's reading of Husserlian **phenomenology** in the context of his **deconstruction** of the **metaphysics of presence**, **speech**, the sign, etc., see especially ***Speech and Phenomena***, as well as Derrida's introduction to Husserl's *Origin of Geometry* and ***The Problem of Genesis in Husserl's Philosophy***, which Derrida wrote as a dissertation in the early 1950s. For Husserl and metaphysics see also 'Form and Meaning' in ***Margins of Philosophy*** (included, too, in the English edition of ***Speech and Phenomena***). See, too, ***Writing and Difference***, especially '"Genesis and Structure" and Phenomenology' and 'Violence and Metaphysics'. See also in ***Margins*** 'The Ends of Man', for Husserl and humanism. For Husserl and intuitionism, see ***On Touching***. See also ***Points***, ***Positions***.

In 'The "World" of the Enlightenment to Come (Exception, Calculation, and Sovereignty)' in ***Rogues***, Derrida reflects on Husserl's thoughts about the apparent failure of European rationalism in the twentieth century. See also ***The Other Heading***.

hymen   See ***Dissemination***.

— I —

'I Have a Taste for the Secret'   An interview with Maurizio Ferraris conducted between 1993 and 1995 in various locations: Paris, Ris-Orangis, Naples and Turin. First published in Italian in 1997. The noted Italian philosopher

Gianni Vattimo contributes to the last part of the discussion, which ranges broadly across a number of abiding themes and issues in Derrida's work. During the exchange, Derrida looks back at a career extending over more than thirty years. He starts by reminding us that, while **deconstruction** remains far from anti-systematic, its defining gesture is to draw attention to the fact that any system depends at bottom on non-systematizable elements which indeed produce and sustain the system's own possibility. Derrida also challenges systematic periodization within the history of **philosophy**. He questions the notion of historical development based upon the idea of a relationship to the past construed as distinct from the present reconciled to itself in the 'now': the latter, involving an accepted definition of contemporaneity, paradoxically belongs to a classical past, whereas those viewed by Derrida as true 'contemporaries' – **Kierkegaard, Nietzsche, Heidegger** – are themselves thinkers of, precisely, the untimely. Thus deconstruction mistrusts periodization as a mode of reading or interpretation and looks instead to the powerfully structuring fissions within a corpus, often discernible at micrological levels, which allow its **singular inventiveness** to persist beyond any set contextualization. For Derrida, an *oeuvre* becomes most interesting at the point where it establishes the conditions of its own legibility, inventing and thus exceeding its own context (**Plato**'s time is scarcely legible, Derrida suggests, without reading Plato). In producing the very **context** in which its readability might live on, such an *oeuvre* is laden with the **performative**-transformative force of the future anterior, and therefore constitutes an appeal to the **other** and the 'to come'. The irruption of a possible yet unanticipatable future on the strength of such singular or radical otherness links to other familiar Derridean themes: the undeconstructibility of **justice** as excessive **messianic** possibility beyond right or law; the inappropriable experience of **death** as imminent possibility imbuing justice with the force of an urgent injunction; a radical thinking of **hospitality** giving itself over to an absolutely indeterminate *arrivant*; Derrida's deep-rooted suspicion of notions of belonging or '**community**' which he sees as reducing the **ethical** commitment to the other, and so on. Readers of this interview will also find fresh rearticulations of Derrida's thinking on the **name**, the **secret, iterability, testimony,** and **logocentricism.**

Derrida reminds us that the difference between *hypomnesis* and *anamnesis* in Plato entails not a dispute between **speech** and **writing**, but

impossibility

a less stably polarized economy of 'good' and 'bad' writing in which the latter comes to haunt the former. As such, one cannot divide or exclude **philosophy** in general from writing in general. Relatedly, Derrida suggests that the criteria of language and translatability are not enough to establish a permanent border between philosophy (or pure philosophical 'thought') on the one hand, and **literature** (or indeed the 'biographical') on the other. Instead, the connection between what Derrida calls the **signature** and the singular experience of thought is made central to the event of writing. Not surprisingly, perhaps, the interview therefore begins to chart a biographical course. It explores Derrida's expulsion from school in **Algeria** on anti-semitic grounds and yet his refusal to identify with **Judaism**, both of which inform Derrida's sense of not-belonging as a matter of ethico-political fidelity and **responsibility** to the other. Derrida reflects on his complex relation to existentialism and **phenomenology** in the 1950s and 1960s, and on the circumstances surrounding the publication of three major works (***Speech and Phenomena***, ***Writing and Difference*** and ***Of Grammatology***) in 1967. He dwells on the experience of international travel in response to a host of academic invitations that in some senses makes of deconstruction an occasional writing, and considers his level of involvement in the events of May 1968 and in a number of counter-institutional initiatives during the 1970s and 1980s. However, in questioning the grounds of accepted or assumed oppositions between 'thought' and 'writing', literature and philosophy, language and its referent (and, indeed, in asserting the dependency of dialectical thinking upon non-dialectizable differences), Derrida strongly affirms rather than disputes the idea that deconstructive performances refuse to give up on the question of truth. Indeed, Derrida reminds us that deconstruction was first of all a putting into question of linguisticism, of the 'linguistic turn' or the authority of linguistics, via the analysis of logocentrism. While questions of language and rhetoric fascinate deconstructive analyses, deconstruction itself demands attentiveness to the call of the other which marks the limit of linguistic construction, reduction or incorporation. This is confirmed by everything that Derrida says about the **event**, singularity, justice, death, the **secret**, hospitality, **testimony**, and so on.

impossibility Derrida famously describes **deconstruction** as 'the experience of the impossible'. However, impossibility in Derrida's thinking is not simply the opposite of possibility. To act in the interests of what is already given as 'possible' – to welcome the welcomable, forgive the forgivable, invent the inventable, or decide the decidable – is, for Derrida, to follow a recognized convention or norm, an established obligation or programme, a set rule or **law**. Thus, he questions whether any **event** of **forgiveness, hospitality, invention** or **decision** genuinely worthy of the name takes place by way of such conditional or limited forms. In contrast, decision in the radical sense is possible only in the midst of a presently undecidable situation; fundamental invention must paradoxically forgo all the resources of that which is 'inventable'; forgiving must venture and test itself in terms of what is profoundly unforgivable; hospitality worthy of the name must remain open to the wholly unwelcomable **other**. Thus, while the 'masterable-possible' (the performance of the 'I can') sets limits on the event or the coming of what is other, it is the 'impossible' that establishes the very conditions of possibility of 'possibility' in a more deep-seated sense. By this thinking, Derrida is not concerned simply to paralyze action-taking or delegitimize conditional possibilities in advance. Rather, it is by reminding us of the originary 'im-possibility' of invention, hospitality, gift, forgiving, decision, that Derrida asks us to continually rethink and transform the 'conditional' in the name of the '**unconditional**', notably in the fields of law, politics, and so forth (where values and ideas of forgiving, hospitality, decision etc. are far from irrelevant). However, to the extent that the 'impossible' is irresolvable, aporetic, or unmasterable, its call is ceaseless, demanding unending vigilance.

In one sense, the 'impossible' therefore names the limits of **presence** or of what is currently 'present'. 'Impossibility' calls up the repressed other as in fact constitutive, an indispensable **supplement** which, try as it might, 'possibility' cannot ultimately forgo. In this way, the 'impossible' may also be thought in terms of the always groundless (or non-present) originality of **différance, trace,** or **arche-writing**, which the metaphysical tradition seeks to repress or exclude, but which in fact grant its conditions of possibility.

See also, for instance, **Aporias**, the **democracy to come, gift,** *Given Time*, *Psyche*.

invagination A term originally from embryology. Invagination refers to the infolding of a portion of an outer layer, surface or edge, so as to

invention

open a pocket. For Derrida, this pocket is not a simple 'inside', nor can it be appropriated as such, but is instead the opening of the 'inside' to the **'other'**. This is a non-simple interaction, not least in the sense that invagination does not simply stage the encounter of preconstituted forms, but instead opens by way of a folding in which neither 'inside' nor 'outside' (the minimal determinants of 'form') acquire stable self-identity. Thus in 'The Law of Genre', found in **Acts of Literature**, the invaginated pocket is not contained by or as an interior, but instead turns out to divide and overflow the 'whole'. In **'Living On'**, invagination is described as an 'inward refolding', an 'inverted reapplication of the outer edge'. However, one must be careful not to assign an essential femininity to invagination, or to refer this term to a pre-sexed nature or biology.

See also the Kantian problem of form in **The Truth in Painting**; mourning, introjection and incorporation in **'Fors'**; and the entry on **sexual difference**.

invention   See especially 'Psyche: Invention of the Other' in the first volume of **Psyche**. Here, (the) invention must, by definition, radically exceed or overflow that which is already possible, but at the same time its inventiveness must be registered and validated in a statutory setting which already exists (a setting which, nevertheless, it may powerfully transform). Thus, invention is at once **singular** and **iterable**.

In 'Psyche' Derrida considers two types of invention: first, the production of technical capabilities by 'putting-together' existing resources in new ways; and second, fabulation, in which new discourses or media are invented for the fresh production of subject matter. Derrida examines these heterogeneous, yet in practice inextricable, notions of invention, in order to reflect on the fact that invention in the radical sense must not limit itself to what is presently or actually 'inventable'. To invent the inventable is to produce that which is already possible. Such invention does not earn its name in fundamental terms. Invention must therefore do the **impossible**: invent the uninventable. Indeed, invention must reinvent the very concept and discourse of invention. This is the task or calling of **deconstruction**. And yet invention must be of the **other**. For if invention is limited to the 'masterable-possible' or the humanly-possible, if it is performed on the strength of the 'I can', it remains tied to what is inventable and thus uninventive in the stronger sense. From this, Derrida argues that the other is not inventable, or an inventable invention; rather, invention is of the other, the other is invention.

ipseity   This term indicates not merely selfhood or individual identity, but more generally self-sameness or self-identification: a being at home with oneself, a self or subject conceived as **present** to itself. In turn, this would imply the capacity of the 'I can' or the standpoint of the 'masterable possible'. Deconstruction puts in question the notion of an ipseity which remains unsupplemented by alterity or the **other**. In other words, it asks about the limits of self-presence. Ipseity is a term that features in **Levinas**'s thought, bearing a complex relation to his thinking of the other, and Derrida's relation to such Levinasian themes often guides his use of the term.

iterability   This word combines the Latin *iter* ('again') with the Sanskrit *itara* ('**other**'). As Derrida notes, every **mark**, each **singular** text or irreplaceable **event** is at once a unique, 'once-and-for all' occurrence and yet manifests or inscribes itself on condition of a possible **re-marking**. Thus, the 'singular' is always repeatable; or, rather, it is iterable, since every repetition (*iter* – 'again') inevitably alters (*itara* – 'other'), just as each **signature** – as the supposed hallmark of identity – nevertheless attains validity only on condition of its inscription at *another* time or in a *different* place. Iterability isn't just a simple add-on, then, an extrinsic and dispensable 'extra' that comes along after the fact of an original form or **presence**. Instead, iterability implies a **supplementarity** that goes all the way down. (Thus, the 'original' or 'master' signature acquires its authority only once it can be compared to subsequent examples, so that an always potentially transformative repeatability or iterability may be discerned at the very *origin* of the signature's identity or its conditions of possibility). For Derrida, **writing** in general is always iterable since, in its very legibility, it always calls to an 'other' beyond those empirically present at the scene of inscription or reading. An always non-present remainder thus lingers irreducibly amid the structural conditions of writing, which therefore remain tied to the inappropriability of the *to come*. As Derrida puts it in **'Signature Event Context'**, this is 'the logic that ties repetition to alterity' – in other words, the logic of iterability.

See also **'Shibboleth'**, **'Signature Event Context'**.

— J —

Jewish, Judaism In *Circumfession*, Derrida speaks of himself as 'last of the Jews'. Derrida's sentence is, however, **undecidable**. It may mean the final Jew, in the sense of the ultimate Jew, or it may speak of the end of the line for Jews. (Here – indeed in both senses – there are echoes of Christ, the Jew/non-Jew. In *Adieu*, there is the anecdote of Derrida once hearing Levinas quip that he was a Jewish Catholic. The complexly entwined inheritance of Jewish and **Christian** traditions must therefore be carefully thought amid this **aporetic** question of the 'last of the Jews'). Alternatively, the phrase may identify Derrida as the least of the Jews. Thus, these words may make of Derrida at once the 'most last' and the 'least last'. Indeed, such a phrase – in its very undecidability – resists the sense of an ending it would otherwise seem to propose. Elsewhere, Derrida remarks that he at once signs this sentence, but also puts it in quotation marks as a typical or stereotypical comment. In *Learning to Live Finally*, moreover, Derrida says that this phrase may be allied to what **Aristotle** says about prayer: 'it is neither true nor false'. (One wonders whether, for Derrida, a prayer could be made of the phrase itself.) Nevertheless, in the same interview – his last – Derrida is quick to say that he will never deny his Jewishness; that, under certain circumstances, despite all his misgivings about 'community' or belonging, he will not shy away from saying 'we Jews'.

For places in Derrida's work where Jewishness or Judaism is at issue, see '**A Silkworm of One's Own**', *Adieu*, *Archive Fever*, *Circumfession*, '**Faith and Knowledge**', '**Force of Law**', *Glas*, hospitality, '**I Have a Taste for the Secret**', justice, *Memoires for Paul de Man*, messianicity, *Monolingualism of the Other*, *Points*, *Psyche*, '**Shibboleth**', *The Truth in Painting*.

Joyce, James (1882–1941) Irish author, playwright and poet. For Derrida on Joyce, see entries on *Acts of Literature*, graft, *Learning to Live Finally*, literature, *Psyche*, sexual difference, yes, yes.

justice In '**Faith and Knowledge**', Derrida discusses **Kant**'s idea of **Christianity** as, in contrast to **Judaism** and Islam, a 'moral' and, effectively, secularizing **religion** – one based, that is, on good deeds, moral conduct and rational action, rather than God's revelation. The 'double' origin of the Abrahamic religions we are therefore given to inherit leads Derrida to the question of the **messianism** which, in different ways, accompanies each of them. For Derrida, it is the desire for justice rather than merely the **law** which arises from messianism in its various forms.

Derrida contrasts law and justice in several ways. Law is constructed and constructable. Moreover, it is **violent** at its origin. Law cannot found itself lawfully, since the very question of legality obviously cannot be put until law has established itself. Yet its violently constructed founding does not so much render law illegitimate – for the foundation of the law is structurally prior to all questions of legitimacy – rather, its constructedness renders law always deconstructible. Law, too, prescribes. It demands dutiful compliance with a given authority, and therefore tends to reduce **decision** or **responsibility** in any radical sense.

Justice, in contrast, cannot be a matter of simply following or applying given laws, even if they appear to be entirely 'just'. The truly 'just' decision, if there is any, must stem from a fundamental responsibility that cannot prop itself up through mere reference to statutory or case law, but which must reinvent itself with the utmost vigilance at each time of asking. Justice, in other words, is allied to the radical decision (a decision that finds its only possibility in the vicinity of that which is not presently decidable). In this sense, justice is aeconomic – the justice of the 'just' decision cannot be calculated in terms of its exchange-value within the economy that is the law. This also means, however, that one cannot *count* on justice – and, for Derrida, justice is ultimately unpresentable to the extent that, once objectified *as such* and thus given as the determining basis for future judgements, justice would be transformed into law, and thereby neutralized *as* justice. One may be able to say with some confidence 'I am lawful', but for Derrida one cannot ever justly say 'I am just', since justice does not itself provide the grounds for such an assured declaration. Yet the '**impossibility**' of justice, in contrast to the already-possible possibility of the law, opens the very possibility of the **future** and the **other** to come (the only possibility worthy of the name).

To put all of this differently, justice cannot be constructed. And since it is unconstructable, Derrida insists upon the undeconstructibility – and, indeed, the indestructibility – of justice.

Justice and law are therefore heterogeneous, but one must nevertheless **negotiate** between them. Justice, the very law of which places it beyond the law, nevertheless cannot hope to be rendered without **force** of law. However, the **unconditionality** of justice calls us to continually rethink and reinvent the conditional forms taken by the law, notably in the interests of the **democracy to come**.

See also **'Faith and Knowledge'**, **'Force of Law'**, **'I Have a Taste for the Secret'**, *Negotiations*.

— K —

Kafka, Franz (1883–1924)   Prague-born Jewish writer. See *Acts of Literature*, **literature**.

Kant, Immanuel (1724–1804)   German philosopher. For Derrida on Kant, see for instance, *Adieu*, **'Faith and Knowledge'**, **'Force of Law'**, **justice**, **messianicity**, *Negotiations*, *On Cosmopolitanism and Forgiveness*, *On Touching*, *Politics of Friendship*, 'Interpretations at War: Kant, the Jew, the German' in *Psyche*, *The Animal That Therefore I Am*, *The Truth in Painting*, 'Mochlos' in *Right to Philosophy*, **university**, *Without Alibi*.

khôra   See 'Khôra' in *On the Name*. See also **affirmation**, **messianicity**, **sexual difference**, **yes, yes**.

Kierkegaard, Søren (1813–1855)   Danish philosopher. See **'I Have a Taste for the Secret'**, *The Ear of the Other*, *The Gift of Death*.

— L —

Lacan, Jacques (1901–1981)   French psychoanalyst and psychiatrist, credited as a key inheritor of Freud. See **logocentrism, psychoanalysis**, 'For the Love of Lacan' in *Resistances of Psychoanalysis*, *The Post Card*.

Latin, Latinity   See **'Demeure'**, *Right to Philosophy*.

law   For literature and law, see *Acts of Literature*, **literature**. (For law and genre, see 'The Law of Genre' in *Acts*.)

For law, politics and violence see *Adieu*, **'Force of Law'**, *Rogues*. (For law and the violence of the proper name, see *Of Grammatology*.)

For European and international law, see *Echographies of Television*, *Learning to Live Finally*, *Negotiations*, *On Cosmopolitanism and Forgiveness*, *Rogues*, **September 11**, **sovereignty**, *Specters of Marx*, *The Other Heading*.

For law, Latinity and Christianity, see **'Demeure'**. For law and the Greek and Jewish traditions, see **'Force of Law'**. For law, revelation and Judaism, see **'A Silkworm of One's Own'**.

For the law of the *demos*, see **demos**, **democracy to come**, *Politics of Friendship*.

For decision beyond the law, see **decision**, **undecidability**.

For law and justice, and the constructedness, force and deconstructibility of law, see **'Force of Law'**. See also **justice**.

For law and unconditionality, see **unconditional**.

For law and forgiveness, see **forgiveness**, *On Cosmopolitanism and Forgiveness*.

For law and hospitality, see **hospitality**, *On Cosmopolitanism and Forgiveness*.

For law and responsibility, see **responsibility**.

For law and testimony, see **testimony**.

On Mandela and law, see 'The Laws of Reflection: Nelson Mandela, in Admiration' in *Psyche*.

For the university and law, see **university**, *Without Alibi*.

For law and alibi, see *Without Alibi*.

For the law of the archive, see *Archive Fever*.

Learning to Live Finally

For the law of mourning, see **The Work of Mourning**.
See also **On the Name**.

Learning to Live Finally   The last interview with Derrida, conducted by Jean Birnbaum and published in La Monde on 19 August 2004. Having confirmed the gravity of his illness, Derrida is reminded of the phrase used in **Specters of Marx** – 'Someone, you or me, comes forward and says: *I would like to learn to live finally*'. After reminding his interviewer of the principal themes of that book – the future necessity of a transformation in international **law** and organizations, and the call for a '**new international**' in the interests of an 'alter-**globalism**' that he reaffirms throughout this discussion – Derrida teases out the defining ambiguities of the phrase in French. In a variety of ways, *appendre à vivre* carries the sense of a lesson given or learned about life. Derrida affirms that he remains ineducable on the question of how to live or, in its classical philosophical corollary, how to die. Nor can he teach others. This affirmation is not to be taken lightly since it resonates with a number of encounters between **deconstruction** and the philosophical tradition (from its classical past, right up to **Heidegger**) on the question of whether **death** can be meaningful in defining life's meaning, or whether **philosophy** has anything to teach on this subject. For Heidegger, death is the most proper or authentic property of *Dasein* as an existing entity, yet Derrida mistrusts any kind of self-directed or appropriative mournfulness for oneself or others as placing a narcissistic restriction on an openness to alterity. For Derrida, instead, death is lived in a writing that will survive its author in order to address an unanticipatable **other**. His language, too – **French** – which gives rise to an experience at once vital and mortal, is his only one yet not his own. These reflections on a certain non-belonging in language, time and mortality allow for fascinating insights to emerge about Derrida's **Jewish** and **Algerian** origins, and the circumstances under which he *will* nevertheless say 'we' – 'we Jews', 'we French', 'we **Europeans**' – in the interests of a tormented, imperfect and divided legacy that nonetheless, for Derrida, still bodes for the **future** (in contrast, for example, to what he calls Arab-Islamic theocratism or American hegemony).

Derrida also dwells on the thought of himself as a survivor of a dying generation (Lacan, Althusser, Levinas, Foucault, Barthes, Deleuze, Lyotard, Kofman) which he refuses to reduce to simple-minded conceptions of

'1968 thought', and rethinks survival as a form of guardianship and **responsibility** to the 'to come', not least in terms of a readership that cannot be presupposed or preformatted by media techniques and **technologies**. In a striking formulation, Derrida confesses that he fears that there will be nothing left after his death, that his books will be reduced to a mere library deposit, and that at the same time he has not yet even begun to be read.

In the interview, Derrida rearticulates his commitment to an **unconditional university**, and advances a proposal that marriage be replaced in the civil and secular sphere by new sorts of contractual unions whose duration and character (number and sex of partners) should not be prescribed. The interview ends with Derrida's reassertion that, far from purveying a bleak nihilism or cynicism or a narrow relativism or **linguisticism**, deconstruction entails an unconditional **affirmation** of life.

Levi-Strauss, Claude (1908–2009)   Brussels-born French anthropologist, closely linked to structuralism. See **Of Grammatology**, **supplement**, **Writing and Difference**.

Levinas, Emmanuel (1906–1995)   Lithuanian philosopher. For Derrida and Levinas, see **Adieu**, **Aporias**, **'Différance'**, **hospitality**, **ipseity**, **Jewish/Judaism**, **Monolingualism of the Other**, 'At This Very Moment in This Work Here I Am' in **Psyche**, **sexual difference**, **The Animal That Therefore I Am**, **The Ear of the Other**, **The Gift of Death**, **The Work of Mourning**, 'Violence and Metaphysics' in **Writing and Difference**.

lie/lying   See especially 'History of the Lie' in **Without Alibi**.

Limited Inc   This volume from 1988 includes **'Signature Event Context'**, Derrida's reply to Searle's response to this essay (regarding **speech act theory**), which is entitled 'Limited Inc a b c . . .', and an afterword by Derrida. See **'Signature Event Context'**, **speech act theory**.

linguistics/linguisticism   **Deconstruction** disputes the **logocentric** and **phonocentric** assumptions of linguistics, notably in the post-

Saussurian guise of a structural linguistics that suggests itself as having gone beyond **metaphysics**. Derrida is keen to assert that deconstruction is not reducible to a narrow textualism, relativism or linguisticism, but instead affirms an '**other**' which cannot be reduced to linguistic construction or determination.

See also entries on *différance*, *'Différance'*, 'I Have a Taste for the Secret', *Learning to Live Finally*, literature, *Margins of Philosophy*, metaphysics of presence, *Monolingualism of the Other*, *Of Grammatology*, *Positions*, *Psyche*, *Right to Philosophy*, 'Signature Event Context', *Speech and Phenomena*, translation, *Writing and Difference*, yes, yes.

literature For Derrida, the possibility of a rigorous distinction between literature and **philosophy** must be questioned. Philosophy takes place on condition of its own inscription and, despite its typical secondarization of language in relation to thought, always calls for reading. Meanwhile, not only do all kinds of ideas about literary value and writing rest upon certain philosophical assumptions passed down through the Western tradition, but the very question of literature ('What is literature?') is itself philosophical. Nevertheless, the relationship between literature and philosophy is an uneasy one, notably to the extent that literary effects do not confine themselves to works of 'literature' but always threaten or tend to overrun textual borders, thus reminding philosophy of its own (repressed) status as **writing**. Indeed, the notion of literature as essentially textual, rhetorical or figural play, ungrounded in the clarity or rigour of thought, is itself based on important philosophical ideas and suppositions (about art, writing, representation, metaphor, authorship, and so on). Thus, such a definition of literature turns out to be something of a projection of philosophy's own concerns. If the opposition set up between philosophy and literature is itself a philosophical one, this does not so much establish the dominance of philosophy (though doubtless this would be philosophy's ambition), but instead suggests that philosophy participates in the very inscription it would wish to transcend, continually requiring the **supplement** of its literary 'other' in order to define and defend itself as such (for Derrida's understanding of philosophy as that which seeks to appropriate its 'outside', see also *Dissemination* and *Margins of Philosophy*; for the 'dangerous supplement', see *Of Grammatology*).

Derrida's interest in literature should not be taken, therefore, to indicate either **deconstruction**'s departure from philosophy or its inherent textualism or relativism. On the contrary, Derrida consistently argued that, while his work attended with utmost vigilance to the 'text' of philosophy, nevertheless the deconstruction of **logocentrism** made possible a certain exposure or openness to an unpresentable, non-linguistic '**other**'. For Derrida, however, literature is not defined by some mysterious or revealable 'essence', but by its instituting in terms of the *right* which modern democracies assign to literature: a 'right to say everything'. From this perspective, literature also raises the question of **law**. The law of literature, the law which gives us literature, also encourages excess and defiance of the law. Put from another viewpoint, the laws of literature remain difficult to determine or delimit by law. (See 'Before the Law' in ***Acts of Literature***.)

The literary text is therefore **singular** in the sense that, always overrunning essential determination, it marks the exceptional **event** of an irreplaceable **signature, date** and inscription. Yet, for Derrida, this event is made possible only by the possibility of literature's **re-marking**, its readability or **iterability** – which is to say, its (self-) transformative potential. As Derrida often suggested, literature – if there is any – may be thought of as that which transforms the very **contexts** and conditions of its own legibility. Literature makes a differential mark, different-from-itself-within-itself, and thus **promises** or calls for a **future**.

Of course, in practice literature's 'right to say everything' is repeatedly repressed, censored or qualified in a variety of different circumstances, and for a large number of reasons. Yet the principle of such a 'right' remains a characterizing feature of such societies, and sets up the problem of literature in specific ways. In ***Demeure***, for instance, Derrida ties literature to a far-from-simple history of **Latinity** that culminates in an increasingly extended secular-**Christian** tradition. Here, literary 'passion' is linked to **testimony** as the irreplaceably singular making of truth. Ultimately inassimilable to evidence, positive knowledge or proof, the 'truth' of such testimony cannot be divorced from the (depthless) **secret** or from **fiction**. Nor can it be separated from the possibility of perjury or **lying**. In 'Passions' (***On the Name***), meanwhile, the right to 'literature'/right *of* 'literature' tasks the writer with **responsibility** at the same time as it profoundly irresponsibilizes him or her. In all these cases, literature is affirmed as perhaps the very trait of the '**democracy to come**' – a coming democracy which continually places

'Living On: Borderlines'

demands on us in the 'here-now' – in the sense that literature (if there is any) continually puts in question its own law, indeed keeps open the issue of its own, **unconditional** responsibility, and is thus given of the potential to resist forms of **sovereignty**, domination and mastery.

Throughout his career, Derrida wrote on a host of 'literary' figures: **Mallarmé**, **Kafka**, **Blanchot**, **Joyce**, **Ponge**, **Celan**, Shakespeare, **Cixous**, and others. (*Acts of Literature* brings together a good selection of these writings, together with an interview by Derrida on 'This Strange Institution Called Literature'.) We may rehearse just some of these. In 'The Double Session', included in **Dissemination**, Derrida affirms the deconstructive force of Mallarmé's *Mimique*, which in its very miming of mimesis puts in question the age-old philosophical understanding of mimesis – one that bases itself on a thinking of 'truth' in terms of **presence**. In **'Living On: Borderlines'** Derrida reads Shelley's *The Triumph of Life* alongside two short texts by Blanchot, in order to reflect upon the survival of literature at its own undecidable limits, and upon its resistance to, and re-marking by, an always impossible yet necessary translation. In 'Before the Law', Derrida reads Kafka's text as always undecidably before the law of itself. 'The Law of Genre' reads Blanchot's *The Madness of the Day* in order to show that the **mark** of belonging to a 'genre' does not itself belong to the genre it marks. This effect is constitutive and irreducible – the very 'law of the law of genre', says Derrida – so that, by law or in principle, genre must endure its own self-contamination. (For these last two texts, see **Acts of Literature**.) **'Shibboleth'** turns on the question of the **date** in Celan as an unsubstitutable mark, a unique incision in language, which nevertheless calls for re-marking at another, always specific and singular date. Thus the text of Celan as a survivor of **Nazism** comes to be read as commemorative, although in a way that *in principle* always traverses and overruns the stultifying grip of official history. Derrida's text on the poetry of Francis Ponge, **Signsponge**, traces Ponge's signature as that which both singularly re-marks and depropriates him in the work. Derrida's writings on Joyce look to an 'originary' **affirmation** which is the very condition of literature. Other texts, from **Cinders** to **Circumfession**, at once re-pose and re-perform the question of literature.

'Living On: Borderlines'   This double-banded text was written for the 1979 collection *Deconstruction and Criticism*, which brought together essays by members of the so-called **Yale School** (Harold Bloom, Paul de Man, Geoffrey Hartman, J. Hillis Miller and Derrida himself) who were each asked by the publisher to write a new piece that took a specific literary example as the occasion to elucidate the main features of their own work. In reply, the contributors proposed Shelley's poem *The Triumph of Life* as a common text.

The upper band of Derrida's contribution, 'Living On', explores the question of the survival or 'living on' of **literature**. Here, Derrida **graft**s onto his reading of Shelley an exploration of two short texts by Maurice **Blanchot**, *La Folie du jour* (*The Madness of the Day*) and *L'Arrêt de mort* (*Death Sentence*) which for Derrida somehow translate the **undecidability** of Shelley's title, the double genitive of which implies both the triumph of life over **death** and death's triumphing over life. This very undecidability brings into view the problem of the 'literary'. The lower band, meanwhile, presents itself as an extended note to the translator of this text. Here, Derrida poses questions concerning the possibility and limits of **translation** (Derrida's contribution was, of course, earmarked for translation from the outset). Just as in writings such as 'Letter to a Japanese Friend', this problem of translation remains inextricable for the very thinking of **deconstruction**. Institutional and disciplinary resistances to deconstruction's thinking of translatability are, for Derrida, bound up with this notion of the 'borderline', which is not only rethought but enacted quite differently at the always undecidable and divided limits of Derrida's double-banded writing. 'Living On: Borderlines' might therefore be read alongside other writings such as 'The Double Session' in ***Dissemination*** and, in ***Points***, 'Che cosè la poesia' (in which the poem is a hedgehog that self-protectively balls itself up in the middle of the road, bristling its spines at the traffic that may traverse its crossing and indeed threaten its existence, although this must be ventured). For it gives us to think a problem which is not confined to this text alone: for Derrida, the writing we might call 'literary' may be read only in terms of a certain reference without referent. Thus, every text precisely *borders* on another, points towards or embarks upon another, yet in a way that ventures beyond those navigational tools and mooring techniques offered by a traditional concept of referentiality. (The original title of the piece, 'Journal de bord', translates more literally as 'shipboard journal'.)

margin 89

logocentrism Taken from the **Greek**, *logos* translates literally as 'word' but includes the broader sense of 'reason' or 'logic'. The *logos* expresses the desire for an ultimate origin, telos, centre or principle of truth which grounds meaning. This desire founds the **metaphysical** tradition, in particular its determination of being in terms of original **presence**. Thus, the concern of the *logos* is to establish a self-sufficient foundation or transcendental signified, for which God would perhaps be the most familiar name. Consequently, logocentrism views all differences as ultimately derivative and recuperable: for instance, **writing** is but a privative version of the living presence enshrined in **speech**. The deconstruction of logocentrism (which sees ***différance*** as the constitutive yet unpresentable '**other**' of the metaphysical tradition) is under way in several of Derrida's major texts, notably those from the mid- to late-1960s or soon afterwards.

Derrida also coins the neologism '**phallogocentrism**'. This **grafts** together logocentrism and phallocentrism, a term used initially by the psychoanalyst Ernest Jones to critique Freud's analytical bias towards the phallus. Derrida brings the term into play in order to deconstruct the Lacanian reference to the phallus as master signifier within the symbolic order.

See also ***Dissemination***, ***Margins of Philosophy***, ***Of Grammatology***, ***Positions***, **'Signature Event Context'**, ***Speech and Phenomena***, ***The Post Card***.

logos See **logocentrism**.

Mallarmé, Stéphane (1842–1898)   French poet and critic. See ***Acts of Literature***, ***Dissemination***.

margin   See ***Margins of Philosophy***.

Margins of Philosophy   This volume, first published in French in 1972, includes a number of seminal texts, among them **'Différance'**, which is also included in the English edition of **Speech and Phenomena**, and **'Signature Event Context'** (*Sec*), which can be found in **Limited Inc**. (See separate entries on these essays.) Throughout the various essays in this volume, Derrida discusses a host of thinkers and writers, among them **Hegel, Husserl, Heidegger, Aristotle, Descartes, Rousseau, Nietzsche, Saussure, Benveniste,** Valéry.

The collection begins with 'Tympan', itself divided into two columns, including a long quotation from the first volume of *Biffures* on the narrower right hand side (Michel Leiris's autobiographical memoir). Three epigraphs from Hegel and lengthy footnotes, including diagrams, contribute to the complex typographical structure of the piece, by means of which a number of margins appear to organize or 'space' the text, margins which both propagate the limits, effects and relations of 'part' and 'whole' and put at issue their very economy. The left-hand column of 'Tympan' places in question the unified structure and closed borders of **philosophy**, from which its **sovereign** mastery is projected so as to permit an apparently limitless appropriation of its *own* 'outside'. Here, the tympanum – the membraneous partition stretched obliquely between the auditory canal and the cavity of the ear – provides the figure in which Derrida allows to reverberate the very question of that barrier which permits a certain transport, letting philosophy receive and comprehend its **'other'**, attuning its ear through strategies of incorporation and hierarchizing privilege. The question, for Derrida, is whether one can penetrate the tympanum in order for the question of philosophy to resonate differently. This, indeed, would involve new conceptions or articulations of the 'outside', since from the beginning philosophy has been concerned to determine and appropriate nothing other than exteriority itself. It would also demand a certain rethinking of the **margin** or limit of philosophy, beyond the movement of dialectical synthesis one finds in Hegel, and so beyond the more predictable interplay of 'inside' and 'outside' which tends to reduce resistance (indeed, the very resistance that permits vibration to *sound*) to mere dialectizable opposition. While Derrida's text never refers explicitly to Leiris's, their oblique relation resounds in the fact that Persephone – the 'subterranean' name assigned by Leiris to the part of his text cited in 'Tympan' – corresponds to the French name for the

Margins of Philosophy

earwig: *perce-oreille*, which means literally ear-piercer. Persephone is everywhere associated with twists, spirals, helixes, curves, floral curls, springs, corkscrews: figures which open, puncture, wind about and course through the linear image of the limit. Thus from the margins of (the very question of) philosophy (as no longer simply a vacant or virginal space to be filled or determined as such), Leiris's text keeps in reserve the question of broaching the ear, in order that something other may be heard than that which names itself philosophy.

Next after '*Différance*' (see separate entry) in the collection is '*Ousia* and *Grammē*: Note on a Note from *Being in Time*', in which a footnote of Heidegger's provides the occasion to review, across the entire philosophical heritage of the West, the determination of being and time in terms of **presence**. Here, the reading of Heidegger permits one to see that every text in the philosophical tradition carries within itself *both* the resources of thought which establish a metaphysical conception of time *and* the means to deconstruct its very concept or conceptuality. From the margins of Heidegger's text, then, the 'unthinkable' other of **metaphysics** resounds at the subterranean level of metaphysics itself, even in the very repression or erasure of its **trace**. Presence, then, is nothing other than the trace of this trace, the obscured remains of an always improper or *différantial* origin. In 'The Pit and the Pyramid: Introduction to Hegel's Semiology', meanwhile, the advent of the Saussurian theory of the sign is situated in terms of the general (although far from simply homogenous) system of metaphysics which treats the sign as a transition or detour on the way to self-presence and absolute knowledge of a **being** or consciousness. As Derrida shows in texts such as ***Of Grammatology*** and *Sec* this conception of the sign orders the hierarchy of thought over speech and speech over writing. Thus, in Hegel and Saussure alike, semiology proceeds under the jurisdiction of psychology construed as a science of the 'soul' or of the 'living'. While linguistics supposedly forms only a part of the field of semiology, its emphasis on phonetic language, and thus upon **speech**, therefore supplies a privileged model for semiology in general as based precisely on this 'metaphysical' theory of the sign. Linguistics, in other words, establishes the teleological paradigm for the entire field of which it is supposedly only a part. (Derrida's essay concludes by exploring the ways in which Hegel disparages non-phonetic writing, notably the Egyptian and Chinese historical models, as too caught up in the essential ambiguity of symbols, too remote from the human voice, poorly equipped to free the spirit from the letter.)

Hegel's semiology receives particular attention in this text since, in aspiring to philosophical completion, the interrogated limits of the Hegelian system will come to expose those of metaphysics itself. Since, throughout the entire text of metaphysics, the sign is maintained in its formal or arbitrary exteriority as that which remains only *in sight of* truth, its body is merely the worldly vessel of the **spirit**, breath, thought or intention that animates it, and which therefore supposedly precedes and outlasts it. Thus, in Hegel, the sign – as that which brings into sight the transcendence and freedom of the animating spirit – is also a tomb. This tomb incarnates or gives life to the body only under the sign of **death**. It announces a death to come. The sign thus recalls in itself the double genitive which structures the **undecidable** readability of Shelley's poem 'The Triumph of Life': life (the life of the spirit) triumphs over a death-bound worldly incarnation to which it is nevertheless beholden for precisely this (spiritual) life. (See **'Living On: Borderlines'**.) The sign as the very monument of life in or after death is also the crypt which consecrates death in life. By recovering this interpretation of the sign from the Hegelian text, Derrida is able to elaborate its irreducible **supplementarity**: the sign is construed as an additional part and yet, at the same time, it is that which indispensably compensates.

In 'The Ends of Man', which dates itself quite precisely from April 1968 (the time of the Vietnam peace talks, the assassination of Martin Luther King, and the build-up to the student protests in Paris) Derrida scans the entire field of French philosophy in its relationship to continental **Europe**, precisely around the question of 'man'. He notes the ebbing tide of humanism and anthropologism in **France** (which one might associate for instance with the waning of existential thought), yet wonders why this trend has not been accompanied by a rereading of figures such as Hegel, Husserl and Heidegger, precisely to question the discovery of humanist themes within their thought. Partly in answer to this question, Derrida argues that the critiques of metaphysical humanism offered by these thinkers remain in thrall of the metaphysical system. Moreover, the pronouncement of the end of man which began to dominate French thought at broadly this time must be treated with extreme caution, Derrida tells us, since such an 'end', construed both as finality and transcendence, is precisely inscribed and prescribed in metaphysics in its various teleological, eschatological or dialectical forms. Indeed, philosophically (or otherwise), 'man' has only ever had meaning in these terms. The 'end' of man or of a metaphysical humanism and anthropologism must therefore be thought otherwise, in a countering movement that plays between an endlessly rigorous **deconstruction** of the existing field on the one hand, and, on the other, the interruptive force of a **decision** to change or displace the terrain, both of which include risks that must continually be played off one against the other.

In 'The Linguistic Circle of Geneva', Derrida reclaims Rousseau as an ancestor of modern linguistic science in order to elaborate a common fund of metaphysical concepts and determinations that must be deconstructed. (Like Saussure, and indeed the Hegel of 'The Pit and the Pyramid', Rousseau gives metaphysical priority to the voice, construing **writing** as secondary, extrinsic and flawed; he affirms the arbitrariness of the sign; and he configures **linguistics**, semiology and psychology in terms of the same deconstructible relations of 'part' and whole'.) As Derrida shows, Rousseau chastises **Condillac** – to whom he is otherwise much indebted – for imagining the institution or inauguration of language as undertaken by a community of inventors who were, effectively, already possessed of sociolinguistic ability or potential. (For Derrida on Condillac, see also *The Archeology of the Frivolous*.) This conception is guilty of question-begging for Rousseau, and requires a more radical conception of origins or 'nature'. Yet Rousseau is faced with two equally problematic conceptions: either that of language's origin in a pre-linguistic 'nature'; or of its self-instituting, self-projecting break with such 'nature'. Rousseau must try to square the circle, which implies that the thought which gives rise to 'speech' may itself need speech to think. Moreover, if what is founded in language is, precisely, the possibility of the 'arbitrary', how might some arbitrary force have intervened from 'outside' nature in order to found this very possibility? How could language be founded arbitrarily when it itself founds the very possibility of the 'arbitrary'? The vicious circles in which Rousseau is caught here resonate provocatively with the Geneva 'Circle' which inhabits the essay's title. To negotiate the circle in its formidable logical contradictions, nature is ultimately thought by Rousseau to depart from *itself*, to interrupt *itself*, in the founding of language. By simultaneously rendering nature 'artificial' and the artificial 'natural', Rousseau's thought, like Hegel's, partakes of the supplement.

'Form and Meaning: A Note on the Phenomenology of Language' (also in the English edition of *Speech and Phenomena*) argues that **phenomenology**, notably that of Husserl, seeks to criticize metaphysical concepts only in the name of a more essential metaphysics. However, just as the intention of a speech act for **Austin** depends for its success upon the conventionality of an established **context**, so phenomenological 'theory' or 'science' requires the objectification of its objects by way of a form, or via a medium that must also be utterly dispensable for scientific 'truth' or meaning to emerge in its full transparency. Thus the logic of the supplement, once again, enters into this reading of Husserl.

In 'The Supplement of Copula: Philosophy Before Linguistics', Derrida shows how Benveniste analyzes the constraints placed upon Aristotelian thought by the **Greek** language. Benveniste argues that metaphysical concepts are produced and informed by the structural possibilities of a specific linguistic system. Such a contention challenges, of course, the claim of metaphysical thought to 'truth' and universality. Thus Aristotelian categories are, for Benveniste, first of all linguistic categories. Yet Derrida notes that the very concept of 'category' is not questioned here. If 'category' is itself primarily a linguistic rather than a philosophical product, a category of language rather than of thought, what authorizes Benveniste to resort to the concept of 'category' in order to displace the philosophical import of Aristotle's categories into the domain of the linguistic? Would not this move, as precisely one of philosophical or conceptual argumentation (rather than one of linguistic fabrication which recognizes itself as such) be 'de-authorized', as it were, by the very implications of the argument it makes? Thus the relations between the categories of the 'linguistic' and the 'philosophical' are not so easily settled. As Derrida shows throughout this volume and in many other texts, linguistics (Benveniste's included) remains as much in the pay of metaphysics as philosophy is informed by the linguistic system. Meanwhile, as Derrida shows, one must consider the ability of non-Indo-European languages without the linguistic resources to formulate 'to be' nevertheless to think its possibility *otherwise*. This points not to a certain lack which pertains on the 'outside' of Western thought, as to the possibility of a supplement to the copula (that which links subject to predicate) which in fact structures the very limits of that thought.

'White Mythology: Metaphor in the Text of Philosophy' asks whether **metaphor** is merely accidental, or instead fundamental to philosophical production. As Derrida recalls, Renan and Nietzsche affirm the metaphorical origin of 'proper' concepts and, for that matter, the very concept of the 'proper' while, in the texts of writers such as Freud and Bergson, the constitutive importance of metaphor is practised or proposed, albeit contradictorily in the interests of an eventual neutralization of metaphoric effects. Hegel also seeks to incorporate metaphor within the dialectical movement of idealization in order at once to apprehend and reduce its constitutive force. This, indeed, is the classic gesture of philosophy and metaphysics. The idea of metaphor as derivative, ancillary and non-serious extends all the way from Aristotle to Austin, from **Socrates** to **Searle**. However, difficulties arise when seeking to describe and comprehend the basic activity of metaphorization. The very concept of metaphor provides a questionable vantage point for thinking metaphoricity. Not only is metaphor classically a prime or, indeed, 'proper' concept within the philosophical tradition and, as such, laden with the residue of metaphysics, but in seeking to allot and determine the general field of which it is simultaneously a part – a field of metaphoricity that by definition and in its tropic movements must be characterized by a certain resistance to unification or totalization in the 'proper' – the concept of metaphor is immediately deconstructible in its relation to the very (non-) object of enquiry which would otherwise seem to give it thematic authority. As a concept it cannot dominate the field in which it might be considered to feature – notably by way of the *metaphoric* origins of its concept. Thus the *metaphor* of metaphor is precisely what is excluded at the point one wishes to use the *concept* of metaphor to comprehend metaphoricity. The conceptual *usage* of metaphor therefore says too much and too little at once, it always overpays and poorly repays according to a logic of usury – of interest, borrowing, and loss – that Derrida pursues throughout the text. The thinking of metaphoricity cannot happen purely and simply within philosophy, if such a thing were ever possible. Indeed, putting the question of 'truth' to metaphor produces some unpromising effects, as Derrida shows. To judge a metaphor 'bad' is to risk doing too much business with it, hazarding a lapse in neutrality or objectivity, yet even the best metaphor cannot be judged entirely 'good' (that is, 'proper' to the object in its revealed fullness) without bringing to an absolute end its very metaphoricity, which thereby eludes thought. Metaphor is, then, the 'unheard' of philosophy, which can only hear (in) its own name. Instead, the otherwise inaudible (re)sounding of metaphor – or the metaphor of metaphor – may be heeded, however obliquely, only in the ear of the 'other' ('Tympan'), or by dint of the with-against movement which repercusses deconstruction's relation to philosophy ('The Ends of Man').

While a thinking of *différance*, trace and supplement extends across *Margins of Philosophy*, one of the volume's principal – and inextricably linked – terms is *'relève'*. This conveys a sense both of lifting or relifting and suppression, of that which simultaneously raises and relieves of function. The Hegelian *Aufhebung* names such a process as one in which a dialectizable element is at once incorporated, put to work, and overcome in the movement of ever higher synthesis or idealization. Phenomenology and linguistic science alike relieve and relift metaphysics according to this same movement, while the philosophical discourse and concept of metaphor aspires to a similar incorporation and overcoming. Derrida also refers to the *relève* of humanism and of 'man' in Hegelian, Husserlian and Heideggerian thought ('The Ends of Man'). Yet such relifting and relieving, when thought of as a process of reinstating at ever greater depth that which one wishes to bring to an exposed surface, is not merely a recurrent feature of the philosophical innovations and struggles which emerge from the history of metaphysics. It is also the risk of deconstruction, the very risk indeed which recurs in its attempts to circumvent this logic, calling Derrida to insist on the utmost vigilance (or the least possible triumphalism) in any deconstructive reading or practice.

mark   See also **re-mark.** For Derrida, each incision in language constitutes a **singular event**, the making of an irreplaceable mark (which is therefore always in some sense signed/dated: see especially **'Shibboleth'**). Yet the singularity of the mark is given on condition of the possibility of its re-marking or **iterability**. (See, too, **Signsponge**.) This constitutive **supplement** of the re-mark therefore divides the mark, or marks its self-difference, at the origin. Every mark is therefore a differential mark, always susceptible or open, perhaps, to the **other** and the **future** to come.

Marx, Karl (1818–1883)   German philosopher, political economist and theorist, sociologist, and revolutionary thinker. See **Marx, Marxism**, and especially *Specters of Marx*.

Marx, Marxism   See especially *Specters of Marx*. See also *Echographies of Television*, 'Faith and Knowledge', 'Force of Law', *Learning to Live Finally*, messianicity, *Negotiations*, *Points*, *Positions*.

Mauss, Marcel (1872–1950)   French sociologist. See **gift**, *Given Time*.

Memoires for Paul de Man   This volume includes a series of three lectures given early in 1984, first at Yale and then at the University of California, Irvine, in the wake of de Man's death. Initially published in English translation in 1986, the reprinted edition of 1989 is famous for including 'Like the Sound of the Sea Deep within a Shell: Paul de Man's War', which originally appeared in *Critical Inquiry* in 1988. Here, Derrida tackles the issue of de Man's wartime journalism. During August 1987, Samuel Weber telephoned Derrida with news that a Belgian doctoral student, Ortwin de Graef, had unearthed articles by de Man from the early 1940s which had appeared in *Le Soir*, a French language newspaper, and also *Het Vlaamsche Land*, a Belgian publication. Both of these were renowned for carrying material that was sympathetic to the German occupation. While de Graef appeared keen to seek Derrida's advice on how to handle these findings, he nevertheless shared his discovery with a number of others in the United States, notably at Yale (where de Man had taught), while also sending a sample to the British journal *Textual Practice*, together with a hastily constructed introduction. Derrida's sense of de Graef, whom he had not yet met, was of a young academic keen to keep some control over an important find, but unsure how to negotiate a situation that was potentially extremely volatile. Weber and Derrida asked de Graef to send to them all the pieces published in French, which were the majority, receiving in reply a collection of 25 from a set of around 125. The basis for this selection was not, Derrida tells us, entirely clear. Hoping to encounter a series of texts which made only minor concessions to the occupier – those of 'omission' or 'abstention', for instance – Derrida was disappointed to find a deeper level of engagement, which in this essay he immediately and forthrightly condemns, while also detecting a complex and somewhat divided discourse of a rather disconcerting nature. Reluctant to evaluate the material too hastily, on the basis of a possibly unrepresentative sample, Derrida nevertheless chose to respond publicly, recognizing that the 'war' over de Man's early writings had already broken out in the media, giving rise not only to the strongest condemnations levelled at the author, but also, by extension, at the supposedly dubious political grounds of deconstruction. For Derrida, this media discourse was both poorly informed and highly motivated, indeed pre-calculated, calling for a more cogent analysis to appear sooner rather than later. By the end of the same month, Derrida had also decided to make the material as public as possible, so that it could be read and debated in complete freedom.

The contents of the articles sent to Derrida were, for him, painfully surprising, since he had found no reason during his twenty-year friendship with de Man to suspect such complicity with 'the very worst'. In this essay, indeed, Derrida wonders why de Man did not speak of the episode more widely and frequently, and speculates that de Man had sufficiently distanced himself from this context, in both his theoretical and public writings (including a written explanation), to make the gesture rather indecently theatrical. Derrida's sense of surprise over the letters was nonetheless compounded, he tells us, since he already knew of de Man's editorship in 1940 (prior to the defeat) of a Brussels journal which had voiced strongly anti-fascist and pro-democratic sentiments. However, on reflection, Derrida recalls in de Man's editorial writing for this same publication a reference to the decadence of Western civilization, and mention of a new 'order' (one, however, that we should not necessarily confuse with the 'new order' of the extreme right), which he found troubling as the 'commonplace' language of many an authoritarian or totalitarian discourse in the making. But, looking again at the text – one published, let us recall, in an explicitly pro-democratic and anti-fascist context – Derrida shows that such commonplaces are not merely stated uncritically, but are instead attributed to a particular type of perspective with which the author does not in fact identify in any straightforward or forthright way. For Derrida, this leaves open the possibility that de Man's editorial strategy and style remarks such commonplaces with a certain irony, producing an over-determined inscription which necessarily implies some remove. For Derrida, this rhetorical strategy should not be too hastily discounted when reading the journalism in question, written after the defeat, which was of course framed on the page by material that subscribed uncritically to the official rhetoric of occupation. By making this point, Derrida is not attempting to exculpate de Man too speedily (indeed, the very idea of putting de Man on trial is for him somewhat miscalculated, not only because de Man was already dead and therefore could not answer the charges, but also because during his lifetime he offered a public explanation which indicated a complete and irreversible break with both the ideological organs of the occupation and the pressures of censorship). Instead, Derrida asks us to note – precisely in contrast to the sort of writing which typically would have surrounded de Man's articles – a non-simple and, in effect, non-conformist stance and style. For Derrida, a double-edged attitude traverses these writings, one which risks putting into question as highly debatable the very opinions and ideas it seems to expound.

In one particular article, however, 'Les Juifs dans la littérature actuelle' (Jews in Present-day Literature), Derrida feels himself confronted by an anti-semitism which – even in terms of this double-edged writing style – would seem inexcusable, one which appears not only to reinforce familiar stereotypes, but that also finds itself able to contemplate without obvious difficulty or distress the founding of a **Jewish** colony outside **Europe**. While condemning such sentiments without hesitation wherever they arise, Derrida nevertheless notes that the entire piece is structured as a denunciation of 'vulgar anti-semitism' and its 'lapidary judgement', based on 'myth', 'error' and mere 'opinion'. While Derrida does not entirely rule out the possibility that such an indictment tacitly preserves the possibility of a more 'cultured' anti-semitic viewpoint, he also insists on another possible interpretation: precisely because the article mentions none other than the 'vulgar' type of prejudice, it may condemn the vulgar nature of anti-semitism *itself*, in other words its essential and wholesale vulgarity. Again, while Derrida acknowledges the obvious charges against de Man here, he once more underlines the deeply non-conformist aspect of any denunciation of anti-semitism in such publications at this time, and wonders about the way this article may effectively have addressed and indicted the other pieces which would have surrounded it on the page.

Derrida notes the juvenile quality of some of the articles in question (de Man was in his early twenties at the time), but also the strong impression of a literary erudition and an artistic culture, at once European and international, making its presence felt. (In a number of texts by Derrida on philosophical nationality and nationalism, the place of Germany in this culture is painstakingly examined – see for instance the '*Geschlecht*' essays in **Psyche**.) Derrida goes on to question the influence of de Man's uncle,

Henri, on these writings, and asks more broadly about the Belgian or, rather, Flemish context in which, while both French and German influences were frequently resisted, anti-French sentiment sometimes manifested itself in terms of a complex identification with a particular future for Germany in Europe (although Derrida can find no trace of an endorsement for **Nazism** in the wartime texts by de Man that he reads, and in places detects a highly ambivalent – that is, more 'pro-French' and indeed sometimes less nationalistic – attitude to the allegiances of such Flemish nationalism). Certainly, rather than excuse the author's youthful immaturity, Derrida is quick to ask of the young de Man that he take his responsibilities, noting that others of a similar age took theirs in resisting the occupying forces, often with grave personal consequences. However, Derrida concludes the text by alluding to the testimonies of two former Belgian resistants who knew de Man during the war. These state that de Man was not thought of as a collaborator, an anti-semite, or a pro-Nazi, and that he offered assistance to the resistants in Belgium.

Near the beginning of his text, Derrida recalls the first words of *Memoires*, those which had been written and published prior to the addition of this essay: 'I have never known how to tell a story'. He observes wryly that de Man's 'war' (both during the occupation years and in the contemporary press) has nevertheless imposed upon him the unanticipatable obligation to tell *this* story. It is an unforeseeable injunction which comes precisely from an **other**, indeed from the one for whom the structure of narrative in general cannot be extricated from allegory (that is, from a discourse of the other, a discourse which always says something other than itself). Responding, taking one's **responsibilities**, in this context is a complicated matter indeed. *Memoires*, too, reads de Man in order to speak of **memory** as always oriented or projected towards a **future** that one cannot see coming. Such a future ties memory to the structure of the **promise**, linking it with a 'to come' which cannot be predicted or guaranteed. And such a promise finds its gravity in **friendship** and **mourning**, since friendship promises and recalls itself in respect of the **singularity** of the other, which is also to say in regard to the **death** and **impossible** mourning of the other. In memory of de Man – that is, right from the beginning as well as after his death and before the unforeseeable events of a future – Derrida seeks to keep the promise that friendship always is. A promise which, however, cannot know exactly what it is promising. Such a

Memoirs of the Blind

friendship does not license one to speak in place of the other, but instead calls the friend to assume responsibilities which are reducible neither to a simple defence or judgement of the other.

The volume opens with 'In Memoriam', also included in **The Work of Mourning**. The subsequent three lectures, rich and varied in their interpretations and arguments, deal with precisely these questions of narration and allegory, memory, the promise and the future, and the impossible mourning of the other, going by way of de Man's readings of Rousseau, Hölderlin, Hegel, Nietzsche and Heidegger, to mention a few. Also at issue, in thinking of de Man's intellectual legacy, is the question of '**deconstruction** in **America**', upon which Derrida was invited to speak at this time. (One story that might be told of de Man is that of a European emigré, nicknamed 'Hölderlin in America' by one of his friends.) However, Derrida resists making this a central theme, and indeed points to the plurality of possible interpretations of 'deconstruction in America', which the phrase itself may never come to dominate or resolve. (For instance, one might also envisage a thinking of America *in* deconstruction, that is 'America' as always already deconstructible and perhaps distinctive in its production of deconstruction-effects. Or else one might propose, as Derrida ventures to do, that America *is* deconstruction – although such a hypothesis is given in a form which immediately challenges the status of 'deconstruction' as a **proper name** and therefore puts into question precisely what it is that 'America' names, or promises to name.) Derrida observes that de Man's interpretation of **Rousseau** in terms of 'textual allegory' forcefully brings out not merely the **fictionality** of political forms and discourses, but their promissory structure, which generates (indeed *recalls*) historical possibility only on condition of a certain **aporia** or unreadability that allegory in fact names. One might speculate that this interpretation of the de Manian legacy in particular has a special contribution to make to the thinking of 'deconstruction in America'.

Memoirs of the Blind: The Self-Portrait and Other Ruins

Published in English in 1993. In this volume Derrida remarks upon a number of images chosen from the prints and drawings department of the Louvre, all of which portray blindness in some way. A fuller account of this book is included in the entry on **The Truth in Painting**.

memory   See *Adieu, Archive Fever, Dissemination, Echographies of Television, Geneses, Genealogies, Genres and Genius, Memoires for Paul de Man, Points, Psyche, Specters of Marx, Without Alibi, Writing and Difference* (especially 'Freud and the Scene of Writing').

messianicity   Between the two sources of the Abrahamic religions identified by **Kant** – a basis in 'faith' or God's historical revelation on the one hand (**Judaism**, Islam), and an orientation towards 'knowledge', morality, good deeds and righteous conduct on the other (**Christianity**) – Derrida detects an enduring messianicity, the structure of which in fact precedes or overflows each religion and every messiah. For readers of Derrida, this messianicity may be linked to originary **affirmation** and the structure of the **promise**; to the '**yes, yes**' and to the **future** or the **other** 'to come' as effect, condition or possibility of *différance*. (In **'Faith and Knowledge'**, where this question of a 'messianic' without messianism arises, such messianicity is treated via an allusion to **khôra** as always non-present 'origin' – here, Derrida refers us to the texts found in *On the Name*.) Derrida thus speaks of a messianicity without the messiah or messianism, one which opens itself to the absolute *arrivant*, the wholly other and the anticipatable future beyond all prophetic discourse. Derrida associates such messianicity with the desire for **justice**. Indeed, this linkage puts in question traditional distinctions between pre- and post-Enlightenment thought, between mysticism and rationality, religion and reason.

In *Specters of Marx*, meanwhile, one such supposedly 'post-Enlightenment' form of knowledge and discourse – **Marxism** – is effectively redescribed by way of its relation to the messianic, to a messianicity 'beyond' or 'without' messianism. Indeed, Derrida suggests that this is especially true of a Marxism still to come, the Marxism which remains after the 'collapse' of Soviet communism. This would be a *spectrally* surviving Marxism, one which could not but *come back to* its relation to messianicity, and to **re-mark** itself in terms of the promise of the future or of the 'other' to come; but one which might be differently disposed than previous Marxisms to prophetic language and utopian thinking (i.e., less inspired by the onto-theological dream of a reincarnated wholeness, a pure identity or ideal 'presence' beyond spectrality itself). Tellingly, a kind of utopianism had re-emerged around the time that Derrida wrote the book, in the form of **Fukuyama**'s pronouncement of the 'end of history' – an 'end' which

metaphysics of presence

supposedly accompanied the defeat of communism by neo-liberalism and free market economics. For Derrida, however, the **spectre**(s) of Marx cannot be exorcized by, or indeed banished from, this 'messianic' discourse of the Fukuyama type (which is itself, Derrida suggests, a ghost story of sorts). Instead, it is precisely on the strength of Marx's 'spectres' that the possibility arises of a Marxism of the 'here-now', a Marxism surprisingly well-equipped to think the 'spectral', 'virtualized', 'disjointed', non-self-identical world of today, not least as a provocation to neo-liberal hegemony. For Derrida, **deconstruction** inherits a certain messianic 'remains' of Marx, in the interests of justice and the **'democracy to come'**.

metaphor   See 'Plato's Pharmacy' in **Dissemination**, 'White Mythology' in **Margins of Philosophy**, 'The Retrait of Metaphor' in **Psyche**, **Of Grammatology**, **'Signature Event Context'**, 'Freud and the Scene of Writing' in **Writing and Difference**. See also 'Khôra' in **On the Name**, **On Touching**, philosophy, phonocentrism, **The Truth in Painting**.

metaphysics, metaphysical   See **metaphysics of presence**.

metaphysics of presence   For Derrida, the Western tradition in its philosophical and historical form assigns principal value to **presence**, and indeed determines **being** in precisely these terms. The metaphysics of presence thus describes the conceptual (but also practical) conditions of possibility within which the thought, texts and histories of this tradition emerge. For such a metaphysical tradition, presence expresses itself in a number of ways: the presence of the subject to itself in thought or speech (but also through its vision or sense of touch); the determination of a being or entity in terms of its presence in time and space; the notion of the original presence of a transcendental signified or ultimate source of meaning, such as God. In Derrida's writing, then, presence is the watchword for a thinking which remains invested in the idea of the self-identity, self-continuity, or self-sufficiency of a being.

Within this metaphysical tradition, presence articulates and elevates itself in terms of a series of oppositions, whereby difference is negatively marked. Thus, as Derrida shows in a number of his major works, while **speech** is seen as the expression of living presence, **writing** in contrast is viewed as a detached and ultimately lifeless form of representation, a mere copy of the original (the spoken word) which, indeed, threatens presence with its supposed 'other' – absence. Writing, in other words, lacks presence; what is different from presence (in this case, from living speech) is therefore construed in terms of lack. Similarly, within the metaphysical tradition, other hierarchies based on the opposition of presence to absence or lack determine not only the history of thought but also cultural relations and practices more broadly. Thus the metaphysics of presence dominates the relation of the masculine to the feminine, nature to culture and technology, and so on. Here, the superior term is always characterized by its purity, plenitude, originality or self-suffiency – its presence – in view of which the subordinate term is determined as such on the basis of its perceived defects or deficiency – its lack.

However, Derrida rethinks difference, not in terms of the opposition and privation of presence, but as originary and constitutive. (Here, we should be quick to note that this does not amount to the substitution of difference for presence as an origin in the classical sense.) Derrida makes this argument in a number of texts. For instance, **Saussurian** linguistics considers the relation of the signifier to the signified to be an arbitrary and relational one. From this viewpoint, language is seen to function as a system of differences or differential values. But, asks Derrida in his essay *'Différance'*, what produces and maintains such differences, what establishes the conditions of possibility for the play of differing and deferring that permits signification to happen? To make a force such as this signify – to give it a determinate value, identity or meaning – would amount to including it (*present*ing it as such) as an element in the system which it supposedly renders possible. Yet neither can such a force (which Derrida nicknames *différance*, since it cannot have a **proper name**) be thought to rise above the field of differences in which it is constitutively at play. Neither exactly present nor absent, *différance* – a difference irreducible to the oppositional thinking characteristic of metaphysics – is thus the non-signifying force or **trace** that cuts across each and every **mark**, the unpresentable and unsystematizable **supplement** or remainder which at once constitutes and overflows the mark's possibility. *Différance*, trace, supplement (to draw upon just some of the subsitutable words Derrida coins in what he describes as an unmasterable series) thus redescribe the entire field which metaphysics seeks to dominate throughout history. Supplementation is that which the metaphysics of presence projects as an inessential and privative attribute, something it could well do without; deprived of the supplement, however, the metaphysical tradition could not constitute itself, as Derrida repeatedly demonstrates.

See also **'Différance'**, *Margins of Philosophy*, *Of Grammatology*, *On Touching*, *Politics of Friendship*, **'Signature Event Context'**, *Speech and Phenomena*.

mimesis   See *Acts of Literature*, *Dissemination*, *Writing and Difference*.

mondialization   See **global, globalization**.

monolingualism   See *Monolingualism of the Other*.

Monolingualism of the Other; or, the Prosthesis of Origin   A short text from 1996 written in more (or perhaps less) than one voice, the form taken by this late work resonates intriguingly with its central **affirmation**: 'I have only one language; it is not mine'. Taking up a sort of interminably divided residence between apparently contradictory statements in order to demonstrate the necessity of each of them, Derrida asserts with the phrase 'We only ever speak one language' his 'own' monolingualism (which is at once irreducibly **singular** to him although never having been 'his' alone), while at the very same time insisting on the impossibility of speaking just *one* language, a single, unified language given as 'natural' or original in a classical sense. French, this 'only' and yet somehow '**other**' language of Derrida's (who consistently felt himself less effective in 'secondary' languages such as English and German), is not for him – as *also* an **Algerian Jew** – to be confused with merely a *foreign* language coming from 'overthere'. Rather – since the distinction between a language, a dialect and an idiom can never be entirely pure or natural – this language, like all others, is to be understood as the site of a violently cross-cutting series of highly charged historical relations of force that tell the story of both the essential disunity in the making of any language, and a contingent language politics of the state, a politics of **linguistic** and geo-cultural imposition conducted by a complex variety of means. Consequently, the determination of a 'single' language will always fall foul of a certain uncountability in the face of this more or less violent, constituting plurality.

To call his 'own' **French** merely a 'foreign' (that is, purely 'outsider') language would, for Derrida, fail to do justice to the essential (political) complexity of this situation. At the same time, since as he demonstrates monolingualism is always imposed or instituted by the other (as precisely 'a prosthesis of origin'), Derrida also disputes the basic possibility of referring to a '**mother** tongue' as a sort of 'natural' linguistic heredity.

As an exemplary figure of the Franco-Maghrebian, Derrida shows how his 'identity' since birth will have remained divided and disordered between, on the one hand, the imposition (and, indeed, forced withdrawal during the 'Occupation') of **European** citizenship and, on the other, an unavoidable cultural, linguistic and historical participation in North Africa which relates complexly to this very same citizenship. (Derrida reflects on the tormented nature of the hyphen that joins and divides the French and Maghrebian, where neither can be taken to imply a straightforward historico-political unity. The hyphen, then, promises or claims a relation that is not simply a given; and yet this hyphen will never be able to silence the **memory** of the concrete forms of **violence** for which it must always stand.) As Derrida shows, French citizenship (which, like any other, is never simply naturally occurring nor granted absolutely) was bestowed upon Algerian Jews in 1870, but withdrawn by the French in 1940, apparently under no pressure from the occupying German forces in France, only to be restored a couple of years later. Derrida reflects on the perhaps unexampled status of these Algerian Jews *as a group* during that period, existing for a time with no other citizenship, and suffering a whole series of related exclusions. (It is worth noting that the legal status of Algerian Muslims and Jews from the mid-nineteenth century throughout the wars and upheavals of the twentieth is discussed by Derrida in 'Pas d'hospitalité', found in ***Of Hospitality***.) As an Algerian Jew, Derrida himself was excluded from State-recognized schooling, but chose to skip classes for a year rather than attend the Jewish lycée created by displaced teachers and students, with which he felt little affinity. *Monolingualism of the Other* includes a carefully woven account of the language politics of the French-Algerian lycée at that time, where Hebrew, Arabic and Berber were actively discouraged rather than entirely forbidden, and indeed those of different neighbourhoods – Jewish, Arabic, and so forth – in French Algeria during the war. Derrida also speaks of the invisibility of Algerian history and geography in the lycée at the expense of an imposed French curriculum; the lack of immediate

mother

resources offered by his surrounding Jewish culture for fashioning identity anew at a certain moment of its historical asphyxiation; and, from the time of the exile of French literary culture to places such as Algiers during the war, of a long-term capitulation to 'good' metropolitan French which intensified as Derrida entered French literature, philosophy and academia, a capitulation which nevertheless exercized itself in the interests of transforming the proper possibility of this 'good' French from the inside.

To host a language is also to become its hostage, says Derrida (in the vein of those texts he wrote at roughly the same time – 1995 and 1996 – by way of an adieu to **Levinas**). Putting **ipseity** before identity, Derrida shows how the 'I' is conditioned by the more originary power of the 'I can', which, however, trembles before a certain terror inside language, that which profoundly threatens the fantasy of total (self-) possession. The supposed master of a language or languages is denatured by language itself as always also a colonizing force. Language cannot be fully appropriated, since it is that which – without any natural property or propriety – jealously (though never fully) appropriates at the site of an always divided cultural, political, historical and linguistic setting. For this reason (one which demands as much as permits the apparently contradictory assertions which open the text), Derrida can never entirely assimilate the language that is nonetheless his 'own', of which he is both host and hostage: French. And this would be true of all languages, all speakers or writers, all linguistic 'masters'. Indeed, the most acute conditions and experiences of colonial imposition are, in one sense, merely high points of this basic situation. Yet such a recognition, far from neutralizing differences between the more extreme and relatively mild versions of a language politics at work, calls us to remember this fundamental state of affairs in order to allow a repoliticization of the stakes in each and every case.

This volume also offers a long footnote on the **ethics** of language – at the intersections of Judaism, **Christianity**, Europe and the other shores of the Mediterranean – found in a number of figures, from the Moroccan Abdelkebir Khatibi to Franz Rosenweig, Gershom Scholem, Hannah Arendt and Emmanuel Levinas.

mother   See *Circumfession*, *Glas*, 'Khôra' in *On the Name*, **sexual difference**. (For mother tongue, see *The Ear of the Other*, *Monolingualism of the Other*.)

mourning See *Adieu, Aporias, Cinders, Glas, Learning to Live Finally, Memoires for Paul de Man,* September 11, *Specters of Marx, The Gift of Death*, and especially *The Work of Mourning*.

— N —

name See *On the Name*, proper name.

Nancy, Jean-Luc (b.1940) French philosopher. See *Echographies of Television, On Touching, Politics of Friendship, Rogues*.

Nazism See, here, entries on *Of Spirit, Memoires for Paul de Man, The Ear of the Other*.

negative theology See *'Différance', On the Name*, 'How to Avoid Speaking: Denials' in *Psyche*.

negotiation In the interview 'Negotiations' (in the volume of the same title), negotiation is linked to 'the impossibility of establishing oneself anywhere': the **impossibility**, that is, of determining a high ground, a permanent footing or self-sufficient basis for thought or judgement. Negotiation is called for, unremittingly, by the self-difference that founds any problem, any text, any event or situation (see *différance*). In other words, negotiation is the **responsibility** called up by the **undecidable** – and in this interview Derrida goes so far as to speak of an **ethics** of negotiation (although of course Derrida's arguments make it clear that one must continually negotiate with such an ethics, in terms of what the 'ethical' may come to mean or how it might be determined).

One may be confronted with the demands of the non-negotiable (the categorical imperative, say), yet nevertheless one must always negotiate with such non-negotiability. In order to avoid mere piety, abstraction, ineffectuality (or, indeed, certain types of exploitation, perversion, misuse), **justice**, the '**unconditional**', must continually transact with the conditional forms of **law**, right or norm that we inherit. In the interests of the **future** or the **democracy to come**, this negotiation calls for the utmost vigilance, and, for Derrida, remains interminable. One can never be done with it, there is no ultimate prize or victory. Negotiation is, then, far from heroic or 'noble', but is instead, as Derrida puts it, 'a little dirty' or 'impure'. You get your hands dirty.

Negotiations: Interventions and Interviews 1971–2001 This large collection contains a wide variety of occasional texts by Derrida which combine so as to give specific, concrete illustration to the reconfiguration of **ethical** and political thought attempted by Derrida over many years. Polemics on behalf of particular figures or issues correspond complexly with the philosophical reformulation of ethico-political questions and problems, as if one might witness thought in action or, better still, action in thought, action *of* thought. There is an open letter to Bill Clinton from 1996 appealing for the conviction to be overturned of the former Black Panther Mumia Abu-Jamal (still held on death row today), whom Derrida regarded as a political prisoner. The volume includes the fragment of a 1971 letter to Jean **Genet** concerning his appeal for the freedom of George Jackson, held at that time in San Quentin Prison and subsequently executed. Such texts might be read alongside Derrida's sustained reflection on the question of capital punishment during the epochal world-political trend of its abolition (the United States constituting a striking and exemplary exception here, of course), and his observations on the reticence of Western philosophy historically to condemn the death penalty. There is also the transcript of an improvised speech given during a demonstration in Nanterre in support of the 'sans-papiers' (literally, those 'without papers'), and another of his 1994 public endorsement of an appeal for civil peace and democracy in **Algeria** on behalf of certain activist organizations in France at that time, which also outlines Derrida's reservations about the specific framing of this appeal. One finds here, too, Derrida's thoughts on intellectual **responsibility** and the possibility of a philosophical rather than programmatic politics in the interests of a renewed sense of responsibility and **decision**. Some texts reflect Derrida's engagement with UNESCO during the 1990s, an engagement which might be seen as part of Derrida's broader commitment to developing international institutions that might better recognize the resources of the philosophical tradition (Derrida himself both questions and transforms a certain Kantian legacy of cosmopolitanism) and which could promote innovations in the field of international relations, **law** and politics (a new 'world contract', as he puts it), notably in view of the techno-scientific structures and economies of knowledge-power that currently drive '**globalization**' in all its discourses and effects.

The interview 'Politics and Friendship' includes Derrida's various recollections of the changing intellectual milieu in **France**, and especially Paris, from the 1950s and 1960s onwards, charting the history of his personal relationship with Althusser and explaining his intellectual differences with Althusserian **Marxism** and the French Communist Party. The interview also contains Derrida's reflections on some of the conditions that shaped – for him and others – the possibilities of reading Husserl, Heidegger, Lacan, and a host of leading French thinkers of the period. Derrida's thoughts on the ethical and legal dimensions of the human genome project in the early 1990s are also to be found in this volume.

There is also a brilliantly perceptive analysis of the text and signing of the Declaration of Independence, which went to establish the constitutional basis of the United States ('Declarations of Independence'). As Derrida points out, the Declaration is signed and authorized by the very 'People' whom it in fact serves to inaugurate or bring into being as a national, constitutional body, thus demonstrating – in the **impossible** anachronicity of both the *après coup* and the future anterior – the intractable **violence** rather than the '**justice**' or 'legality' of the founding act. The relationship of **deconstruction** to actuality and to what is most 'timely' is discussed in 'The Deconstruction of Actuality', an interview given to the journal *Passages*. Here, far from referring simply to a given 'present' or **presence** or to a self-evident reality, actuality for Derrida is always constituted by complex effects of **différance** that are negotiated (both impossibly and necessarily) by the selective making of 'truths'. This analysis thus gives rise to two suggestive neologisms on Derrida's part, **artifactuality** and **actu-virtuality**. The collection opens with a lengthy interview, 'Negotiations', which discusses Derrida's role in the activist grouping **Greph**, which sought to oppose the proposed government reform of philosophical education in France in the 1970s, and the part he took in founding and directing the Collège international de philosophie (**Ciph**) in the early 1980s. In this context, Derrida reflects on the ethics and politics of **negotiation**, indeed upon negotiation as a way to transform the definition of 'politics' and

Of Grammatology

'ethics' in concept and practice. Never pure or concludable, but never avoidable either, negotiation earns its name not through negotiating (with) what is merely negotiable. (Here we find a similar logic to the one which says that, by operating in a preconstituted field of possibility, **forgiveness** of the forgiveable or **hospitality** extended to the welcomable guest or **invention** of the inventible does nothing justly worth the name.) Rather, it is by engaging the *non-negotiable* in negotiation that the prospect remains open of responsibility and decision. One name for this 'non-negotiable' might be *justice* (as, precisely, the 'undeconstructible' in whose name **deconstruction** nevertheless happens). Justice is non-negotiable, then, but one must nonetheless always engage it in negotiation, negotiate everywhere (with) its non-negotiability, in the interests of the **democracy to come**.

new international See *Spectres of Marx*.

Nietzsche, Friedrich (1844–1900) German philosopher. See *'Différance'*, **'Faith and Knowledge'**, **gift**, *Margins of Philosophy*, *Memoires for Paul de Man*, *Politics of Friendship*, *Spurs*, *The Ear of the Other*, *Writing and Difference*.

non-response See *On the Name*.

Of Grammatology A seminal work, famously sharing its year of publication – 1967 – with two other major texts by Derrida, ***Writing and Difference*** and ***Speech and Phenomena***. The volume is divided into two main parts. 'Writing before the Letter' sees Derrida outline a 'grammatological' notion of **writing** as distinct from its traditional conception in the West. In its classical concept, writing is predominantly considered a **technical** form of representation serving in instrumental, auxiliary and thus derivative fashion to translate on to some lifeless substrate a phonetic language which, in living **speech**, finds its full **presence** and immediacy as the essential correlative of thought. Derrida distinguishes between the Western tradition's sense of 'good' and 'bad' writing: the 'good' entails the inscription of divinity in the soul, in nature or in the religious book; whereas the 'bad' soullessly contrives and corrupts, monstrously crossing the divine breath with a prosthetic, unnatural, technical body. **Phonocentrism** is therefore Derrida's name for the priority given to a conception of the unity of sound and sense which at once produces the self-presence of the subject in living speech and weds such speech to the realm of the soul or the divine. Writing in its 'bad' form as fallen exteriority, meanwhile, carries within itself only the principle of **death** and a pejorative sense of difference. For Derrida, phonocentrism thus supports the determination of being as presence, and is on the most intimate inside of what he calls the epoch of the **logos** (which, in short, names the idea – always ultimately **onto-theological** – that words refer essentially to things, an idea which dictates that writing is ultimately effaced in the living unity of speech and soul, truth, God).

The classical determination of writing as principally a secondary region of language, then, establishes a sequential and hierarchical order of precedence which runs from the thinking mind to spoken words to written form. From this perspective, writing is thought to function merely as the signifier of the signifier, while living speech considered in its full and original presence yields authentic access to the signified, and thus to truth. Derrida powerfully **deconstructs** such a **metaphysics** of language by demonstrating that, far from transcending and thus anchoring the entire field of language, the signified in its conception or determination always already depends on its function as a signifier (thus Derrida wants to think this deconstructibility of the signifier-signified distinction in terms of his conception of the **trace**); he furthermore draws attention to the deep paradox that the classical understanding of (divine) living speech operates essentially by means of **metaphor** (years later, of course, he will tie together in a single inextricable knot the very possibility of **testimony**, **fiction** and **lying**). Constitutive of the West's very history, Derrida suggests that such a metaphysics of language reaches its point of closure, while perhaps not coming to its end, amidst the long-term development of new techniques of communication and information, and indeed alongside

Of Grammatology

newly emerging forms of science and mathematics, which erode the priority of phonetic-alphabetic language and its determination of writing as instrumental and representative.

Part of Derrida's purpose in this section of the volume is to question the extent to which **linguistic** science, notably that of the **Saussurian** kind, may go beyond or break with this enduring metaphysics of language. First of all, he distances a grammatological concept of writing from its scientific conception, on the grounds that the very idea of science arises in the logocentric and phonocentric era of the West. Furthermore, identifying language as the object of scientific enquiry assumes and presupposes that the latter might separate itself objectively from the former as merely a technical, external and auxiliary instrument rather than the very condition or element of science itself. Such 'scientific' thinking remains up to its neck in the metaphysical determination of writing which, in its quest for positive knowledge, it would presumably wish to overcome. Derrida shows how Saussure in fact reasserts the priority of speech over writing in determining the object of linguistic science. Phonocentric and logocentric thinking, going back as far as **Plato**, are reinforced in Saussure's concept of writing as merely the technical and historical exterior of the true linguistic object (the spoken word). For Derrida, Saussure's theory of the sign's arbitrariness strongly participates in the long-established order of relations in which the graphic comes to be associated with artificiality, displacement and violence. However, just as in 'Structure, Sign, and Play' (see **Writing and Difference**) the possible event of a rupture entailed by the advent of **structuralism** remains to come, so for Derrida the assertion of the arbitrariness of the sign by Saussure invites, if unwittingly, a conception of writing (or **arche-writing**) in terms of **différance**, a thinking of spacing and of the institution of the trace, which in turn exposes the very limits of the Saussurian definition of the linguistic object as tied ultimately to the metaphysical or onto-theological tradition that in fact produces linguistic 'science'. It is this metaphysics, indeed, which determines all the oppositions – signifier/signified, speech/writing, nature/culture, prior/derivative, inside/outside, presence/absence, identity/difference, diachronic/synchronic – which form the basis or element of Saussurian thought. For this reason, deconstruction is grossly misunderstood as seeking merely to reverse the order of priority implicit in such dualisms. (Derrida constantly had to refute simple-minded accusations that he preferred writing over speech.) Rather, a deconstructive grammatology entails a modified conception of writing as an 'origin' without presence, a movement occurring outside the categories of intentionality or the subject. Arche-writing, as Derrida suggests, founds language in its spatio-temporal play as never fully systematic, objectifiable, conceptualizable, idealizable. This thought of language moves us from the dreams and desires of 'science' to questions of the institution and historicity of the field, in its always partial and violent imposition.

The second section of the volume, 'Nature, Culture, Writing' presents a reading of Jean-Jacques **Rousseau** and, indeed, those such as Claude **Levi-Strauss** whom Derrida suggests follow in the wake of his thought. Derrida finds in Rousseau a systematic repression of writing that, for him, characterizes the entire tradition of metaphysics. For Rousseau, voice plays a determining role in assuring the subject's self-presence. Through speech, the subject is able to attest to its presence, indeed to secure (self-) consciousness of that presence through an essentially unmediated experience that is here named **auto-affection**. In contrast to speech as the immediate (self-) expression of living presence, then, writing is assigned a secondary role by Rousseau as merely the **supplement** of spoken language. To the extent that writing may be seen to divide and dislocate presence, however, it is for Rousseau a 'dangerous supplement' that always threatens to corrupt the integrity of the subject and speech. Viewed as merely a material technology and external substrate for the extended representation of language (language that is to be understood as essentially oral in origin), writing puts at risk the living presence inherent in speech. As a technical invention which supervenes upon language in its essential form, writing threatens to corrupt the spoken word: by mediating the living presence at the origin of language itself (that is, speech as the expression of a subject or consciousness), it cannot but risk becoming a – deathly and deadly – substitute for it. Rousseau's thinking here produces at once a myth of origins, a representation of 'nature' (and, indeed, of the 'Fall'), a theory of language, and a political philosophy. In contrast to modern societies, primitive forms of social organization are idealized by Rousseau as based purely on spoken interactions which, via the organic immediacy of (self-) expression, precede the possibility of division and conflict figured by the advent of writing.

Derrida, however, puts in question Rousseau's narrative concerning the relation of writing to speech. He endeavours to show how writing supplements speech not merely as a subsequent addition to what is already fully present in itself, but as an essential trait that intervenes constitutively at the very origin of that which it supplements. For Derrida, then, Rousseau's 'dangerous supplement' of writing – construed in terms of an extrinsic and always potentially destructive 'add-on' – everywhere supplements *itself*, in the sense that it comes at the price of another supplementarity at work, an originary supplementation which produces difference at the origin of all metaphysical values and priorities (presence, consciousness, speech, and so on).

Thus, writing is obviously the indispensable condition of self-revelation in Rousseau's own **autobiography** (access to the self-presence of the autobiographical subject is secured precisely via graphic inscription), and indeed Rousseau himself acknowledges its value in the self-narration that constitutes his *Confessions*. Meanwhile, Derrida traces this deconstructive logic of the supplement throughout Rousseau's writing. In *Émile*, Rousseau advocates educational reforms that cannot but supplement the supposed self-sufficiency of nature epitomized by maternal love (a love which, if it indeed conveys and confirms nature's self-reliance, should not require supplementation). In the *Confessions*, meanwhile, masturbation is at once a dangerous supplement to 'naturally' fulfilling sexual relations – and, thus, something to which Rousseau resorts in order to relieve sexual frustration – and yet it is also an **auto-affective** act by means of which the onanist seeks untroubled self-satisfaction. (Sexual frustration persists, however, since the dangerous supplement of masturbation conjures an image of self-presence which is no less fictive than that which derives from the idea of totally fulfilling intercourse with another). In 'The Essay on the Origin of Languages in which something is said about Melody and Musical Imitation' (a supposedly minor text on which Derrida concentrates in some detail here), Rousseau attempts to distinguish melody, as the pure, direct and natural expression of passion, from harmony, as the calculated production of non-discordant relations. Yet in representing melody as an *imitation* of nature, however faithful it may be, Rousseau permits us to read melody as itself produced by a certain spacing, interval, difference or, indeed, supplementarity. In other words, melody emerges via a process through which, in a sense, it *harmonizes* with nature. From this perspective, harmony is less a contrived 'add-on' to melody, than the very source of its supposed natural simplicity and immediacy. Similarly, Rousseau considers passionate expression to be the source of language (this he associates with the southern tongues), whereas language as an instrument of need (which Rousseau finds in the northern tongues) is characterized by him as a potentially deadening or corrupting addition to the original. Southern languages are thus defined by 'accent' (a lively and expressive resonance that comes close to song), whereas the languages of the north may be characterized in terms of 'articulation' (suggesting lucidity, precision, the ability to designate, but also lifeless utility). Yet elsewhere Rousseau acknowledges that language emerges and functions on the strength of convention, notably the production of signs, which itself implies that 'accent' is supplemented at its origin by 'articulation' (construed in terms of the production of differences which permit language to designate). Need is thus that which – rather than ruinously corrupting 'nature' – supplements passion at its very origin, both in the sense that Rousseau effectively *needs* passion to found his narrative of the origins of language, and because 'accent' turns out to find its very conditions of possibility in 'articulation'.

In all these cases, the supplement at once augments an ideal or original presence or plenitude, and exposes lack and self-difference at the origin. Thus the supplement is not simply a potentially threatening addition to and foreign substitute for the original, but rather it is constitutively – yet also deconstructively – at work in the production of all the concepts and values which characterize the metaphysics of presence. (In this respect, the supplement is part of the series without a 'proper' or master name which includes *différance*. See, for instance, **Dissemination** and **'Différance'**.)

Through Derrida's reading of Levi-Strauss in the second part of *Of Grammatology*, the supplementarity of the speech-writing relation is brilliantly exposed. Derrida sees Levi-Strauss's structuralist anthropology as descended from Rousseau. In *Tristes tropiques*, Levi-Strauss investigates what he sees as the pre-literate culture of the Nambikwara tribe. For Levi-Strauss, writing is that which arrives from the 'outside' to violate the peace and tranquility of this otherwise unspoilt, essentially 'oral' society. Yet Derrida shows how the **violence** of 'writing' is already a structural feature of Nambikwara culture. For the tribe is already defined, in part and in whole, by the institution of proper names. Such names appropriate and depropriate more or less violently: the **proper name** is the mark by which one is identified, yet it is also that which depropriates me from the outset, since the proper name is destined to outlast me, to substitute for me in my

Of Spirit 117

absence. Thus, through a separation which is both eventual and original, the proper name announces my absence, my death, from the beginning. The proper name as a form of violent inscription rather than pure expression thus marks the advent of writing at the very origin of tribal identity. (Here, we are talking about 'writing' in its most basic sense, rather than in a narrowly empirical way. This broader definition goes beyond the metaphysics of *logos*, by which writing is construed in terms of the empirical emergence of a technical possibility that ruinously supplements speech. Thus, throughout the texts of this period, one of Derrida's key moves is to insist upon an enlarged or fundamental conception of writing that permits deconstruction to counter narratives of the corrupting passage from nature to culture, speech to writing, and so forth. For writing in its enlarged sense – arche-writing or originary writing – is what permits the production of differences that allow such oppositions to emerge in the first place). Writing's violence is at once compounded and attemptedly concealed by the law which prohibits the disclosure of tribal members' proper names to outsiders. By depicting such revelation to foreigners as a shocking impropriety, tribal law feigns to protect the propriety of the name (a propriety which is always fictive). As Derrida shows, however, this name finds its very possibility in difference, mediation, writing, law, violence, all of which inhabit Nambikwara culture from the outset rather than befalling a supposed state of 'nature' in artificial and extrinsic ways. The apparent critique of Western civilization's values which underpins Levi-Strauss's anthropological project is thus, Derrida contends, another example of the Western tradition of **logocentrism**.

Of Hospitality (2000)   A text with Anne Dufourmantelle. See ***Adieu***, **On Cosmopolitanism and Forgiveness**. See also **hospitality**.

Of Spirit: Heidegger and the Question   This is the text of a lecture given in 1987 at a conference held in Paris by the Collège international de philosophie which contributes powerfully to Derrida's engagement with Martin **Heidegger**, begun earlier with those readings found in such texts as '*Ousia* and *Grammē*' and 'The Ends of Man' in ***Margins of Philosophy***, and continued in the series of essays on Heidegger grouped around the word '**Geschlecht**' (a polysemic and untranslatable term meaning variously race, lineage, stock, generation, sex, thus pointing towards Derrida's sustained reading of Heidegger according to questions of philosophical nationality and nationalism).

Whereas in *Being and Time* (1927) Heidegger advises that the term **'spirit'** should be avoided by philosophy as just too metaphysical to help with, let's say, the question of the Being of an entity such as *Dasein*, in the 1933 Rectorship Address at Freiburg University he is to be found acclaiming nothing other than the **German** 'spirit'. (It was not until the early 1950s that Heidegger made telling his retreat from this particular usage.) However, in contrast to experts, followers and detractors alike of Heidegger's philosophy, Derrida suggests that the theme of 'spirit' in fact hauntingly pervades Heidegger's thought, whether in the form of avoidance or appropriation (Derrida suggests the difficulty of separating or opposing the two). Moreover, instead of offering merely an overlooked addition to the critical vocabulary of Heideggerianism, 'spirit' for Derrida demands a fresh programme and new protocols for reading Heidegger's corpus in inevitably unconventional and disruptive ways. Indeed for Derrida 'spirit' might even establish a more powerful and originary (albeit unacknowledged) resource for Heidegger's thinking – and for thinking about Heidegger – than that of the Heideggerian 'question' itself. 'Spirit' – albeit an *other* spirit, other than the 'spirit' which gets, in Derrida's terms, self-affirmingly 're-Germanized' or, for that matter, re-**onto-theologized** – may indeed give the Heideggerian 'question' its (unquestioned) possibility, as perhaps the very resource of **deconstruction**.

Derrida's painstaking analysis of 'spirit' obviously reopens the question of Heidegger's **Nazism**, notably at a time when the Chilean writer Victor Farías made renewed charges concerning the *essential* (that is, not merely contingent or accidental) Nazism of Heidegger's philosophy. Derrida himself responded to Farías (see **Points**) in 'Heidegger, the Philosopher's Hell' and 'Comment donner raison? How to Concede, with Reasons?', questioning the scholarship of Farías, and suggesting that his study made no real contribution to the sum of existing knowledge about Heidegger. Of course, since these exchanges occurred around the time of the so-called **de Man** affair (occasioned by the uncovering of de Man's wartime journalism in a pro-Nazi Belgian newspaper), retrospectively the two 'controversies' have become somewhat merged, rather unhelpfully, amid talk of a deconstruction sorely pricked by charges of an essential complicity with fascism.

One implication of Derrida's text is that the unexpelled, inadequately deconstructed metaphysical residue of 'spirit' may play a certain part in Heidegger's catastrophic flirtation with Nazism. (One aim of the text is to trace the consequences of those philosophical distinctions to which Heidegger resorts – however unconvincingly from a deconstructive viewpoint – in order to distinguish the essence of thought in relation to **animality** and **technicality**.) However, Derrida is concerned neither to partly exculpate Heidegger by distinguishing a spiritualistic from a biologistic (that is, genetic-racist) Nazism, nor to condemn the language or thinking of 'spirit' as *necessarily* Nazistic (elsewhere in the text, Derrida observes that 'spirit' is also a part of the humanistic discourse which, for better or worse, has historically provided an important resource for resisting anti-democratic and totalitarian ideologies of all kinds, although not without running the risk of drawing from the very same conceptual fund that in fact allows them to acquire force). If the question of 'spirit' is not Heidegger's alone, but engages a broader philosophical and literary tradition including Hegel, Schelling, Hölderlin, Trakl, Valéry, Husserl and others (not to mention the religious and cultural legacies of the ancient and Christian worlds), Derrida resists the implication – drawn subsequently by Richard Wolin – that deconstruction practices certain types of relativistic slippage which lose the essential difference between Nazism and non-Nazism. Instead, we might see Derrida's approach in *Of Spirit* as more highly attuned to the transformative confrontation of Nazism with the German, **European** and classical tradition. (It is in this sense, among others, that the text contributes strongly to Derrida's long-standing investigation of the threads that tie together **philosophy**, nationality and nationalism.) For that matter, the line of enquiry to be found in *Of Spirit* may also equip us to become more cautious about the possibility of resorting uncritically to this very same legacy to provide resistance to the spectres of fascism.

On Cosmopolitanism and Forgiveness   This volume includes 'On Cosmopolitanism', presented at Strasbourg in 1996 to the International Parliament of Writers, which Derrida helped establish, and 'On Forgiveness', a text from 1999 which responds to questions from the French journal *Le Monde des débats*. The language of reconciliation in post-apartheid South Africa provides one impetus for the discussion Derrida embarks upon in the latter essay.

Derrida found himself writing 'On Cosmopolitanism' at a time when many were quick to pronounce the end of the city as a classical ideal within the Western tradition. In his seminal work *Homo Sacer* (1995), for instance, Giorgio Agamben argues that it is the concentration camp rather than the city that comes to define the topolitical destiny of modern Western society; while, following Hannah Arendt, Agamben also suggests that the refugee, rather than the citizen, provides the model for the contemporary human being, as a form of bare life caught in a biopolitical relationship with modern forms of sovereignty. Derrida instead wonders about the possibility of a novel reinvention of the city as a place of refuge which might itself force a renewal of international **law** and a transformation of the juridical formation and political orientation of the state. In other words, the city of refuge could only belong to the state and reinscribe its identity and purpose within international law on the strength of a deep reformation of, precisely, their forms of **sovereignty**. (Derrida shrewdly follows Arendt in seeing international law in its current guise as largely the product of deals struck between powerful sovereign states.) Indeed, Derrida locates at the very heart of the International Parliament of Writers's constitution precisely this aspiration to affirm cities of refuge. He does so in the name of a new cosmopolitics which itself innovates with the dense histories of the right to asylum.

Derrida tracks the history of modern forms of statelessness, speaking of a progressive abolition during the twentieth century of the right to asylum, as itself a principle enshrined both in Enlightenment and French Revolutionary thought, particularly in the wake of two World Wars and the diasporas occurring at the close of the colonial period. Derrida speaks of a dwindling respect for refugees claiming asylum status continuing through the 1980s and early 1990s. (One should therefore cross-reference this essay with texts such as 'Derelictions of the Right to Justice' found in **Negotiations**, which records Derrida's improvised speech during a 1996 demonstration in support of the *sans-papiers* in France.) Derrida challenges the way in which the refugee question is often deliberately confused with a perceived problem concerning immigration, in order not only to erode the principle but to impede the practical possibility of asylum. For instance, Derrida charts attempts to strangulate the economic opportunities of refugees in the name of a supposedly valid deterrent against opportunistic migration. He also tells how the state's inability to deal with new forms of statelessness

On Cosmopolitanism and Forgiveness 121

either legally or politically has resulted in the conferral of hitherto unprecedented police powers operating independently of individual governments.

In examining the history of cities of refuge, Derrida contrasts the impact of a Hebraic tradition of welcoming innocents with both the medieval tradition, which accords sovereignty to the city in order to determine more restrictive laws of **hospitality**, and the legacies of Pauline **Christianity** and **Greek** stoicism inherited by Enlightenment thought. In **Kant**, hospitality is limited to the right of visitation, thus excluding the right of residence, while the effort to give rigorous definition to hospitality in terms of its law effectively reties the conditions of hospitality to the model of state sovereignty. Derrida finds these limitations problematic, since what except an **unconditional** hospitality would truly be worthy of its name? For Derrida, genuine hospitality must be absolute, asymmetrical and unmasterable, going beyond even the capacity to welcome or the ability to receive. For to receive and welcome what can indeed be received and welcomed annuls the **gift** and **event** of the hospitable in the midst of an already prescribed relation and calculated exchange with a knowable, anticipatable guest. The unmasterable nature of unconditional hospitality thus places it beyond the reach of sovereignty and its forms of right and law. In this way, it belongs to the **secret**. However, Derrida concludes this essay by advocating a new **negotiation** in international law, and in the law of the city and the state, between the principle of an unconditional hospitality (for no other would truly be worth its name) and the lawful conditions of a right to hospitality, which necessarily modulate this principle as an otherwise too abstract ideal constantly at risk of ideological perversion or ineffectual piety. (In 'Pas d'hospitalité', included in *Of Hospitality*, Derrida speaks of this negotiation in terms of the **aporia** or antinomy of hospitality. Unconditional and conditional hospitality vie antagonistically and indeed asymmetrically, according to a 'strange hierarchy' which rescores at once their heterogeneity and indissociability.)

Derrida begins 'On Forgiveness', meanwhile, by charting the effect of an Abrahamic religious heritage upon what he calls a near **global** geopolitical scene of **forgiveness** since the Second World War. Its idiom is universal and international, Derrida tells us, so that non-Abrahamic cultures nevertheless partake of its particular language of **confession** and repentance (witness post-war Japanese appeals for forgiveness, for instance). Derrida identifies the dominant features of this culture of forgiveness with a certain

christianization beyond secular disenchantment that is therefore no longer in need of the Christian **religion**. One of its effects is the burgeoning discourse of 'crimes against humanity' which in principle permits the entirety of humankind to accuse itself, leaving no innocent bystander in a position to arbitrate or judge. Meanwhile, Derrida notes the irony that the concepts of 'human right' and 'crime against humanity' acquire their very possibility only from a **European** revolutionary history that is also one of massive violence and cruelty.

For Derrida, forgiveness of the forgivable – of what might be considered forgivable according to morality, norms or culture – is in some respects necessary and understandable, and certainly preferable to a brutal refusal of the various types of reconciliation we have available to us. Yet such forgiveness does not live up to its name. Forgiveness of this sort is ultimately a prescribed, already possible response which falls short of the necessarily **singular** event of forgiving, which to truly justify itself must be absolutely **inventive**, entirely exceptional and irruptive, beyond the measure of right, law, normality or morality. What instead calls for forgiveness is therefore only the unforgiveable, just as **decision** is called for only in the face of the undecideable as precisely that which cannot be reduced to an existing field or programme of relations or values. Forgiveness cannot be reduced to a *meaning* that our existing ethico-juridico-politico-philosophico-historico-cultural knowledge equips us to understand, and thus belongs in a certain way to the secret; nor in any simple sense can it be mediated or moderated by a third party such as the state, which largely anticipates its meaning and outcome in advance (although see here also the question of the 'third' in **Adieu**); therefore forgiveness cannot take place in view of a normalizing finality or directed purpose. If one forgives only on condition that the forgiven person repents and is rehabilitated, then in effect forgiveness is extended not to the guilty party but only to a reformed and thus quite different other. Thus forgiving ultimately annuls itself in the therapeutic finality of a concluded forgiveness. The conditions of possibility of forgiveness, like those of the gift, are thus its conditions of **impossibility**. In forgiving, one must do the unmasterable-impossible (the only thing that in fact can be done, since to do what is already masterable-possible is in a sense to do nothing at all) – forgive the unforgiveable.

Derrida examines our christianized Abrahamic heritage (culminating in the universal geopolitical scene of forgiveness today) as fundamentally divided between a concept of forgiving's unconditionality on the one hand and, on the other, the practical effectivity of a conditioned forgiveness taking its place alongside an ensemble of values (implicitly exchange values) including punishment, atonement, rehabilitation and reconciliation. If Derrida insists on the necessity of alluding to an unconditional and an-economical forgiveness, however, this is not in the name of an idealistic purism. Rather, irreducible as it may be to conditioned forms of forgiveness, unconditional forgiving as a point of absolute reference remains vital in regulating the decisions and responsibilities we take in the ethico-political field (not least to combat a certain effect of conditioned forgiveness in confirming sovereign power and mastery). Nor, without such concrete decisions and responsibilities, could this absolute pole (unconditional forgiveness) begin to detach itself from mere piety or from the possibility of perverse manipulation. Yet, each time of asking, singular transactions between the conditional and unconditional poles of forgiveness always take place without ultimate justification. This can be put differently: to **negotiate** with forgiveness in this way, to decide on the undecideable, is doubtless necessary but always unforgiveable.

On the Name   This volume includes three texts which were published simultaneously in French in 1993, albeit in separately bound but matching books: 'Passions: "An Oblique Offering"', 'Sauf le nom (Post-Scriptum)' and 'Khôra'.

In 'Passions' Derrida begins by reflecting on the invitation by David Wood which occasions his text, an invitation to contribute to *Derrida: A Critical Reader*. In order to do justice to this invite, Derrida insists he cannot respond in merely a polite or dutiful fashion. To the extent that it would remain largely rule-bound or ordered by convention, such a well-behaved response might, paradoxically, offend against **friendship** by mixing up friendliness with duty. Mere politeness therefore risks an impolite violation of friendship, and thus to be more truly responsive and responsible to the **other**, the laws and norms which govern the response (including those which found a discourse on **responsibility**) must tremble under the weight of a certain contradiction which demands *more* and *less* responsibility at once. Here, Derrida sounds a note of caution to those, fired by rumours of **deconstruction**'s nihilism or amoralism, who endeavour to rethink deconstruction as an **ethics**, at least in the traditional sense. For a discourse on responsibility cannot proceed merely *responsibly*, in good moral conscience or with confident ethical justification, in a direct, frontal and unequivocal relationship to the object it proposes or places before itself: 'responsibility'. To put it differently, *one cannot take responsibility for oneself* (Derrida would, of course, ask us to attend to the multiple syntactic charge of this phrase). Responsibility is always for and of the *other*, since any conception of a 'masterable-possible' responsibility (I can *be* responsible or know what responsibility *is*) implies an already performable and thus pre-programmed sense of responsibility which, precisely, annuls responsibility and responsiveness. Following this line of thinking, the problem of taking responsibility in and for one's **name** (which is not the same thing as oneself) must also be taken into account, notably since the name is destined to outlast rather than return to its bearer.

In this text, Derrida also asks the question of the **non-response**. In one sense, according to a classical philosophical objection to its possibility, the non-response takes its place within the field of possibility of responsibility itself. In this argument, non-response is always a sort of response, for example of the kind that one might prefer in place of an inadequate or premature response (this, indeed, might be the most polite and thus most dutiful response of the non-response). Yet, to the extent that the non-response remains irreducible to positive knowledge, it can always madden the demand for responsibility in its more dogmatic or dutiful guise. Nevertheless, at the same time responsibility must recognize and accept the non-response as valid within its own terms. Non-response therefore implies a certain interruption within the field of responsibility which, however, does not supervene as merely an anomaly or exception. Non-response, in other words, names the deconstructibility of responsibility, but also the possibility of its transformation in the interests of, let us say, the **democracy to come**. In the last part of the essay, Derrida therefore turns to a consideration of the nonphenomenalizable **secret** as that which cannot be reduced to a mere *problem* that might be resolved by resorting to acts of disclosure or revelation, or indeed by representing the secret in terms of dissimulation or conscious deception by a subject. Such an unaccountable and depthless secret in its nonresponsive response exceeds the determined play of oppositions (truth/lying, speech/silence, hidden/revealed) which typically give shape to the demands of morality, religion, politics and law. Finally, Derrida confirms that his taste for the secret is what is at stake in a certain liking for

literature on his part. The latter is not to be confused with a particular genre or canon of texts, but is instead for Derrida the condition of a democracy which secures in principle *the right to say everything*. Such a right invites **fictions** that we might call irresponsible (the author is authorized to write without responsibility to anyone) or which remain fundamentally nonresponsive in terms of the conventions and modalities of power, knowledge, responsibility and duty – which, however, precisely institute such a right. In the sense that literature resists the evidential or informational construal of truth (truth as proveable or positive knowledge), literature can say everything without ever giving up the secret. Here, in 'view' of literature's secret, Derrida affirms a hyperbolic and original condition of democracy which resists the historically limited form and concept of democracy we inherit today: a 'democracy' which demands particular kinds of accountability, scrutiny, oath-taking, **confession** and so forth (while also, we might add, justifying lawful exceptions, frequently in the interests of certain powers and privileges).

'Sauf le nom (Post-Scriptum)' includes Derrida's response to **negative theology** (also called apophasis or the *via negativa*) which is frequently understood to speak of God principally in terms of negation or of what it is not possible to say about God. Often allied to forms of mysticism outside orthodox religious dogma, apophasis would seem to drift towards atheism, although as Derrida points out atheism always takes its cue from the prior terms of theism(s). Derrida would seem to be interested in negative theology to the extent that it calls for a rethinking of **metaphysics** (which must also entail a rethinking of language in or as a relation to God, death, absence or non-presence) that itself puts into question the traditional operations of ontological thought, cognitive reason, positive knowledge, linguistic reference, and so forth. 'Sauf le nom' translates as 'save his name' but also 'safe, his name': this **undecidable** or **untranslatable** phrase asks whether God's name, and nothing but his name, is saved by negative theology, or whether, in preserving something like the thought of a nonphenomenizable secret, negative theology saves all but the name of God in his very name. Finally – like the non-response or the secret – negative theology ought not to be thought of as merely 'outside' the orthodox tradition it resists, but rather as tracing out its always deconstructible limits or its self-difference, thus expropriating the 'proper' in itself. As the text recognizes, such a thinking has implications for new conceptions of politics, law and democracy within/against our inherited traditions.

'Khôra' extends Derrida's interest in what is nonphenomenizable within and beyond the ontology or **onto-theology** of metaphysics. In the *Timaeus* **Plato** speaks of khôra as belonging to a third genus or 'place' beyond all categorial oppositions (such as **logos**/mythos or sensible/intelligible). As the 'place' of the original inscription of forms, khôra gives place to all oppositions and thus, it would seem, eludes the reach and **law** of all that it situates or puts in place. Thus placing itself beyond all that might be named on condition of binary or dialectical determination, khôra thus names a certain incapacity for naming (itself). Yet the name 'khôra' is also the site of a variety of **metaphorical** inscriptions that occur, in Plato and after him, where khôra's irreducible difference maddens thought and writing. Such metaphoricity or tropological rendition of khôra extends from its very inscription as 'place', 'location', 'region' or 'country' to the images given of khôra by Timaeus as '**mother**', 'nurse', 'receptacle', 'imprint-bearer'. Such tropological determinations of khôra are formed, however, only from the inscribed forms that khôra itself forms. It is as if the tropological determination of khôra presumes that khôra could be found in a place *that it itself must give place to* (without, for all that, giving anything that might be received in the name of khôra). Hence, khôra cannot be thought to *support* its own interpretation in this way. As Derrida has argued throughout these texts, one cannot therefore attribute, to those names proposed to express or determine whatever may precede questions of an ontological kind, a simple 'proper' (property, propriety). 'Mother', one such 'exemplary' name (as a tropological translation of khôra), names (improperly) nothing but an irreducible difference. Such a difference cannot, however, acquire a definitive place or value within the field of oppositions constituting **metaphysics** or, in other words, the entire historic-philosophical tradition of the West. Thus 'mother' is the tropological projection of a **phallogocentric** discourse, yet it is also that which – in precisely its improper naming of an irreducible difference – unsettles the very (historico-anthropo-theological) definition of 'mother' and, for that matter, 'father'.

The discourse on khôra gives rise to a certain *mise en abyme* which itself necessarily raises the question of the politics of the site, for instance that of the city or the state. By reading the figure of **Socrates** as one who seeks to imitate the placeless place-giving or place-making of khôra, Derrida speculates on the relations of **philosophy**, politics and the state (calling up the figure of the 'father' as much as the 'mother') as at once constitutive and deconstructible.

On Touching – Jean-Luc Nancy In this volume, Derrida undertakes a far-reaching survey of the philosophical discourse surrounding the sense of touch, from Plato, Aristotle and the Gospels all the way through to **Nancy** himself. Along the way, Derrida offers careful readings of a host of philosophers of 'touch', including Descartes, Berkeley, Kant, Husserl, Bergson, Levinas, Heidegger, Merleau-Ponty and Deleuze.

In ***Margins of Philosophy***, ***Dissemination*** and other earlier works, Derrida reminds us that the founding gesture of **philosophy** is its attempt to think its own 'outside', to appropriate to itself all that it finds at its borders. Put differently, philosophy hopes to control its (sense of) contact with the '**other**', an 'other' it must at once encounter, engage, overcome, isolate and transcend. Far from remaining a physical triviality quite removed from the lofty domains of pure thought, a certain 'touching' therefore goes to the very heart of philosophy – if, indeed, it were possible to touch the heart or go to the heart of touching . . .

For what is at the *heart* of touch? Contact as that which happens *between* bodies or surfaces is, in a sense, nothing in itself. Touch, indeed, *intervenes* between other objects. It cannot be reduced to an 'object' in its own right (in this sense, one might say that 'touch' recalls **différance** as the interval which 'spaces' or structures differentiality). This renders highly problematic all reference to '*the*' sense of touch. For one may be able to touch, but one cannot touch touch (itself). Indeed, strictly speaking, the very condition of touching is the experience of the limit rather than of the body in a wholehearted sense (one never touches the deep interiority but only the border that gives the 'thing' its spatiality and thus offers the very possibility of contact). The limit, however, is not in itself an appropriable 'object' or 'thing'. A limit is not a 'ground' to be occupied, a 'place' in which one might dwell, or a domestic interior in which one might abide. It is rather – and precisely – their threshold. One only ever touches a limit, therefore, since touch is just this experience of the limit; and yet the limit itself remains untouchable or intangible as an appropriable entity, a body 'proper', or a (self-) present form. Thus, the sense of touch poses significant problems for a philosophical discourse wedded to the thinking of **presence**. (Nor are such problems about 'touching' easily inherited within or beyond philosophy, as Derrida knows only too well, since inheritance itself implies the same problem of contact at the limit with the 'other', and thus of the 'untouchable-touchable'.) But neither is touch an optional extra with which **metaphysics** can easily dispense since, as Derrida's early work repeatedly affirms, the relation to the 'outside' or 'limit' of philosophy is in fact the originary **supplement** or supplementing origin of philosophy's entire project. (To touch is always to touch oneself, of course, since one cannot touch the other without experiencing the contact – one's own contact – oneself. Philosophy's relation to the 'other' is thus always **auto-affective**, although necessarily it is impurely or improperly so, being always also hetero-affective, receiving its touch from the other, even the other 'self' that touches itself, taking itself as its own 'object'.) Moreover, since by definition touch at one and the same time reduces distance through an intimate proximity and yet presses against a resisting limit, the question always remains whether touching strokes or strikes the other. Throughout the tradition of Western philosophy, touch therefore remains undecidable, aporetic, indispensable yet ultimately ungovernable.

For in what *sense* might philosophy take the sense of touch? Touch is one of the senses. It is perhaps the sense which permeates and connects all other senses, each depending on a certain nearness or proximity. Touch, in other words, may be nothing other than sense itself. (Indeed, while one can survive the loss of other senses – sight, hearing, taste, smell – lack of the sense of touch signals **death**: death is at the end of touching.) The question of the *sense* of the sense of touch therefore remains inextricably *touched* (maddened as much as affected) by the topic it hopes to master and transcend. 'Sense' (in the *sense* of '**reason**') is itself implicated in the (philosophical) discourse of the senses, and so cannot supply a 'neutral' or 'objective' term or concept from which to arbitrate the question in which it already figures. Nor can the question of the *sense* of sense be dismissed as merely an inopportune metaphor, an unfortunate figure of speech, in order to purify the philosophical project that is here at hand. (Indeed, the topic of the hand in the philosophy of 'touch' is one to which Derrida pays a great deal of attention, both in this volume and in the body of essays going under the general heading of '**Geschlecht**'. Like **metaphor**, the hand is the prosthetic supplement of philosophy itself.) Why is the *sense* of sense not easily dismissed as mere metaphor? Metaphor names a process of substitution or deferral by which certain terms are brought into contact with one another while seeking to reserve for themselves identifiably separate functions or properties, although of course **deconstruction** continually exposes the limitations of this polar stability: the 'literal' cannot itself go untouched by an always possible metaphorical perversion. Metaphor – and, for that matter, its supposedly 'literal' counterpart – cannot in other words be excluded from the problem of touch.

Here, then, Derrida puts in question the immediacy typically associated with touch (whose 'sense' we think too immediately, directly or literally). He questions the access supposedly given by touch to either the (self-)presence of oneself or of another. Thus, in the company of Nancy, Derrida's writing resists those ontologies that would, in thinking being as presence, seek to go to the heart of touch: among them, Derrida mentions transcendental idealism (the intuitionism of **Kant** or **Husserl**) and empirical realism, which together not only represent the extreme poles of the philosophy of touch, but in fact share an irrecusable affinity in putting 'presence' at the origin. (Thus idealism and empiricism 'touch' on one another in unavoidable yet ambivalent ways.) This affinity, indeed, can be glimpsed in every **Christianized** discourse of the flesh. Indeed, Derrida's book is much less a thesis which aims to extend itself with unscathed virility into the very body or corpus of Nancy's work, than it is an attempt – alongside Nancy – to think a more 'tactful' thought of touch (one which respects the untouchability of touch while touching upon it). This tactfulness is, precisely, a way for Derrida to approach Nancy himself, to touch perhaps more tactfully (more and less touchingly) upon him. Such an attempt in all its complexity affects every modality of writing to be found here. At stake is a freedom (in Nancy's sense) beyond the masterable-possible intentionality of a subject, the one who says or thinks, with steadfast virility, 'I can': Derrida tries to write 'on' Nancy in a way that preserves rather than dispels the possibility of this freedom. Here are immense difficulties: the **law** of tact itself warns one against too much touching, despite the fact that touching is always already undecidably excessive, playing or pressing at the limits of both strike and stroke. Touch, indeed, is evermore tactful/tactless in its resisting touch of that which invites or repels touching.

Nancy thinks of touch, beyond the simple immediacy of contact, of closeness, continuity or access to (a) presence, in terms of an always doubled process of sharing, of an interruptive partition that in fact allows participation, apportioning or partaking. This thinking of sharing recurs at intervals throughout his philosophy (like its syncopated heartbeat), most famously in Nancy's conception of an inoperative **community**. Such sharing once more recalls the differing/deferring movement of Derridean *différance*. Thus, sharing would not itself be put to work by an original presence since it is precisely sharing (as interposition, spacing, apportioning) that would produce the differentiality in all its forms which in fact intervenes in all of philosophy's terms or concepts, including those of 'origin' and 'presence', making them possible from the outset. If such 'sharing' is at the heart of the matter of touching, this 'heart' cannot therefore be construed in terms of a simple or natural interiority or self-present origin. There is no proper 'heart' to the discourse of touch (one always touches the surface, not the heart, or only ever the surface of the heart, or the surface of one of its chambers, and so on – however deeply one penetrates, one is always touching surface). Nancy himself fell gravely ill in the late-1980s and underwent a heart transplant, about which Derrida speaks in this volume (noting that it remains unknown to him whether the transplanted heart was that of a man or a woman, the latter indeed producing higher rates of success). Against the image of a single, irreplaceable and always virile heart, then, Nancy's thought of sharing must give rise to a thinking of the supplement or prosthesis at the origin, the 'non-self-same' at the heart of the heart; which is to say, a thinking of the **technicity** of bodies and, for that matter, of gendered bodies.

onto-theology   See especially ***'Différance'**, **Of Grammatology***.

other   This term is so prevalent across Derrida's vast *oeuvre* as to defy comprehensive, text-by-text tracking. It also participates, of course, in the heading of a number of Derrida's writings (***Psyche: Inventions of the Other**, **The Ear of the Other**, **The Other Heading*** . . .) – a participation which indeed profoundly alters their bearing, putting into question the normative sense of direction and purpose (heading) associated with traditional argumentation or 'thetic' exposition. In other words, the 'other' enters in precisely as a condition of the **writing** and bearing of deconstructive texts. Inclusion in the title affirms a certain limit of entitlement, so far as the 'text' of **deconstruction** is concerned.

other

Throughout Derrida's writings, the 'other' is not simply an oppositional or binary 'other' against which a dominant term or entity defines and defends itself (e.g., 'woman' as the other of 'man', 'black' as the other of 'white', and so on). This is the case even though one feature of deconstructive engagement is an intervention in the hierarchical operations of binary structures (presence/absence, masculine/feminine, nature/culture, **speech/ writing**, etc.) in order to re-elaborate the functioning of the subordinated term. Derrida recognizes that binary oppositions always effectively produce hierarchies, hierarchies which deconstruction seeks to question and transform by demonstrating the constitutive importance of the subordinate term as irreducible **supplement**. In the process, however, the excluded, repressed or 'secondarized' term is so profoundly redescribed that it can no longer be restricted to one side of the opposition in which it participates, since it in fact comes to make that opposition possible in the first place (see **writing, supplement**, etc.).

The 'other' in Derrida therefore comes to be 'other' than the 'other' of an oppositional difference. Derrida's profound rethinking of the structures of opposition that characterize the **metaphysical** tradition (a tradition which determines being as **presence** and which thereby construes difference in terms of absence or 'lack') exposes us to the thought of an entirely heterogeneous 'other', that which overflows as much as it constitutes the possibility of all terms, values, relations or oppositions. Throughout Derrida's work, there are many 'nicknames' for this 'other', an 'other' that, for unavoidable reasons, eludes a **proper name**. Derrida's thinking of ***différance*** posits the 'originarity' of a non-present remainder, that which produces and maintains all differences while relating to them neither as a simple presence nor in terms of a stable absence. His **affirmation** of deconstruction as the 'experience of the **impossible**' entails an openness to the 'other' which I cannot welcome, appropriate, invent, decide on or master; an 'other', however, from which is received any **decision, invention, responsibility, hospitality** or **forgiveness** worthy of the name. Derrida's appeal to the '**democracy to come**' also calls up the 'other' beyond presence/ absence. Since the ***demos*** includes, however impossibly, the asymmetrical and irreconcilable demands of freedom and equality, democracy is radically unfulfillable as such, and is thus always structurally open to the 'other' – an 'other' which, far from awaiting us as the unified ideal of a programmable future, presses upon us (with all the force of its self-difference) in the 'here-now'. Derrida's thinking of an originary yet always double affirmation – **'yes, yes'** – is, too, a thinking of a non-simple non-present remainder that structures all possibility. **Literature**, meanwhile, makes a differential **mark**, different-from-itself-within-itself, **re-marking** itself for a **future** or an 'other' to come. **Justice** is the undeconstructible 'other' that calls for ceaseless vigilance and continual transformative engagement with the **law** in its always constructed and conditional form. **Event, secret**, affirmation, the **'unconditional'**, responsibility, **singularity, iterability, promise, spectre, messianicity** without messianism, **sexual difference, trace, translation** – none may be thought without recourse to this radical difference or heterogeneity of the wholly other 'other'. ***Tout autre est tout autre*** (every other (one) is every (bit) other): in ***The Gift of Death***, the responsibility beyond responsibility to which Abraham is called by the wholly 'other' is at once entirely singular and inescapable for all. Responsibility towards the 'other' unavoidably entails an always unjustifiable irresponsibility toward others than this 'other'. Such a thinking of *tout autre est tout autre* marks the limits of all **ethical** thought and yet calls, precisely, for its 'other' (other-of-itself).

— **P** —

Paper Machine First published in French in 2001. Here Derrida examines the impact on writing and thought of more recent **technological** developments such as word processing, and thinks hard about the connections between paper and machine tool (pen, typewriter, computer) in a number of contexts and settings. Perhaps foremost, however, he takes this investigation as the occasion to question a conventional thinking about paper (and about the era of paper) according to which it is viewed as simply a passive and secondary substrate in relation to the thought that inspires writing and the process by which it is conducted.

While Derrida himself is at great pains to recover its intricate history, paper is not for him merely an extrinsically determined technological convenience, something that comes along afterwards according to the same

metaphysical hierarchy which names **writing** as a poor relation to **speech**. Paper is not just an extrinsic support for the psychic or imaginative process which joins itself to bodies, instruments and materials only in order that, through writing, evanescent thoughts may be deposited and **archived**. (For this reason, indeed, neither can paper be thought too hastily according to a stable chronology in which historical and technological advances presage its inevitable end.) Instead, for Derrida, 'paper' itself provides the very figure for considering the paradoxical divisibility of its host of traits, *feuilles* or folds. Paper's supposed function as a stable surface, to which might cling the traces or marks coming along from the outside, is regarded by Derrida as part of a discourse that is laden with assumptions. This discourse becomes problematic at the point when we ask whether in saying 'paper' we mean the empirical body that bears the name, or whether we are already resorting to a rhetorical figure. The problem is apparent, in other words, when we come to understand that the notion of an empirical *body* that *bears* the name of paper already gives itself over to a figure of speech, so that reference to the 'empirical' here is not in fact supported merely 'empirically', any more than the thought of paper is supported solely by its own empirical 'body' as an extrinsic substrate.

Tracing paper through its past, present and future, Derrida starts out from the word *'biblion'*, the original meaning of which is tied less to the notion of a **book** or *oeuvre*, instead designating a support for writing – paper, bark, tablets. If in **Greek** the linked word *'bibliotheke'* – forerunner to *bibliothèque* or library – means the slot for a book or its place of deposit, the supposed imposition of a tranquil permanence which accompanies the *bibliotheke* in fact only takes place in the wake of a word that itself gathers according to the logic of metonymy, which, less than securely depositing or storing, opens itself unstably to a number of potential shifts, differences, deferrals and slippages. The library, for Derrida, is in its modern guise a place and concept in which we find brought together a powerfully instituting metonymic series running from author, thesis, book, archive and institution, to state deposit, statute and nation-state. This is a highly charged associative chain, of course, but one which remains susceptible to practical **deconstruction**, since the constitutive linkages are wrought by means of part standing for whole, giving rise to an exemplarity which also borders onto the logic of the **supplement**.

Elsewhere in *Paper Machine* Derrida observes that paper-centric norms, conventions, figures and language continue to pervade the discourse of computer programmes (themselves bearing paper-centric names such as 'Office' or 'Notebook'), confronting us on-screen with pages, paragraphs and margins, asking us to cut, paste and clip, and so on. Moreover, the frequently assumed gradual decline or withdrawal (*retrait*) of paper must be set against real statistics demonstrating a general expansion in its production and circulation. Added to which, Derrida's activist intervention in the plight of the *sans-papiers* in France exposes the very real, continuing cost of being without paper(s). Nevertheless, Derrida wonders about the future of the *bibliothèque* in view of the rise of computerization and electronic media that together encourage new sorts of documents, texts and archives to be produced, all of which seem to move us away from the book form and the culture of paper. What, indeed, is the future of the book? Is there a book still to come, once libraries become spaces (perhaps without conventional geography) that are dominated by electronic texts without paper support, texts which make possible a radical reorganization of textual processes themselves, as well as potentializing a deep transformation in the relations of writing and book to body and place, aggravating further the structuring metonyms of book and library? For Derrida, a simple idea of the traditional archive's demise is perhaps not altogether in keeping with his notion in 'The Principle of Reason' (see **Right to Philosophy**) of what the archive most faithfully guards or double-keeps: that which it does not have and which is not yet.

pas   In 'Pas', reprinted in *Parages*, where Derrida writes on **Blanchot**, he puns on '*pas*' as meaning both 'step' and 'not' ('*pas sans pas*'). This implies a self-differential movement akin to the double gesture of **deconstruction** (see **Margins of Philosophy**, **Positions** and **Writing and Difference**).

performativity   As Derrida tells us, **speech act theory** makes an important, if questionable, distinction between constative language – as that which states or describes – and performative language – as that which enacts or does. Speech act theorist J. L. **Austin**'s favourite example of performative utterance (one to which Derrida refers in **'Signature Event Context'**) is the marriage vow, in which the words 'I do' have no intrinsic

performativity 135

meaning or reference, but instead cause something to happen. To the extent that the concept of performativity places the accent on the transformation of a given state of affairs, Derrida is frequently characterized in terms of his interest in performatives, over and above constatives which we might think of as conserving the idea of a 'truth' or 'meaning' prior to language (language, then, as mere representation or description). However, we must be careful here. For one thing, Derrida is highly critical of speech act theory's insistence on the idea that performatives are optimally effective in highly conventional settings bound by established codes, required actions and instituted roles. For Derrida, no **context** is so fully 'saturated', closed or complete that we could ever rely entirely on the outcome of the performative acts it may occasion, just as no word or concept is so absolutely communicable that we could wholly depend on the results of its usage. For speech act theory, performativity is construed as a form of action-taking in which the speaker must fully comprehend the context surrounding his utterances in order to successfully enact his intentions within it. In other words, performative discourse is, for speech act theory, nothing other than the scene of the 'masterable-possible' performed by a volitional subject. Yet for Derrida, such already-possible possibility is, precisely, non-transformative: it annuls the chance of the **singular event**; it diminishes any **decision** worthy of its name; it impedes the coming of the **other** or the **future**. In contrast, for Derrida, it is the experience of the *impossible* (uninventable **invention**, unreckonable **gift**, **hospitality** beyond welcome, **forgiveness** of the unforgivable) that, by taking us beyond a predetermined or preprogrammed situation, gives *possibility* the only chance worthy of the name.

In any case, Derrida challenges the possibility of a rigorous distinction between the 'performative' and the 'constative'. From his earliest writings, Derrida disputes the idea that language might ever simply state or describe. His entire critique of **logocentrism** and **phonocentrism** aligns such a concept of language with the **metaphysics of presence**. Indeed, for Derrida, the priority accorded to **speech** within the metaphysical tradition provides the critical background for his own **deconstruction** of speech act theory. At some level, then, constative language always performs, institutes, forces, aims to do; while every performative utterance bears a certain (impure) relation to referentiality. In 'Signature Event Context' Derrida shows how all language, whether constative or performative, is always exposed to the risk of infelicity or contamination by the **other**, its 'serious' intention inherently parasitized by the possibility of the 'non-serious' (**fiction**, theatricality, **metaphor**, irony). Thus, we might say that Derrida's always provisional interest in performativity as a working concept insists on the powerful **remainder** of the unmasterable, the other, the intractable possibility of the 'non-serious', the irreducible chance of non-arrival or **destinerrance**.

perhaps   See, for instance, Derrida's discussion of the 'perhaps' in ***Politics of Friendship*** (while Derrida often makes much of the Nietzschean inheritance of this word, for further reading one might also compare the 'as if' in ***Without Alibi***.) The perhaps in Derrida may also be linked to the **undecidable**, the **impossible**, the **future**, **messianicity**, **spectre**, etc.

phallogocentrism   See **logocentrism**.

pharmakon   See especially 'Plato's Pharmacy' in ***Dissemination***.

phenomenology   In philosophy, the study of phenomena as they appear to consciousness. Phenomenology is the study of structures of consciousness as experienced from the first-person point of view (a point of view, however, which is not just individual, since phenomenology is concerned to analyse phenomena as they appear in acts of consciousness, on the basis of a systematic and generalizable 'science'). Edmund **Husserl** is credited as the father of phenomenology, while developers and criticizers have included **Heidegger**, Merleau-Ponty, Sartre, **Levinas** and **Ricoeur**. Derrida's early work in particular included a sustained concentration on Husserl and phenomenology, on the basis of demonstrating the continuing influence of a **metaphysics of presence**, **phonocentrism**, **logocentrism**, etc.

See especially ***Speech and Phenomena***, also Derrida's introduction to Husserl's *Origin of Geometry* and ***The Problem of Genesis in Husserl's Philosophy***. On Husserl and metaphysics see, too, 'Form and Meaning' in ***Margins of Philosophy*** (included also in the English edition of ***Speech and Phenomena***). Also ***Writing and Difference***, especially '"Genesis and Structure" and Phenomenology' and 'Violence and Metaphysics'. For

Husserl and humanism see 'The Ends of Man' in **Margins**. For Husserl and intuitionism, see **On Touching**. See also **Points, Positions**.

For Levinas and phenomenology, see **Adieu**.

philosophy When speaking of philosophy, Derrida is usually alluding to the **metaphysical** tradition which determines **being** as **presence**. This tradition gives rise to the intellectual history and cultural politics of **Europe** and the West. For Derrida, philosophy in general names itself in terms of the transcendence of thought over language, empiricity and biography. It announces the priority of the concept over inscription, the pure 'word' over perverse **metaphoricity**. And it thereby understands truth as the revelation of Being in its original **presence**. Thus, in order to found itself in relation to an essential ground that is 'proper' to itself, philosophy must surpass and overcome all that is merely extrinsic or prefatory to its own arrival as such. In **Dissemination**, Derrida therefore speaks of philosophy as that which continually seeks to appropriate (wholly ingest or stably exclude) its 'outside' – an 'outside' which he thinks of as being constitutive in its continual **supplementation** of philosophy as always *on the way* to its own self-completion. (See also 'Tympan' in **Margins of Philosophy**.) In this sense, philosophy turns out to be no more than the preface it hoped to go beyond. To put this differently, the philosophical 'system' (not merely particular philosophical systems devised by specific philosophers, but philosophy's disposition towards systematicity in general) turns out to depend on an irreducible supplement of non-systematizable traces. Yet this also gives philosophy its chance in terms of an ultimately unsuturable opening to the **'other'** as absolute arrivant, an opening to the 'to come' as unanticipatable, unprogrammable **future**. An opening, too, to the **'democracy to come'** as that which unendingly resists **sovereign** power and determination. This is an exposure which, despite itself, philosophy must endure. Thus, **deconstruction** does not simply oppose itself to philosophy – on the contrary, it insists that philosophical debate remain open. Indeed, during the 1970s and 1980s, Derrida defended philosophy against government plans to limit its role within **French** national education. While he did not frame his intervention in terms of an unquestioning defence of philosophy in its canonical form, Derrida's objection to the attacks upon it was articulated in terms of a desire to question and resist 'a certain unformulated philosophy' which, in fact, spurred government policy from the beginning. For Derrida, there is in this sense no space outside of or free from 'philosophy', but only a certain countering of one philosophy with another (or, better still, a countering of 'philosophy' with the other-of-itself). In **Writing and Difference**, indeed, he more than once suggests the impossibility of dispensing entirely with metaphysics, and indeed powerfully exposes the return of metaphysical thought in precisely those discourses that want most to overcome the philosophical tradition. Yet if 'philosophy' as metaphysics is indeed unavoidable, neither can one go *right to* philosophy, outside of the institutional conditions or 'systems' which, however, never entirely limit or contain philosophy as such (see here **Right to Philosophy**). If one cannot simply 'do without' philosophy or metaphysics, there is only the chance to deconstruct, rethink and transform philosophy in view of its ultimately irrepressible opening to the 'other'. (Here, the very limits of philosophy in relation to its 'outside' – whether we call it 'politics', 'culture', 'society', or 'reality' – would be open to question and transformation.)

See also **Dissemination**, **'I Have a Taste for the Secret'**, **Margins of Philosophy**, **Right to Philosophy**, **university**, **Writing and Difference**. For philosophy and literature, see **literature**.

phonocentrism Phonocentrism names the priority given to **speech** over **writing** within the **metaphysical** tradition. Here, while speech is imbued with living **presence**, in that it may be considered a form of full and immediate expression, writing represents a fall into alienated exteriority, being a lifeless instrument of recording, archiving or memorialization. Writing is a mere prosthetic, a 'dangerous **supplement**' (as Rousseau puts it) which threatens to replace the living with the dead, to substitute the absent for the present, to elevate the artificial and **technical** over the natural, and thereby to supplant identity and unity with **violence** and difference. For Derrida, phonocentrism supports the metaphysical determination of **being** as presence, since it assumes that the self-identity of the subject is expressed in living speech; and because it marries the spoken 'word' to the soul or **spirit**, and thus to an **onto-theological** origin or transcendental signified beyond all difference.

In **Of Grammatology**, Derrida powerfully deconstructs Western phonocentrism by demonstrating that speech is a function of writing in the larger sense he wishes to establish: that the signified must first of all function as a signifier; that the notion of living speech expresses or rather inscribes itself in inextricably **metaphorical** terms; and that writing (the violent inscription of the **proper name**) in fact founds the very possibility of 'pre-literate' cultures – cultures prized for their supposed naturalness, fullness, authenticity and immediacy. In his essay **'Différance'**, meanwhile, Derrida suggests that the (always unstable) distinction between speech and writing is itself a condition of a non-signifying and non-systematizable remainder – *différance* – that can be dominated by neither term of this classical opposition.

See also **Dissemination, Margins of Philosophy, Positions, 'Signature Event Context', Speech and Phenomena**.

Plato (428/427BC–348/347BC)   Classical Greek philosopher. See **Dissemination**, especially 'Plato's Pharmacy'. See also **The Post Card**. See too **'I Have a Taste for the Secret'**, 'Khôra' in **On the Name**. For Platonism, see for instance **The Gift of Death, Writing and Difference**.

plus d'un   See for instance **Specters of Marx**.

Points . . . Interviews, 1974–1994   This 1995 volume includes twenty-three interviews conducted with Derrida over a twenty-year period, presented in broadly chronological sequence. In the earliest of these, Derrida offers replies on the **singular** and idiomatic nature of his texts (in particular, **Glas**), reflecting on the ways in which the 'theoretical' or potentially programmatic dimensions of his work are continually overrun by the scene of **writing** and reading in which it comes to be inscribed ('Between Brackets I' and 'Ja, or the *faux-bond* II'). Here, Derrida offers fresh explanations of his interest in the **signature**, the **proper name**, the institution, and **mourning**. (Indeed, Derrida's thinking of the signature and proper name crops up time and again in this collection, notably in regard to the literary and philosophical traditions and texts which interest him.) Later, he ruminates on the intellectual milieu that led him to **Husserl**, **Mallarmé**, **Blanchot** and others, and considers the impact of Marxism, **structuralism** and **psychoanalysis** during the 1960s ('The Almost Nothing of the Unpresentable'). Questions are also answered on **deconstruction**, *différance*, **Of Grammatology, The Post Card** and other texts from the 1960s and 1970s.

In another interview from the early-1980s, Derrida speaks about the **university** institution, the **Greph** and the International College of Philosophy or **Ciph** ('Of a Certain Collège International de Philosophie Still to Come'). The relation of **literature** to **philosophy** and the nature of Derrida's own writing is addressed with accompanying reflections on his upbringing in **Algeria** and entry into **French** intellectual culture ('Unsealing ("the old new language")', 'There is No *One* Narcissism', 'A "Madness" Must Watch Over Thinking'). Derrida's theoretical and activist engagement with the question of philosophy teaching and the academic institution arises throughout the dialogues from this period. (See also, in this volume, 'Once Again from the Top: Of the Right to Philosophy'.) In other interviews, the issue of Derrida's 'voice', deconstructive discourse, the question of writing and the philosophical 'text' come to the fore ('Dialangues', 'Is There a Philosophical Language?'). The relationship of deconstruction to **memory** and to decision is also dealt with.

In a correspondence from 1982–83, it is the question of **sexual difference** that takes centre-stage. Elsewhere, the relation of deconstruction and philosophy to journalism, media culture and the public sphere is discussed ('Language (*Le Monde* on the Telephone)', 'There is No *One* Narcissism'). Derrida also broaches the question of **Heidegger**'s relation to National Socialism ('Heidegger, the Philosophers' Hell', 'How to Concede, with Reasons?', 'Eating Well'), with some of the discussion going by way of references to *Of Spirit* and other of his texts on this thinker. Derrida also remarks on (his) **Judaism**, and on **'Shibboleth'**, *Cinders* and the poetry of Paul **Celan** ('There is No *One* Narcissism', 'Passages – from Traumatism to Promise'). There are also interviews on 'The Rhetoric of Drugs', on Derrida's engagement with **Ponge** ('Counter-Signatures'), and deconstruction's thinking of the subject, set against a wide philosophical backdrop ('Eating Well'). In the latter, **responsibility**, **hospitality**, the relation to the **other**, and the human and the **animal** are all put in question.

The collection includes 'Choreographies', also published in *The Ear of the Other*, and 'Che cos'è la poesia?', in which the poem is depicted by Derrida as a hedgehog balling itself up in the middle of the road as a self-protective act in the face of the traffic against which it must nevertheless venture itself. (See, too, in this volume, 'Istrice 2', which also includes an extended discussion of Heidegger.)

Picking up on themes addressed in 'Language (*Le Monde* on the

Telephone)' and 'There is No One Narcissism', *Points* concludes with interviews on two 'affairs'. One surrounded the honorary doctorate that Cambridge University proposed to award Derrida in 1992, which met with fierce opposition from certain quarters. While the non-placet vote that ensued went in favour of the award, the affair fuelled the negative stereotyping of deconstruction in the media. In this interview, Derrida seeks not only to correct several of the misrepresentations of deconstruction that abounded at this time, but to reflect on why they should have arisen in the first place. As such, he embarks on an analysis of what might motivate the systematic and **violent** misreading or non-reading of deconstructive texts ('Honoris Causa: "This is *also* extremely funny"'). The other controversy concerned Derrida's objections to an unauthorized, poor-quality translation of 'Heidegger, the Philosopher's Hell' by Richard Wolin, undertaken for a volume that Wolin himself edited. This volume included an introduction which contained, as Derrida's interviewer Peggy Kamuf puts it, 'ill-informed' and 'bad-faith' interpretations of Derrida's relationship to Heidegger, notably in the wake of questions about Heidegger's engagement with National Socialism. In a long article appearing in *The New York Review of Books*, Thomas Sheehan had defended Wolin against Derrida's complaints. An exchange followed in the same publication, including individual and collective letters in support of Derrida. In interview, however, Derrida is ultimately less interested in personal vendetta and invective (although he is unstinting in correcting errors as he finds them), than in the analysis of what links the supposedly 'scholarly' critique of deconstruction to certain public and media discourses. The interview on this 'affair' that concludes *Points* ('The Work of Intellectuals and the Press') was undertaken especially for this volume. (In regard to these last two interviews, see also 'Towards an Ethics of Deconstruction' in **Limited Inc**.)

Politics of Friendship Published in French in 1996. This volume finds its starting point in Derrida's seminar presented under the same title, which took place at the École des Hautes Études en Sciences Sociales in Paris during 1988–89. In the foreword, Derrida describes the volume as itself 'the foreword to a book I would one day wish to write'. *Politics of Friendship* is guided by Derrida's sustained reflection on a statement attributed to **Aristotle** by his biographer Diogenes Laertius: 'O philoi, oudeis philos'. Reading the omega as a vocative, this may be translated as 'O my friends, there is no friend'. For Derrida, the phrase is referred to Aristotle in a way that is reminiscent of a sort of rumour that spreads throughout Western **philosophy**. It therefore crops up in a number of guises throughout the centuries. Famously cited by Montaigne in 'On Friendship', which also provides the occasion for a reading of Cicero on the question of the friend, Derrida pursues the reference to **friendship** through an entire chain of readings which traverse the philosophical tradition. Thus, Politics of Friendship calls on the texts of **Plato**, Cicero, Montaigne, **Kant**, Blake, Hölderlin, **Nietzsche**, **Heidegger**, **Blanchot** and **Nancy**, among others.

The phrase attributed to Aristotle seems highly ambivalent or contradictory. For it appears to be internally split between the constative and **performative**, between that which it would *mean-to-say* and that which it actually seems to *do* with language. How can one announce the fundamental absence of the friend through a direct appeal to one's friends? How could one dare to call on one's friends to tell them of an utter lack of friendship? Yet for Derrida the **undecidable** conditions that inhabit this curious phrase may in fact open up the possibility of another **future** for 'friendship' – both philosophically and politically – which may perhaps go beyond the fraternal tradition that establishes a certain restricted model of friendship as the basis for familial, social and political relations generally (determining in the process the relations of **sexual difference** and of the 'human' to '**animal**', as Derrida is quick to add). For Derrida, this fraternal model is carried over from the **Greek** into **Christian**, Republican, 'national' and 'democratic' traditions. It is perhaps at the very origin of the 'political' in the Western sense. (As Derrida shows, Carl Schmitt wanted to argue that politics itself comes to an end with the demise of the friend–enemy relation. This would be an ending, indeed, which Nietzsche's 'O enemies, there are no enemies' appears to announce or anticipate, although perhaps with the same ambivalence that surrounds the phrase attributed to Aristotle, one that it seemingly puts into reverse, although in other ways confirms. Schmitt's position, however, is one that Derrida seeks to put in question through his own attempt to rethink the relation of the friend to the '**other**', not least in the interests of the '**democracy to come**'.)

In *Politics of Friendship*, the question of the *number* of friends that one might count upon (a problem that is indeed implied by the various possibilities of translating the phrase credited to Aristotle) brings up the idea of a 'countable unity', a contained and accountable set of relations – social, civic,

Politics of Friendship

ethnic, religious, ethical, legal – which effectively form the basis of the fraternal political tradition. Derrida does not merely critique this model of fraternity, in which friendship is rare, limited and knowable. He also seeks to draw out, from within its deconstructible possibilities, another conception of friendship. This 'other' friendship is, indeed, tied to Derrida's inventive sense of the 'democracy to come', a democracy which is not conceived in terms of a reckonable **presence** that one might foresee on the horizon of the **future**, but which inscribes itself in the 'here-now' only on condition of that which remains *non-presentable* in regard to the fraternal 'self-example' which democracy makes of itself in its traditional political guise.

This 'other', then, is a hyperbolic, incalculable or **im-possible** friendship which has as its very medium the boundless unknown of the stranger rather than the self-exemplarity of the brother (the latter always tending towards narcissistic identification and appropriation of alterities). Such an 'other' notion of friendship finds its conditions of emergence, first of all, in a post-Kantian tradition which emphasizes respect as a measure of the distance that relates friend to friend, and subsequently in those post-Nietzschean writings which radically extend this distance so as to highlight the absolute dislocation and incalculable **singularity** of each and every other. In the latter, since the common condition – if there is any – pertains precisely to a lack of common measure, bond or reciprocity, we are given to think the im-possibility of a 'relation without relation', picked up by Bataille's notion of '**community** without community', Blanchot's 'unavowable community', and Nancy's 'inoperative community'. Derrida's *Politics of Friendship* can be read as a critical engagement with this tradition of writing. Ultimately, the volume presses for continual **negotiation** – and inventive **decision** and **responsibility** – between the seemingly irreconcilable laws of the 'political'. It does so in the interests of the 'democracy to come'. For, in classical terms, the '**demos**' which establishes the origin of the Western political model requires *on the one hand* respect for the irreducible singularity of anyone, prior to the discourse of a subject, citizen, state, or people, but *on the other* a fundamental equality which can only pertain in view of some type of universal ratiocination or general '**law**' (the latter establishing, in one sense, the limit of freedom and, in another, its very medium or possibility). This is what Derrida elsewhere calls the impossible *there is* of the demos. In *Politics of Friendship* this situation is described as 'tragically irreconcilable and forever wounding', yet it also gives rise to an experience of the impossible in the 'here-now' that exposes us to what may arrive or happen, to the other and the **event**.

Thus, it is the 'perhaps' that provides the very medium of another friendship to be found 'within-beyond' the fraternal tradition, a friendship to come which cannot yet know – and is still to decide – what it means by the name. (From its very beginning, let us recall, *Politics of Friendship* announces a 'text' on friendship still to come, for reasons that the book itself continually suggests.)

Ponge, Francis (1899–1988)   French poet and essayist. See especially *Signsponge*.

Positions   This volume includes the three earliest interviews with Derrida, published between 1967 and 1971. In general, they provide the occasion for Derrida to re-elaborate the concerns of his early publications in the context of the various issues and debates which preoccupied critical thinking and discourse at that time. In the first, 'Implications', Derrida answers questions about the major works by him which appeared during that year: **Of Grammatology**, **Speech and Phenomena** and **Writing and Difference**. Here, Derrida reflects on the extent to which each of these texts might be included in the other, or might be read so as to interrupt and rearticulate the other. He describes how such writings therefore challenge the supposed unity of the **book**, putting in question its status as a closed or total system. Indeed, Derrida speaks of **deconstruction**'s attentiveness towards an **undecidable** or asystematic reserve that is the very condition of all systems or systematicities. In this interview, Derrida goes on to give illuminating accounts of his thinking of **différance**, **trace**, **arche-writing**, **logocentrism**, the **metaphysics of presence**, and so forth, offering responses to a series of questions about his readings of **Rousseau, Saussure, Husserl, Heidegger** and others. In particular, Derrida locates deconstruction at the limit of **philosophy**, neither simply 'outside' or 'beyond' the metaphysical tradition, nor readily presentable or recuperable within its historical field, but instead engaged in a more original questioning of this tradition's resources in the interests of a **future** that may be still to come. In 'Semiology and Grammatology', Derrida enters into dialogue with the well-known thinker Julia Kristeva. Here, once more alluding to his recent publications, Derrida reasserts the metaphysical basis

Positions 145

of the conception of the sign found in structural **linguistics** and semiology after Saussure; and elucidates deconstruction's enlarged conception of **writing** as itself more basic than the phonetic model in which the priority of living **speech** is asserted over written discourse. This interview includes an extended discussion of *différance*, and of Derrida's reading of Husserl, notably in relation to the major publications of 1967. In the final interview, 'Positions', *différance* is re-elaborated in relation to Derrida's reading of Hegel and, more broadly, in the context of **Dissemination**, on which he had been recently working. It is in this interview, too, that Derrida explains the double strategy of deconstruction: in the first instance, deconstruction must devote itself to overturning the always **violent** hierarchies that structure binary oppositions within the metaphysical tradition, not least by demonstrating ways in which the minor or excluded term establishes the very possibility of its dominant partner; second, however, deconstruction must move beyond a simple inversion of oppositional terms in order to deconstruct the basic systems or structures which give rise to them, indeed to posit at their 'origin' that non-systematizable reserve (*différance*, trace, arche-writing) which is at once unpresentable within, and constitutive of, their entire field. As the interview progresses, Derrida attempts once again to explain his relationship to the Heideggerian 'text', a text which is at once extremely important for deconstructive thought and yet, Derrida suggests, still too embroiled in the metaphysics of presence to resemble the project which he himself wishes to undertake. Derrida refers the reader to a series of broadly contemporaneous writings on his part ('White Mythology', '*Ousia* and *Grammē*', and so forth) which develop his reading of Heidegger. In this interview, Derrida also answers questions on the relation of historicity itself to the metaphysical construal of history, and speculates on the limits and possibilities of a new conceptualization of history, which as he well knows always risks reappropriation by the metaphysical tradition. (Derrida here treats in similar vein the question of 'materialism' that was so important for contemporaneous critical discourses.) This discussion leads to some remarks on Althusser, **Hegel** and, indeed, some intriguing comments on **Marxism** – a Marxism 'to come' that, some three decades later, will be the concern of **Specters of Marx**. Towards the interview's end, Derrida advances some comments on the relation of deconstruction to **psychoanalysis**, a question that imposes itself on many texts over several decades.

postal effect, principle See **destinerrance**, 'Telepathy' in *Psyche*, and especially *The Post Card*.

presence, present See **metaphysics of presence**.

promise The promise responds to the **future** and the **other**. It is **performative** in as much as it entails a pledge, an **affirmation** or giving that is not simply identical to or exhausted by its specific content. Even if the promise is not kept, its gesture retains a certain significance. (Indeed, Derrida's thinking of an 'originary' affirmation before all language is, too, a thinking of the promise.) For that matter, since the promise that carries itself out ceases to be a promise any longer, the force and structure of the promise has precisely to do with its effective self-difference. It also has to do with a certain 'disjointed' temporality irreducible to **presence** (a promise that fulfils itself is a promise no more). Thus the promise remains structurally open to the possibility of an '**other**' beyond itself, a heterogeneous 'other' to come. As Derrida observed, a promise always promises to be kept, i.e. it commits itself, beyond 'ideal' or 'abstract' thought or language, to the production of effective actions and events. This is a most important reminder of how the promise features in deconstructive thought. Nevertheless, promises may always be broken, deliberately or not, and one cannot always – if ever – know what one is promising (see Derrida's reflections on the promise of friendship he offers de Man). Nor can one know for sure that one will be the same person (and, thus, the same 'promiser') whose promise calls to be kept in the future. In other words, going back to Derrida's relationship to **speech act theory**, one might say that the promise is a special (or, perhaps better, an exemplary) kind of performative which remains irreducible to the 'masterable-possible', and thus keeps open possibility in a more radical sense.

For promise and testimony see *Echographies of Television*, **testimony**. For promise and signature see **signature**. For iterability and promise see **'Signature Event Context'**. For promise and lie see *Without Alibi*. For circumcision and promise see *Circumfession*. For promise and profession see 'The University Without Condition' in *Without Alibi*, **testimony**. For promise and affirmation see 'A Number of Yes' in *Psyche* and 'Ulysses Gramophone'. For promise, faith and justice see **'Faith and Knowledge'**. For promise, memory and friendship see *Memoires for*

Paul de Man. For literature and promise see **Acts of Literature**, **'Demeure'**.

For promise and invention see **Psyche**. For promise and founding see **'Force of Law'**. For promise and America see **Memoires for Paul de Man**. For promise and Europe see **The Other Heading**.

See also **democracy to come, future, literature, messianicity, other, singularity**.

proper name   For Derrida on the proper name, see *Of Grammatology*, 'Des tours de Babel' in *Psyche*, *The Ear of the Other*, *The Post Card*, signature, *Signsponge*, *The Work of Mourning*, translation. See also **Cinders, Circumfession, On the Name, 'Shibboleth', Specters of Marx**.

Psyche: Inventions of the Other   First published in 1987. This large collection, initially of twenty-six essays included in a single volume, but reprinted in a second two-part edition with the addition of two further pieces, covers a period in Derrida's writing from the late-1970s and 1980s. In the author's preface and an accompanying note, Derrida tells us that, with the exception of essays devoted to the question of the university institution gathered separately in ***Right to Philosophy***, *Psyche* includes a body of work that complements or supplements his other publications from this period – according, however, to the imposition of a certain *distractedness*. It is only via this motif, indeed, that Derrida indicates the linkages between the various pieces included in the collection. As he observes, a recurrent feature among these texts is the quasi-epistolary occasionality of an address to another, or a writing for others, the **performative** dimensions of which frequently enter in as a condition of the text itself. Thus it is the question of *invention* (for and of the **other**) upon which Derrida dwells in his preface, and which guides the initial essay, 'Psyche: Invention of the Other'. In speaking of invention Derrida hopes, of course, to be as inventive as possible. This involves the complex task of producing a text which, if it is indeed to invent, must both suspend or overflow the established discourse and concept of invention that may be applied to it, and yet at the same time appeal to the other for authorization of its inventiveness. (Of course, while making transformative claims, such an appeal to the other must inevitably draw, however inventively, on the resources of a common linguistic and discursive stock.) By definition, invention – whether that of a technical device or a certain discourse – goes some way to disrupting or transforming the established state of things. An invention worthy of its name must be **eventful**. It must somehow inaugurate, beyond existing programmes, conventions, or operational possibilities. Yet inventions also require validation and legitimation in public and institutional contexts that are in some sense already given. (Although the most inventive inventions may well transform these contexts, possibly from top to bottom.) Without a statutory setting, Derrida asserts, there would be no invention; and yet, by definition, invention must flout the statutory in order to earn its name. Moreover, if inventions are to fulfil their **promise** as inventive for a **future** to come, or indeed *of* the future itself, a certain reproducibility or transmissibility must be inscribed at the origin or advent of the invention. In other words, this repeatability (in or for a future to come) at once constitutes, projects and divides the very originality of the invention.

Derrida draws attention to two types of invention which he believes dominate the field of inventive possibility today, although they relate to one another in complex ways. First, there is the invention which introduces a new **technical** or functional possibility, such as one might associate with the production of machines, devices or instruments. Second, there is the invention which fabulates, via the production of new discourses, narratives, or fictions (or at any rate through the invention of their possibility). One must endeavour to recognize the inter-implications among these two types. Fabulating invention in the broad field of culture – let's say, via a political or media discourse of some kind – and invention in the techno-industrial field – with all its links to the fields one might name, for convenience, under the general heading of 'war' – often go hand in hand. And yet Derrida wants to chart a history (from, roughly, the seventeenth century onwards) in which invention as the productive devising of technical apparatuses – culminating in the contemporary international race for patents – has come to dominate the discourse or interpretation of invention itself, at the expense of invention's other sense: that of the invention or fabulation of truth. While these two registers of invention are inextricable in practice, Derrida argues that they remain fundamentally heterogeneous, to the extent that technical invention re-disposes a 'found' subject matter, whereas the invention of truth establishes the very medium in which subject matter may be newly brought forth. Derrida's reading of **Ponge**'s 'Fable', in concert with several

Psyche: Inventions of the Other

references to the texts of **Paul de Man**, serves to **negotiate** this difference along a number of lines.

Indeed, the heterogeneity of invention's two types gives us to think of invention anew. If, in its historical sense, invention has come to be understood as a human 'putting-together' in new ways of available resources, as distinct from creation ex nihilo in the divine sense, nevertheless to invent in the manner of such a 'putting-together' implies the invention of that which is always already possible – or inventable – as invention. To invent the inventable is, like forgiving the forgiveable or welcoming the welcomeable, to operate within an existent field of possibility. In this respect, it is uninventive in the stronger sense. Invention truly worthy of its name must therefore do the **impossible**: it must invent the uninventable, indeed reinvent the very concept and discourse of invention. This, indeed, is the task of **deconstruction**. And yet invention must be of the other. For if invention is of the order of the masterable-possible or the humanly possible, limited just to the performativity of the 'I can', it remains tied to the inventable rather than the uninventable invention. It gives up on the very impossibility, beyond all horizon of expectation, that gives invention its deeper possibility. The other is not, then, inventable; rather, and as such, it is invention itself, the invention that comes to invent and reinvent us.

Needless to say, *Psyche* includes several seminal essays from this period in Derrida's writing. 'The Retreat of Metaphor' is occasioned by Paul **Ricoeur**'s engagement with Derrida's 1971 essay, 'White Mythology: Metaphor in the Text of Philosophy' (see **Margins of Philosophy**). Specifically, a note referring to **Heidegger** in this text provides the grounds for discussion. Here, Derrida describes Ricoeur's objections to his treatment of Heidegger in a way that recalls the *from/to-Sec* effect which in **Limited Inc** Derrida ascribes to **Searle**'s fierce criticisms of **'Signature Event Context'**: that is to say, the grounds of Ricoeur's objections, Derrida insists, are in fact formulated by the very text he wishes to criticize. (Derrida points out that in 'White Mythology' he questions rather than assumes metaphorical *usage*, pursuing the usurious surpluses rather than the finitely utile qualities of **metaphor**; whereas Ricoeur, Derrida feels, ultimately limits the analysis offered in 'White Mythology' to merely the problems raised by the notion of usage as wear-and-tear.) In 'The Retrait of Metaphor', Derrida once again shows how a treatment of metaphor cannot avoid being affected or treated by metaphor itself. Any discourse on metaphor is always *not without* metaphor. A treatise on metaphor cannot therefore isolate, transcend and dominate its object purely and simply. Metaphor everywhere overflows its limit, and yet remains unsettlingly elusive, withdrawing from the very scene of its critical rendition. Since metaphor is, in a sense, at once everywhere and nowhere to be found, the borders between the 'metaphorical' and the 'proper' or 'literal' begin to falter. Metaphor retreats and returns, as the always **supplementary** trait both of the 'metaphorical' and the 'literal' in their very concepts and discourses. Put differently, the *retrait* or re-tracing/re-treating of metaphor here neither presents us simply with a super-abundance of what we typically mean by metaphor, nor offers up metaphoricity as the object of a 'literal' or 'proper' (that is, 'theoretical') rendition.

'Envoi', another text which returns to Heidegger, asks whether there is an entirely representable concept of representation, or whether what we mean (or think we mean) by 'representation' is itself reducible to a representation that would conform to the 'theory' of representation itself, a 'theory' which is of course up to its neck in the **metaphysics of presence**. For Heidegger, the **Greek** world did not originally have a conception of representation in the modern sense, in that it did not have a relation to the 'what is' based on the interposition of an image or representation as 'we' would understand it. (Indeed, such a conception of representation proposes a representation for a self or subject (individually or collectively), a 'me' or 'we', which in fact governs the formulation of the previous sentence – my own – in the sense of organizing its propositional 'content', precisely, as a representation. In other words, one might speculate that, for Heidegger, such a sentence about the Greek world – for all its possible merits – might in fact be unintelligible to the Greeks.) Instead, this representation of 'representation' emerges more recently. Indeed, 'representation' as a history and system (indeed, giving us our very concepts of 'history' and 'system') finds its modern conditions, for Heidegger, with the advent of a certain Cartesianism. As such, it is not fully representable but must itself be subjected to a thinking of translatability and, for that matter, untranslatability.

In 'Des tours de Babel' this question of **translation** takes centre stage. Babel as a **proper name** remains, strictly speaking, untranslatable, and as such would seem to be outside the relational system of language for which,

Psyche: Inventions of the Other 151

nevertheless, it remains a basic constituent (for what would language be that could not name?). Moreover, Babel as a seemingly untranslatable proper name is also the very name that, in the biblical story, inaugurates translation's necessity. The title of Derrida's essay, too, at once resists translation and yet, precisely in its **undecidable** legibility, calls for it. 'Tours' means towers but also turns – the turn of a phrase, trope or trick. Of course, 'des' and 'tour' together sound the same as 'détour'. Such errant pluralities impel and discourage translation at once. Derrida proceeds to a consideration of Walter **Benjamin**'s 'The Task of the Translator', in particular examining Benjaminian language or, in other words, the translatability of his discourse on translation. (Derrida reads Maurice de Gandillac's translation of Benjamin's essay in order to write a text that is in fact already earmarked for translation.) No amount of theoretical elaboration on the subject of translation can achieve a dominating transcendence over the Babel effect itself.

'At This Very Moment in This Work Here I Am' engages once more with the work of Emmanuel **Levinas**. Without subscribing to the entirety of Levinas's thought, Derrida prizes his thinking of the primacy of the other, and elaborates the implications of such thought for the question of the **signature** and seal under which Levinas's text is constituted. Derrida's essay itself takes the form of an extended interlocution with a feminine addressee, from whom in fact the text is itself as much received as it is elicited. The question of **sexual difference** thus comes to be inscribed upon that of the signature and seal of a writing, a sexual difference which cannot be comprehended from a prior position of disinterested authorship or authority, its 'otherness' restricted to a mere opposition dominated by a neutral term (such a term, in its very domination, would always tend to subscribe to the 'masculine').

'Telepathy', so we are told in a footnote, contains the text found in assorted cards and letters that should have appeared in 'Envois', the first section of **The Post Card**. However, this material – all of it **dated** from the same week in July 1979 – was apparently mislaid until too late on in the publication process. Indeed, Derrida professes to include here only a portion of the rediscovered writing. We are not therefore in the midst of a scene of wholly restored presence, or of the full rehabilitation of a merely *temporarily* missing part. (Such a scenario, indeed, would correspond to a certain telepathic fantasy: wanting to overcome all the distances and discrepancies interposed by the technicality, contingency or 'externality' of language and writing, one might dream of a telepathy which restored an entirely uninterrupted, plenitudinous communion.) Rather, the very conditions of this text's staging call for the elaboration of an altogether different problematic. Much of the piece concerns **Freud**'s interest in **telepathy**, worked out in a series of undelivered or, as Derrida would therefore have it, 'fake' lectures. (As 'fake', perhaps, as 'Telepathy' itself, in its always stalling, withholding or otherwise errant fabulation.) As in 'Envois', then, the very medium or condition of the **postal** effect – that of the delivery of a discourse or text to an addressee – is the possibility of non-arrival, a possible non-arrival mimed by the purported circumstances of the composition of 'Telepathy' itself. And it is doubtless in terms of this very same problematic of (non-) arrival that one must seek to treat Freud's own expressions of interest in the doctrine of telepathy; an interest that, for the more 'rationalist' wing of the psychoanalytic movement, would look to have gone badly astray.

In the midst of such issues, Derrida therefore warns us to guard against the naïve assumption that telepathy would guarantee an unmediated and, thus, assured communication beyond the interposition of a postal or telecommunications system (or, put differently, before the advent of **writing** in its enlarged, deconstructive sense). For by dint of its very name, telepathy registers a distance within the self-presence of a subject; a distance that is, precisely, not to be understood as outside the sphere of the technical supplement. Telepathy, in other words, may itself name in more original form the problem of the advent of entire tele-technical networks that one might associate with the very predicament of modernity. Reading Freud in a certain deconstructive manner, indeed, one might even conjecture that telepathy constitutes an originary technicity now largely superseded or enveloped by other forms of communication, although still re-emergent under certain conditions, for instance in the characteristically nineteenth-century prospect of the mob. Here, the fantasy of telepathic immediacy morphs into the nightmarish (and, indeed, always theatrically connived) scenario of spontaneous coalescence, taking place under the sign of a near *inhuman* self-relation – itself made possible by an all too technicized social world. Thus, as Derrida points out, the telephone (as the technical device which enables a rapid proliferation of supposedly immediate communications) plays its inextricable part in Freud's writing on

Psyche: Inventions of the Other

telepathy, as indeed do séances and mediums as an irreducible technical supplement. (In **Archive Fever**, of course, Derrida will conjecture that the advent of email, as a technical supplement one should not be too quick to relegate to the status of a secondary or extrinsic phenomenon, would have transformed the discourse of **psychoanalysis** from top to bottom.)

Other well-known essays in the first volume of *Psyche* include 'Racism's Last Word', written for the opening, in 1983, of an exhibition aiming to become a museum to Apartheid, still very much in effect in South Africa at that time (Derrida shows how its continued existence depended upon tacit and material support from a number of quarters internationally). Also included is 'No Apocalypse, Not Now', given at a 1984 conference on 'Nuclear Criticism', in which Derrida discusses the arms race, notably in conjunction with questions of invention, speed, the techno-political-military complex, and the fabulation of *total* nuclear destruction as an unprecedented event to come and, in the strict sense, always an invention beyond 'presence', that is beyond actual experience or the possibility of human validation. (This text may therefore be read alongside Derrida's 'Of an Apocalyptic Tone Recently Adopted in Philosophy'. From one perspective, the **apocalyptic** tone of modern thought can be located in terms of the most conservative types of thinking and discourse rooted deeply in the Western metaphysical tradition. For, as Derrida observes, apocalyptic discourse articulates itself by way of scenes of revelation, presenting itself in terms of a process of truth's unveiling. However, as Derrida also notes here, the final veil of the apocalypse can never be lifted. (This is what the prospect of total nuclear destruction intimates.) What the 'apocalyptic' gives us to think today and perhaps tomorrow, then, is, for Derrida, the prospect of a dispatch or message whose destination always remains to come, always remaining undecided as a condition of its very form or possibility: *the 'apocalyptic' cannot know where it is heading*. Whether one thinks back to his earlier writings on **différance**, **trace**, **arche-writing**, supplement, and so forth, or whether one recalls his thinking in *The Post Card* of the constitutive possibility of non-arrival as irreducible to the postal effect, one can appreciate why it is that Derrida affirms the very structure of the **mark**, or of writing in general, to be 'apocalyptic' in this sense.)

Also included in this volume of *Psyche* is 'My Chances/*Mes Chances*', in which the thinking of chance, from the Greek world to the psychoanalytic text, is examined.

The second volume also contains a number of highly significant texts, including writings on Peter Eisenman, Bernard Tschumi and architecture, the International College of Philosophy (**Ciph**), aphorisms, and *Romeo and Juliet*. 'Letter to a Japanese Friend', which opens the volume, was written to Toshihiko Izutsu, a renowned Islamologist, on the subject of the possible translation into Japanese of the word 'deconstruction'. Derrida observes that already in French – in German, English and American, too – this term is engulfed by problems of translation. As an adaptation of the Heideggerian words *Destruktion* or *Abbau*, 'deconstruction' turns out, in good French, to carry the sense of a certain disassembling of the parts of a mechanical, formal, linguistic or architectural construction. However, Derrida is quick to point out that the thinking of deconstruction should not be confined to a horizon dominated by the motif of the machine, the construction or the structure. Indeed, while deconstruction established itself in part as a reappraisal of **structuralism** (so that, in a sense, its context was granted by a dominant structuralist paradigm), nevertheless its thinking of, let us say, dissemination, *différance* or trace powerfully resists full integration within architectural, mechanistic or systematic models of thought. Deconstruction cannot therefore be considered a *method* in the classical sense. Nor should it be confused with *analysis* or *critique*, since in its basic tendency the former aspires to disclose an essential ground, while the latter in effect presumes an extraterritorial standpoint as the condition of its judgements. For that matter, deconstruction cannot be thought merely in terms of an *act* prosecuted by an intending *subject*. (Such concepts of *act* and *subject* are indeed put into question as the very task of deconstruction.) For Derrida, deconstruction does not just come along afterwards, imposing itself from the 'outside', as it were. Rather, deconstructibility is already 'in' whatever may come to be deconstructed. Yet any possible definition of deconstruction (as that which might establish a ground for thinking its 'inherent' form or character) would itself remain deconstructible through and through, notably insofar as the nominal form of the word prompts the onto-logic of the third person present indicative (S *is* P), which deconstruction everywhere seeks to rethink or reconstitute otherwise. For Derrida, the force or value of the word 'deconstruction' must instead be thought in terms of a non-closed series of other, replaceable yet necessarily non-identical terms ('writing', 'trace', '*différance*', 'supplement', '**pharmakon**', and so forth) that are put to work in deconstruction and which put deconstruction to work. The

Psyche: Inventions of the Other

question of this chain of substitutions once more raises the problem of translation and translatability, of course. 'Deconstruction' can never dominate or overcome such a problem, but instead gives it another name, calling us to think the very question of translation otherwise.

Psyche also includes the first two essays in the '**Geschlecht**' series, where Derrida returns to Heidegger in the context of a project on philosophical nationality and nationalism. Not easily translatable across the family of **European** or other languages, the German word '*Geschlecht*' nonetheless suggests a **family** of terms including sex, race, stock, generation, lineage, species, genre . . . and family. This presents us with a first problem, in that 'family' turns out to be a substitutable part of the series which it would also seem to gather together as an overarching motif, its replaceability reactivating the very problem of translation which imposes itself on supposed linguistic 'families'. In others words, in *Geschlecht* we find gathered what cannot be fully gathered.

The first essay in the '*Geschlecht*' family turns attention to the question of whether Heidegger totally dismisses the question of sexual difference as inessential to the thinking of Being. While his apparent silence on the subject seems to suggest philosophical haughtiness in relation to the pervasive nature of modern discourses on sexuality, Derrida shows how the neutrality of *Dasein* does not so much determine itself in terms of negative resistance to sexual differentiation, but instead disposes itself more positively as the primal source of every sexuality. In Heidegger, Derrida argues, *Dasein* is not so much pallidly sexless, as (elusively) potent with the very possibility of the 'sexual', embodying in its disseminal structure the very dispersing multiplicity that gives us the 'sexual'.

The second '*Geschlecht*' essay, 'Heidegger's Hand', examines the idea, in the German philosophical tradition, of an essential **German** idiom beyond empirical nationality, and investigates the specific dynamics of a Heideggerian thinking of *Geschlecht* in the context of Heidegger's understanding of technology, politics, language and humanity (in questionable distinction to **animality**). Here, Derrida dwells on Heidegger's characterization of thought as a type of (human) handiwork that crafts, signs, gives or teaches in ways that resist the economic rationality and techno-bureaucratic professionalization of institutions, politics or states. 'The Laws of Reflection: Nelson Mandela, in Admiration', written during the time of Mandela's imprisonment, characterizes its subject as the exemplary guardian of democratic tradition and **law**, indeed as the very *conscience* of this tradition, the one who persistently confronts South Africa's white minority with the principles or laws of democracy that apartheid systematically betrays. Mandela's 'conscience' not only preserves the **memory** of democratic traditions, then, but bears witness to the future of a **democracy to come**. 'How to Avoid Speaking: Denials' explores the limits of (speaking of) deconstruction's possible relations with **negative theology**. In this respect, as well as by speaking of (the limits of speaking of) **khôra**, this essay may be linked to the texts included in **On The Name**. In 'A Number of Yes', in which Derrida explores the work of Michel de Certeau, what is of interest is the 'yes' to language as that which precedes all questioning, all discourse and, indeed, every subject. Every possible utterance – whether affirmative or critical, positive or negative – cannot but acquiesce to this situation, or in other words cannot but say 'yes' (in whatever it says) to this pregiven or, rather, *presupposed* 'yes' to which one always answers or responds. Put differently, this 'first' yes is precisely *fabulated* as an origin by the utterance which (even if its discourse is radically negative) cannot help but say 'yes' to it. It is as if the second 'yes', at each time of asking, is what presupposes and therefore gives us the 'first', which, if it is as much a condition as the source of the second 'yes', begins to find its possibility only in the innumerable and incalculable 'yesses' disseminated across the general yet non-closed space of what Derrida in his early texts calls writing in its enlarged sense. For this reason the '**yes, yes**' or, better still, all the 'yesses' beyond-within this scene of the 'yes, yes' cannot be reduced to the self-same object of a **linguistic** theory, even if they somehow describe the very condition of language. The situation of this 'number of yes' can neither be grasped ontologically nor empirically, and no science, **phenomenology**, or predicative discourse can do it justice. Instead, this story of the 'yes' at the very limits of **philosophy** is only ever the fable that, before the **logos**, appears as *almost* originary, the original 'yes' inhabited from the first by the (innumerable) possibility of repetition. (The question of the 'yes, yes' is also raised in **'Ulysses Gramophone: Hear Say Yes in Joyce'**. In this essay, Derrida countersigns both the Joycean text which offers so many coincidental connections that link Derrida to *Ulysses* (compelling his reading to draw towards a deconstructive affirmation rather than classical analysis or critique), and the phrase of Molly Bloom's ('Yes I said yes I will Yes') which, for Derrida, itself provides a further signature. Here, again, we find ourselves in the midst of an unreckonable 'number of yes', somewhere between the near originary 'first' that nevertheless always supposes or demands its repetition in another, and the proliferal 'yesses' which **countersign** the 'first' on the borderlines of **memory** and invention.)

In 'Interpretations at War: Kant, the Jew, the German', the last essay in the collection, Derrida continues his interest in philosophical nationality and nationalism by examining the writings of Hermann Cohen and Franz Rosenzweig. In particular, Cohen's *Deutschtum und Judentum* (1915) posits a deep alliance between **Judaism** and Hellenism. Since the cosmopolitical spread of Platonism which in fact establishes **Christianity** as a **religion** is also the fundamental source of Germanness, Judaism in its very intimacy with the Greek cannot be excluded from the German genealogy or psyche. The privileged relation to Hellenism prized in a German tradition right up to Heidegger is therefore part of a heritage that is also Judeo-Christian, Judeo-Protestant and indeed Judeo-German. (**Kant** therefore finds his place precisely within the cosmopolitical space of this overdetermined heritage.) At the time of writing, Cohen wanted to prevent a war between the United States and Germany, and this text addressed itself in part to American Jews, to whom it presented Germany as much less an enemy than a kindred spirit. But Cohen's thesis reverberates through history, both before and after its time. Would Cohen not have seen the entire history of the twentieth century, culminating in its two so-called World Wars, as nothing other than a family feud, a deranged war within the **spirit**? Whether or not one accepts Cohen's analysis, Derrida shows how his arguments do not establish themselves on an empirical or factual basis, but may instead be thought of as a symptom of the situation they seek to describe, a reflection of the (deranged) 'psyche' they seek to reflect or reconstitute. The 'world **logocentricism**' of this entangled legacy – that of a Greek-Jewish-Christian-German psyche – interests Derrida in other of his texts on *mondialization*, religion and world Christianization.

psychoanalysis   Derrida's interest in psychoanalysis spans a large number of texts. Certain affinities between **deconstruction** and psychoanalysis were often suggested to Derrida and, in some prefatory comments to 'Freud and the Scene of Writing', found in ***Writing and Difference***, he acknowledges some connections between the two. The interminable repression of **writing**, *différance*, **trace**, **supplement** or non-present **remainder** which deconstruction gives us to think is recalled in the psychoanalytic conception of a 'repressed' that returns in the form of a symptom. The idea of an identity divided – yet constituted, too – by its own **re-marking** or repeatability not only calls up certain psychoanalytic themes but, indeed, reminds us of some of psychoanalysis's analytical models (or, perhaps better still, some of the *problems* of analysis with which it is confronted). Moreover, for the Derrida of 'Freud and the Scene of Writing', **Freud**'s understanding of the psychic apparatus as a writing 'machine' suggests psychoanalysis's resistance to the **phonocentric** tradition inherited by **phenomenology** and **linguistics**, and perhaps draws close to Derrida's conception of a 'general writing' which cannot be dominated by **speech**, **presence**, etc. However, in the same early essay on psychoanalysis, Derrida's prefatory remarks differentiate his own work from psychoanalysis on the basis that the latter still remains too in thrall of **metaphysics**. Consequently, in a later text, 'Le Facteur de la vérité', included in ***The Post Card***, Derrida argues that **Lacan**'s seminar on Poe's 'The Purloined Letter' continues to be funded by the metaphysical construal of truth as revelation, a revelation which it is the task or destiny of psychoanalysis to deliver – in the form, here, of restoring the letter's 'lack' to its proper place: the truth of the phallus as the signified. (See also 'For the Love of Lacan', a still-later text found in ***Resistances to Psychoanalysis***.) In Derrida's *The Post Card*, then, we find another **postal** principle at work, that of a disseminating *différance* which cannot be surely 'posted' to an ultimate addressee or destination, but which is marked instead by the irreducible and constitutive possibility of non-arrival. (In 'To Speculate – on "Freud"', Derrida therefore puts in question the idea of 'Freud' as the ultimate addressee of psychoanalysis, the **proper name** to which psychoanalysis must restitute itself.)

In *Resistances of Psychoanalysis*, the resistance to psychoanalysis offered by deconstruction (or, for that matter, any other discourse) is to be thought only alongside psychoanalysis's own conception of 'resistance-to-analysis', which implies a resistance *internal* to psychoanalysis itself. Analysis and resistance are, in other words, intensely knotted together in the very movement or production of psychoanalysis, since each depend on and supplement the other. The title of Derrida's book is therefore marked by a double genitive: resistances *of* psychoanalysis implies at once the resistance

religion

offered to psychoanalysis both by its opponents and analysands, and the resistance which it gives itself as perhaps the very condition of its possibility (the fraught institutional history of psychoanalysis – its internal conflicts, feuds and factionalisms – in some sense embodies this constitutive self-resistance). Deconstruction's complex relation to psychoanalysis – neither simply oppositional nor identificatory – must be thought in terms of such resistance, a resistance which both challenges and constitutes, questions and affirms.

For the relationship of the psychoanalytic archive to the psychoanalytic thinking of the psyche *as* archive, or psychoanalysis's relation to its own technical conditions of possibility, see **Archive Fever**. For Foucault's 'resistance' to psychoanalysis, see **Resistances of Psychoanalysis**. For psychoanalysis as a possible source of resistance to the forms of sovereignty which give us the death penalty, see **Without Alibi**. Of course, much could also be said about psychoanalytic traces and resistances where Derrida seeks to think **mourning, memory**, etc. Psychoanalysis may be borne in mind everywhere that Derrida treats **sexual difference** and in view of coinages such as **phallogocentricism**.

— R —

relève See **Margins of Philosophy**.

religion   While there has been considerable discussion over Derrida's interest in debates about religion (and the so-called return of religion), what is certain is that his analyses of complexly entwined religious legacies, notably those of the Abrahamic religions (Judaism, Christianity, Islam), intersect powerfully with his **deconstruction** of the **metaphysical** tradition, and his redescription of some of the founding concepts of Western religion, philosophy and culture (**justice, messianicity, presence, gift, forgiveness, responsibility, hospitality**, etc.) in the interests of another **future**. See also **Aporias, 'Demeure', 'Faith and Knowledge', justice, messianicity, On Cosmopolitanism and Forgiveness, Psyche, The Gift of Death**.

remains, remainder   Another term in Derrida's writing employed to call into question the **metaphysical** determination of **being** as **presence**. Through his thinking of the **supplement, trace, *différance*, writing**, and so on, Derrida opens thought to the possibility of the '**other**', construed not as a presence that is destined to arrive or return intact, but as a non-present or non-self-identical remainder that is in fact constitutively at work throughout the metaphysical tradition itself (even if such a remainder is continually repressed by metaphysics).

re-mark, re-marking   See **mark**.

Resistances of Psychoanalysis   Derrida prefaces this collection of three lectures from the early 1990s (originally published in French, 1996) by noting an increasing resistance to **psychoanalysis**, both at academic and institutional levels and more widely across the various spheres of society and culture. His project, however, is to rethink this supposed opposition between psychoanalysis and its would-be adversaries, not only by suggesting that the various analyses resistant to psychoanalysis inevitably call up the psychoanalytic understanding of 'resistance-to-analysis', but also by affirming a resistance internal to psychoanalysis itself, an **auto-immunitary** resistance to itself (and, thus, an inherent divisibility of itself) found at its own origin. In the first essay, 'Resistances', Derrida therefore observes that psychoanalysis is drawn to, and indeed thinks or forms itself precisely in the vicinity of, that which resists or exceeds analysis. For example, the interpretability of dreams is, for psychoanalysis, everywhere jeopardized by the extent to which the dream devises for itself a veneer-like impression of intelligible or representable meaning. This not only throws analysis off the scent of the work of the dream in all its heterogeneity and difference, but suggests more radically that any wakeful or rational analysis might merely be a ruse of the dream. Every dream therefore leads back to an insoluble and unfathomable 'navel' which psychoanalysis itself analyzes as ultimately unanalyzable. Analysis and its resistance (resistance of analysis/analysis of resistance) are therefore indissolubly knotted in this very 'navel'. Each emerge as non-self-identically split and doubled with the other. Each is incalculably *divisible with* rather than simply opposed to the other. (Similarly, Derrida suggests that repetition-compulsion may be thought of as both resistant to analysis and *analytic* in its very structure.

Resistances of Psychoanalysis

From this perspective, resistance to psychoanalysis cannot be thought outside of the resistance *of* psychoanalysis – a resistance of itself to itself, indeed of and to 'self' as 'other', a resistance of the '**other**' of itself to itself.) Thus, analysis – psychoanalysis – cannot acquire the conceptual unity or self-identity which would be needed in order for it to be posited as a stable 'object' simply to be resisted, critiqued or condemned. **Deconstruction**, if there is any, might indeed name the hyperbolicism of an interminably self-resistant analysis – that is to say, an analysis which, rather than hoping to unveil 'presence' or 'truth' at the origin, thinks a more originary resistance to analysis as that which gives all possibility of critical thought, analytical discourse, or for that matter linguistic discrimination. (See, for instance, **'Différance'**.)

In 'For the Love of Lacan' Derrida salutes psychoanalysis as a form of thinking that remains resistant to dominant cultural programmes, institutions and media discourses bent on certain types of reductive and normalizing representation. He acknowledges the Lacanian text as an indispensable influence on philosophical and critical thought in the latter part of the twentieth century. Yet, referring back to the reading he undertook in **The Post Card** of **Lacan**'s 'Seminar on "the Purloined Letter"', Derrida reiterates what he sees as the deconstructible facets of Lacan's discourse: the commitment to truth as unveiling; the priority given to **speech** in terms of its supposed relation to presence, plenitude and truth, in contrast to the ostensibly mechanical, '**technical**' and auxiliary nature of the **archive** or record; the **phonocentrism** of the Lacanian text in its construal of language (a feature of his discourse that Lacan sought to recast after 1968); the transcendental position of the phallus and the **phallogocentrism** of Lacanian psychoanalysis; the reappropriating return of the letter to the 'proper' as its proper destination, or in other words, its reposting to an origin which precedes the advent of a certain 'lack' (as Derrida suggests, this aspect of Lacanian thought most closely divides it from deconstruction, since, for Derrida, the irreducible possibility of non-arrival is constitutive of the letter itself); the inability to reckon with the **fictional** or **literary** dimension of narration; and the extent to which the effects of the double in Poe's tale are neglected in Lacan's reading.

In the final text of the volume, '"To Do Justice to Freud": The History of Madness in the Age of Psychoanalysis', Derrida reconsiders his relationship to the work of Michel **Foucault**, some thirty years after the publication of

Foucault's *Madness and Civilization*. Derrida's 1963 essay on this text, 'Cogito and the History of Madness', subsequently reprinted in **Writing and Difference**, led to a strong and somewhat bitter debate between the two thinkers, one which clouded their friendship for many years. Since this particular lecture was presented after Foucault's death, thus allowing him no opportunity to respond, Derrida is extremely hesitant to reopen the debate in its original form, but nonetheless raises the question of the (resistant) relationship of psychoanalytic discourse to the Foucauldian text on 'madness'. For Derrida, Foucault is unduly hasty in seeking to 'objectify' psychoanalysis historically, failing to see that his own work emerges from an intellectual milieu which cannot so easily extricate itself from psychoanalytic influences. Psychoanalysis, in other words, cannot be reduced to a simple 'object' of Foucaultian discourse, since it must be taken to inform that discourse to some extent; nor can psychoanalysis be partitioned historically by such a discourse if it enters into its own historical conditions of possibility. Foucault's complex and often contradictory approach to psychoanalysis is reread by Derrida in terms of the resistances which psychoanalysis itself offers to a reductive presumption of its self-identity. Indeed, psychoanalysis's resistance of its supposed 'self-sameness' opens the possibility of a certain deconstruction of Foucault. For this somewhat maddening resistance not only challenges the objectification of psychoanalysis as an identifiable historical form but, by extension, provokes the question of the very possibility of an 'age' of madness. In other words, the self-difference of the 'psychoanalytic' which begins to seep into Foucault's text at precisely those moments he attempts to identify psychoanalysis *as such* threatens to disturb not only his image of psychoanalysis as an 'object' of critical representation, but also the epistemic categories or historical classifications which underpin the Foucauldian project itself. Nonetheless, Derrida salutes Foucault for acknowledging difficulties in his conception of the *episteme*. For Derrida, such difficulties do not merely give rise to a paralyzing impasse in Foucault's work, but instead provide the always heterogeneous and divided resources which make possible the **event** of thought.

responsibility Derrida is frequently quick to distinguish responsibility from morality, duty or even **ethics** in a traditional sense. For Derrida, the possibility of responsibility is diminished when one follows an already established code, convention, programme, **law**, rule or norm. Thus, any responsibility worthy of its name arises on condition of an **undecidable** or **aporetic** situation, rather than in view of settled obligations or given demands and justifications. Responsibility's milieu, in other words, is not that of an already possible possibility. It is rather that of the experience of the **impossible** which, for Derrida, intimately accompanies **deconstruction** itself. (As Derrida suggests in *On the Name*, since the responsibility which interests him precisely cannot be reduced to the order of the 'masterable-possible', in fundamental terms responsibility is always *of the other*.) However, it is the experience of the impossible or the undecidable that gives genuine **decision** (decision of or for the other) its very chance or possibility. Responsibility is thus radically heightened at the point at which predetermined duties and expectations come to be suspended, but paradoxically this suspension of established responsibilities irresponsibilizes responsibility itself. (Put differently, it is a certain breaking with law that gives responsibility its law.) However, one must **negotiate** this aporetic situation in the interests of new forms of responsibility to come.

For responsibility and aporia, see **Aporias**. For responsibility, justice and law, see **'Force of Law'** (see also **'Faith and Knowledge'**). For responsibility and the non-response, see 'Passions' in *On the Name*. For the irreducible secrecy at the origin of Western responsibility, or the irresponsibility of responsibility, see *The Gift of Death*.

retrait   See 'The Retrait of Metaphor' in *Psyche*.

Ricoeur, Paul (1913–2005)   French philosopher influenced by **phenomenology**. See 'The Retrait of Metaphor' in *Psyche*.

Right to Philosophy   Originally published in French, 1990. Appears in two volumes in English translation (see Bibliography under the titles *Who's Afraid of Philosophy?* and *Eyes of the University*). *Right to Philosophy* demonstrates Derrida's engagement from the 1970s onwards with **French** political debates about the reform of national education and the future of **philosophy** teaching in the **university** in France and beyond. The work includes various texts which undertake to analyze and intervene in the question of the institutional conditions and possibilities of philosophy as both an historical legacy and current provocation to the **future**. Through scrupulous reading of a famous letter by **Hegel**, Derrida examines the question of age in teaching, in answer to contemporaneous debates about the age at which philosophy should be taught in France. He scrutinizes the concept of a 'teaching body' as it plays between the body (and mind) of the professor, the faculty *corps* and the national body or bodies. Derrida also reflects on 'class' in education: the classroom, the student body, but also the socio-economic conception of 'class' as it intersects with the education system. The second volume opens by looking at the role played by supposedly 'natural' languages in the historical developments that link education and state in France.

In one of the pieces included in the second volume, 'Punctuations: The Time of a Thesis', which provides the text for his successful oral defence for *doctorat d'état* in 1980, Derrida looks back at the development of his research from the late 1960s onwards, and notes that the very implications of his thinking called for a transformation in the rhetoric and mode of his writing, in the form of its discursive address and its particular intervention in dominant university discourses – a transformation which was to resist conformity to the established norms of a thetic presentation, resulting indeed in such innovative texts as **Glas**. Derrida saw that the discursive models and practices which regulated scholarly and academic institutions in France powerfully intersected with the dominant discursive field inhabited, let us say, by media and government forces, as well as by military, economic and technological powers. For him, indissoluble ties could be discerned between the university institution in its present functions and the near-encyclopaedic system of a certain ontology and **metaphysics** (one that he associates in his thesis defence with **logocentricism**) which was always going to have very real social and political effects. Meanwhile, in another essay collected in the volume, 'The Principle of Reason: the University in the Eyes of its Pupils', Derrida observes how scientific and technological advances arising from ostensibly fundamental research often come to serve the interests of the state, the military, the secret service or the police. (Much later on, in 'The University Without Condition', Derrida notes how the humanities' prized ideal of autonomy often encourages, however unwittingly, funding decisions in the university which favour science and technology and thus actually help to reproduce the power nexus to which he draws our attention.) In the interests of approaching and analyzing all the more effectively this highly charged matrix of forces and powers,

Derrida therefore seeks to adjust significantly the frames, structures and norms that govern the institutional space he inhabits and engages, a space which intersects complexly with its 'outside'. However, Derrida is not so naïve as to suppose that any claim, demand or desire to suspend absolutely the various forms of legitimacy, authority, competence or tradition that accompany the established university model might produce satisfactorily effective results. On the contrary, he suspects such a purist brand of radicalism may actually buy into several of the metaphysical assumptions which underpin the inherited order, and thus, through its own naïveté, that such an approach might allow for a surreptitious and thus all the more powerful reinscription of the dominant field. However, for Derrida, philosophy's asymmetrical contract with the university – neither belonging nor not-belonging to the institution as a part of the whole, the *universitas,* which it itself allots – makes possible an opening on to the very question of the structure and effects of the university space, not least in its relations with the wider world (although Derrida is always most vigilant about the very fragile and **deconstructible** relationship between the supposed 'inside' and 'outside' of the institution). In other words, it is philosophy's 'with-against' relation to the university that perhaps ultimately interests Derrida in his interventions in political debates about French educational reform during this period. Derrida is less concerned with a straightforward defence of philosophy in its accepted scholarly guise than in transformative moves and gestures which make possible the '**other**' of philosophy itself. The question of the right to philosophy – whether one can ever proceed to the 'philosophical' directly as much as whether philosophy is a duty, privilege or justification (itself a question not well served by excessive 'directness') – is posed by Derrida in this very context.

Not surprisingly, then, in 1975 Derrida co-founded the **Greph** (Group de Recherches sur L'Enseignment Philosophique, or Research Group on the Teaching of Philosophy), a group committed both to theoretical investigation and activist intervention, partly in answer to the 1973–74 CAPES report, which Derrida and others saw as linked to a broader political and ideological attack on philosophical education taken up by the French government under the general sponsorship of a matrix of economic, political and techno-industrial and techno-military powers. The proposed Haby reforms of 1975 focused this attack on philosophy teaching in French secondary schools. In response, in 1979 the Greph convened an Estates

General, bringing together in a large amphitheatre in the Sorbonne over 1,200 individuals from a variety of backgrounds and with an array of interests in the debate. Through an elected committee, this meeting passed several resolutions that sought to preserve and extend philosophy teaching in France. In a televised appearance, the education minister for the Giscard government replied by anxiously offering reassurances. By 1981, Mitterand's socialists swept to power on a platform that included proposals by the Greph and the Estates General. While an extension of philosophy teaching in the French education system was not ultimately forthcoming, the new government put in motion an initiative to establish an international college of philosophy in France. Derrida took a leading role in the difficult process of negotiation and consultation that lead to its inauguration in 1983. A series of texts and documents relating to this history can be found in the appendices to the second volume of *Right to Philosophy*. The Collège international de philosophie (**Ciph**), of which Derrida was the first director, was to retain a strong degree of independence despite state funding, and devoted itself to research on and in philosophy in broad intersection with an array of other disciplines, notably to develop fields and topics marginalized in other institutions. The principal characteristics of the college were to be a declared and statutory internationality and the absence of chairs and permanent positions.

As well as conveying a detailed sense of this series of events, and the thinking on Derrida's part which both prompted and reacted to them, *Right to Philosophy* includes several essays by Derrida that are well known in their own right, many returning to the legacies and writings of philosophers such as **Descartes**, **Kant**, **Hegel** and **Heidegger** in order to rethink philosophy's traditions, institutional conditions and futures. In 'Where a Teaching Body Begins and How It Ends', Derrida reflects on his own role as a teacher at the École Normale, a post he occupied for many years, analyzing the complex array of forces and interests that surround the ENS, those which determine the professional function of the *agrégé-répétiteur* (or repeater of the set curriculum) and the expectations placed upon candidates for the *agrégation*, and which contribute more widely to the history and question of French national education and philosophical instruction. Here, the forces in tension with one another that constitute the historico-ideologico-politico-institutional field of pedagogy mean that there can never be a single, self-identical and homogenous teaching body suspending within itself the conflicts and contradictions which shape it, so that the always over-determined teaching body includes a **spectral** (or **actuvirtual**) **supplement** of itself as other than itself, one that cannot simply be 'gathered' in the interests of illumination or enlightened knowledge and education. Thus, the teaching body is always, deconstructibly, marked by a certain reserve or remainder, in its performances (which Derrida is at pains to foreground) as much as in its concept. In this essay, Derrida also implies that the '**linguistic** turn' associated with the rise of contemporary theory risks giving merely a second wind to the traditional image and function of the university.

In 'The Age of Hegel' Derrida investigates, against the backdrop of national proposals for contemporary reform, the question of the age and time for philosophy, both in Hegel's own thought and life and in an era characterized by a state bureaucracy engaged in the process of prising philosophical study from clerical control in order to nationalize education. Here, the role of memorization – both of philosophy and of a philosophical past – is put firmly into question. In 'Mochlos', meanwhile, Derrida's reading of Kant's *The Conflict of the Faculties* exposes the intractable divisions of the modern university, reflecting upon the aporia of founding or instituting which profoundly unsettles the Enlightenment justification and rationale for the university, despite the parliamentary model proposed by Kant to seek redress and rebalance in the face of its insoluble conflicts. Yet, here, Derrida affirms another thought of the institution, better equipped to assume the effects of its own deconstructibility. In 'The Principle of Reason', where he returns to his reading of Heidegger, Derrida addresses colleagues at Cornell as the occasion to think about the topolitical scenography of the institution as one that is caught – in the aporia of its founding and justification – between the barrier and abyss, between an impossible desire for autonomy and self-protection on the university's part and an uncloseable exposure to what is abyssal in its very grounds. This involves a new thought of the university's 'vision', less wedded to a notion of clear sight, enlightened knowledge and transparent representation, and advocating instead a certain strategic rhythm for thinking in and about the university, suggested by the blinking of an eye. Here, Derrida also rethinks the role and status of the professor as a guardian of knowledge, who paradoxically must preserve what he does not yet have and what cannot yet be, precisely in order to keep faith with the university and not to lose the chance of its as yet unknowable **future** amid the efforts of a dry conservation.

Lastly, the first part of the second volume examines Descartes's decision to write his *Discourse on Method* in French. This is interpreted as a crucial instance in a triple-phased language politics of the French state, from the seventeenth century through the revolutionary period to the present. Descartes's French, and the French of the French state (rather than of the people) from this time onwards, seeks to dispel idiomaticity and therefore outwit forms of linguistico-political resistance by presenting itself as a linguistic medium cleansed of all ambiguity, a language of common good sense which articulates itself, first of all, in the pure **present** of a Cartesian philosophy undivided between classical and natural languages (Latin and French). Yet Derrida argues that the subsequent Latin translation by Descartes of *Discourse on Method* in fact confirms the conceptual and linguistic-philosophic conventions that govern the original text, so that in a more profound sense the translation precedes – and divides – the original. While, unlike Hegel, Descartes never had to serve a state-organized education system, Derrida weighs the impact of Descartes's thought and writing amid the legacies of the history he wants to tell, and dwells on the question of **translation** in so far as it affects and limits the supposed mastery of language, education, pedagogy and state.

Rogues: Two Essays on Reason   French publication, 2003. This volume, appearing in English in 2005, comprises two texts. In the first, 'The Reason of the Strongest (Are There Rogue States?)', originally presented at Cerisy-la-Salle in 2002, Derrida speaks of the recent emergence of the phrase 'Etat voyou', adopted in certain quarters of the **French** media and political field as an approximate translation of the Anglo-American term, 'rogue state'. The origins of the latter he traces from its more limited usage in an earlier phase of the Cold War to its greater prominence in the 1980s and 1990s, notably during the Clinton presidency, when it became more powerfully linked with the denunciation of so-called state-sponsored international terrorism. At the point of greatest intensification of its usage, however, the very term was already destined for a certain obsolescence. With the decline of the managed political 'game' between the two superpowers of the USA and the USSR that established a particular world order in the post-war period, threats to the security and well-being of a new world order organized around the precedence of the United States became more and more difficult to imagine in terms of a state form. Indeed, Derrida suggests that the intensified usage of the very phrase 'rogue states' became symptomatic of the anxiety occasioned by the weakening of those traditional political categories based on the historical concept and form of the state which had hitherto established the regulatory horizon of international relations. (In other words, to associate 'new' 'mass' 'terroristic' threats with the evil of a 'rogue state', or to continue resorting to tirades against 'state-sponsored' terrorism, perhaps only avoids acknowledging the prospect of a more fearful menace that is no longer *of* the 'state', although it may have appropriated its very worst weapons.) In this essay, Derrida acknowledges the force of Noam Chomsky's argument in *Rogue States* (2000), that – based on the generally accepted criteria that go to define a 'rogue state' – all the evidence points towards the United States itself as the most 'roguish' of them all. (Chomsky has not been alone in making this case.) However, while in their very form of empirical case-making the scathing indictments against the US by Chomsky and others imply the ideal of a state that might behave less 'roguishly', Derrida goes further by insisting that, in their most legitimate sovereignty, all states are fundamentally 'voyou' or 'roguish'. Such an argument as Derrida's does not, however, lead to political despair, nihilism or an abdication of critical **responsibility**, but on the contrary seeks to be all the more responsible in adjusting or modulating differently the conception of what needs to be done, notably in the field of international **law**, in order to address precisely such insights into both the pervasive roguishness of the state, and at the same time the declining fortunes of its historical form.

Traditionally, the state in its 'democratic' form has been conceptualized in terms of notions of autonomy, self-determination and self-representation; in other words, in terms of a **sovereign** capacity to give to oneself (or itself) law, power, freedom and decision. This supposed auto-foundational circle, based on the performable-masterable-possible of 'I can', Derrida calls '**ipseity**'. Ipseity thus names one, perhaps predominating principle of legitimate sovereignty, that of the *autos*, with which Derrida contrasts another principle underpinning the sovereignty of democracy, that of the **demos**. This implies the irreducible legitimacy of the other, 'each one', 'anyone', 'no matter who'. This principle in its very irreducibility disrupts ipseity's ipseity from the outset, and moreover puts into question the legitimacy it gives itself as the auto-foundational principle of the democratic state.

Derrida undertakes a lengthy analysis in which he traces the unstable borderline between the enshrined principle and value of democratic freedom on the one hand, and, on the other, the ever-present potential this itself entails for liberty-taking, freewheeling license, wantonness or roguishness. (Derrida, indeed, finds the political origin of the voyous or rogue in, precisely, the popular and democratic traditions of modern Western states and cities, traditions it roguishly reflects.) Moreover, since this principle of freedom is enshrined in the very *concept* of democracy, in contrast to other sorts of sovereignties, or other political or theocratic forms, there will never have been a single version or interpretation of the 'democratic' that could lay claim to total and exclusive legitimacy. Thus, not only are all democratic states somewhat 'roguish' in claiming (as they nevertheless expediently must) to be fully legitimate or sovereign; another 'truth' of democracy is that it will never have been reducible to a regime or, for that matter, a constitution. Democracy will never have had a proper meaning as such (which amounts to remarking a certain, and necessary, shortfall or shortcoming of its ipseity). For Derrida, the freedom of play, the indetermination or undecidability at work in the very concept of democracy leaves open the chance of a **future**, both for the concept itself and for **singular decisions** and responsibilities which are to be taken necessarily beyond a fully progammable (or appropriable) political machine or masterful sovereignty. Such a future – or in Derrida's terms, the 'to-come' (and the '**democracy to come**') – is not just *in* the future. It is not to be thought of as something we might hope for 'some fine day'. Instead, it imposes itself with absolute urgency in the very form (or form-beyond-form) which democracy (or the democratic imperative) takes, precisely, here and now. Indeed, since by definition (or, at any rate, by a certain definition not reducible merely to the *autos*) democracy cannot give itself a proper meaning, or cannot inscribe itself purely within the self-same, it makes little sense to appeal to any notion of the democratic *ideal*.

By permitting liberty-taking with/as the very form of democratic freedom, democracy thus suffers a sort of **autoimmune** disorder. Using examples from certain Arab or Islamic nation-states, Derrida shows that it is perfectly possible to use democratic principles and techniques – such as free speech and elections – in order to bring democracy to an end. One can *democratically*, and in the very name of democracy, vote democracy out of existence. (Equally, the defence of democracy against the continual threat of its perversion or demise often results in its proponents resorting to the most undemocratic techniques. In this, democracy deteriorates precisely as it tries to safeguard itself.) Yet, since this necessarily suicidal trait of democracy is what opens it to an alterity beyond the self-same, democracy's autoimmunity is also what gives it the possibility of a future. Since democracy cannot be reduced to the sovereignty and ipseity of a giving of license and legitimacy to oneself, Derrida reaffirms his faith in the (admittedly flawed and sometimes ineffectual) international bodies, laws and declarations which assert a democratic principle somewhat at odds with the 'democratic' demands of sovereign nation-states, those that often aggress *in fact* against the freedom and equality of the marginal or the oppressed. (Of course, we must recall that powerful sovereign states can, with more or less subtle **violence**, appropriate these international bodies and laws to legitimize and thus further their own ends – Derrida shows how the United Nations's Security Council has maintained the sovereign power of world-leading nation-states.)

Freedom and equality, the two great pillars of democracy, are complexly related in conceptual terms, as Derrida points out. While equality typically maintains itself in terms of measureable or calculable relation, freedom in its essential concept is aligned largely with the **unconditional** and the indivisible. Freedom is irreducible to what is relative in the other. However, beginning with **Aristotle**'s idea that the freedom of each alike in democracy provides the basis for its claims to equality among all, Derrida notes that the terms do not always confront one another in rivalrous opposition. Yet Aristotle's attempted reconciliation of freedom and equality means, paradoxically, that one can no longer measure or calculate equal relations on the strength of a freedom that continues to insist on its unconditionality. The exchange relation between equality and freedom is, therefore, once more subjected to what is incalculable. (This text also includes Derrida's reservations about Jean-Luc **Nancy**'s adoption of the term 'fraternity' to describe an equality of sharing which continues to respect the incalculable or incommensurable. For Derrida, fraternalism in its political history has too frequently led back to supposed rights of birth, to blood and land, to nation, patriliny and deity, and thus ultimately in practice to the forms of sovereignty he sees as deconstructible and calling for **deconstruction**.)

Constituted deconstructively in the play between *autos* and *demos*, freedom and equality, ipseity and the other, sovereignty and voyou, a thinking of democracy (and thus, inseparably, of the 'political' as a concept that is coterminous with its history) turns out to require a thinking of **différance**. Equally, and for this very reason, Derrida's thinking of *différance* was always, he tells us, a thinking of the political. Since (somewhat against itself) by its own definition democracy cannot grant itself a proper or self-same meaning, it can never have a pure form in the **present**, or a purely present form. The thinking of *différance* that this calls for implies that *différance* was always already a way to think the singular complexity of the 'political' and the 'democratic'.

The second essay in the volume, 'The "World" of the Enlightenment to Come (Exception, Calculation, and Sovereignty)', sees Derrida struggle with the surprising phrase that he gives himself to think: 'To save the honour of reason'. This 'honour' of **reason** (which would seem to exceed a narrow or purely instrumental rationality of reason) is read against the backdrop of **Husserl**'s writings during the period which saw the rise of fascism. In considering fascism's emergence in **Europe**, Husserl acknowledges the apparent failure of European rationalism, and yet calls for a certain heroism of reason that might assist in Europe's rebirth. However, precisely in its 'heroic' form, reason would then not limit itself merely to the tautological self-definition of rationality's rationalism (an apparently pure and unanswerable exchange which produces insufficient reserves to resist the worst abuses of the European tradition), but would draw instead on some more incalculable element in its very definition or grounding. In this essay, as he seeks to continue with this thought of saving the honour of reason, Derrida endeavours to think the relation between sovereignty (including state sovereignty, and the power to decide the law and exceptions to the law) and the unconditional. Both seem to originate in what is absolute and indivisible. Yet Derrida argues that the unconditional must be separated from sovereignty, precisely in the name of reason. In contrast to the ipseity of sovereignty (an absolute 'I can'), the unconditional – unconditional giving and forgiving, unconditional hospitality, the unconditional event, invention, decision – depends, if one thinks rationally about it, upon the suspension of the masterable-possible. If I already have within my 'self' the capacity to forgive, give, decide, invent, be hospitable, then no forgiveness, giving, decision, invention or hospitality worth its name will have come to pass. No event will have taken place. The unconditional sees ipseity tremble before the coming of an other it cannot predict, programme, appropriate or contain. Derrida asks us to think about the inseparably antagonistic interplay of sovereignty and the unconditional at the very limits of reason. This interplay divides reason, causing its autoimmunity, but giving it the chance of a future, too. What is most 'reasonable' in this (unsituatable) situation is the continual task of singular **negotiations**, each time of asking, between sovereignty and the unconditional. Such negotiations (without horizon or programme) would be undertaken in the name of a certain **giving** and **forgiving**, and in the name of **hospitalities**, **inventions** and decisions to come, which answer to the most pressing international political circumstances. In the very transformations these imply, Derrida suggests such negotiation is already under way.

Rousseau, Jean-Jacques (1712–1778)   Genevan-born philosopher and writer. For Derrida on Rousseau, see *Margins of Philosophy*, *Memoires for Paul de Man*, *Of Grammatology*, supplement, *Without Alibi*, writing.

— S —

St Augustine (354–430)   Latin church father, Berber philosopher and theologian. Influenced by Neo-Platonism. See *Circumfession*, confession, testimony, *Without Alibi*.

Saussure, Ferdinand de (1857–1913)   Swiss linguist. For Derrida on Saussure, see *différance*, *'Différance'*, linguistics/linguisticism, *Margins of Philosophy*, metaphysics of presence, *Of Grammatology*, *Positions*, trace, writing.

Searle, John (b. 1932)   American philosopher and speech act theorist. See *'Signature Event Context'*, speech act theory.

secret In an interview with Maurizio Ferraris during the 1990s, Derrida confesses his taste for the secret. However, one should not be quick to confuse this 'taste' with a desire for a deeper, revealed truth, since for Derrida the construal of truth in terms of revelation remains a determining feature of the **metaphysics of presence**, and thus of Western **philosophy** in general. Instead, Derrida's analysis of the structure of the secret may be linked to his thinking of ***différance*** as the non-signifying, non-present **remainder** which traverses each **mark**, every system, every relation or entity (and which thus founds the metaphysical tradition in its very deconstructibility). The **event** – of **decision, invention, hospitality**, of the **gift** and **forgiveness**, and so on – is tied to the secret, in that it remains irreducibly resistant to present or 'already-possible' possibilities, to objectification or phenomenologization, and indeed to 'theoretical' elaboration as such (hence, Derrida frequently uses formulations such as 'the gift, if there is any . . .', 'the decision, if there is any . . .'). For Derrida, then, the unconstructable, uninventable, unanticipatable, absolutely '**other**' is at stake in 'the experience of the **impossible**' which itself calls for deconstructive, transformative engagement with the conditional forms that politics and **law**, for instance, give us. While in 'Passions', therefore, **responsibility** is always of the other (since responsibility discharged in the name of one's existing capacities or resources represents a diminution of decision and responsibility), in ***The Gift of Death*** European responsibility is tied to the secret. The 'secret' here is not merely a concealed or repressed 'origin', but a constitutive difference (for instance, between the 'truth' and impossibility of death *as such*) that comes to structure the entire cultural and philosophical legacy in which responsibility finds at once its possibility, its limits, and perhaps its **future**.

Deconstruction's taste for the secret is also inextricable with its openness to an 'originary' **affirmation**. The '**yes, yes**' which gives the conditions of possibility for all discourse – whether 'negative' or not, 'critical' or not – is tied to a depthless secret: that of the first 'yes' that is always also fabulated as 'origin' by each and every 'second'.

See **'I Have a Taste for the Secret'**, *On Cosmopolitanism and Forgiveness*, *The Gift of Death* and *On the Name*.

September 11 In an interview with Giovanni Borradori conducted just a few weeks after the attacks in the United States on the World Trade

Center and the Pentagon, Derrida dwells on Borradori's initial suggestion that September 11, 2001 produced the impression of a major **event**. With great incision, he explores how this impression might be comprehended in terms of the inter-relationship of highly determined political, military and media interests and powers. In particular, the ritualized invocation of the **name** to which the 'event' was so quickly reduced – '9/11' – sought to numb the trauma via a work of **mourning** while maintaining a mechanical repetition which, in the end, inhibited careful analysis of a kind which might have hindered certain vested interests in the government, military and elsewhere from stealing a march on the interpretative process and thus occupying the rhetorical high ground. Despite the fact that the United States had not been attacked on American soil for almost two centuries, Derrida wonders about the uniqueness and surprise of this event, given the numerous attempts to target American interests abroad (Derrida notes in passing the difficulty, today, of distinguishing fully between the domestic or national territory of the United States and American interests more generally); given, too, the infamous Oklahoma City bombing in 1995 (while McVeigh and Nichols were US nationals, the perpetrators of '9/11' were also, in a sense, home-grown – trained on American soil, launching the attack from within by utilizing US technology, being themselves produced by a longer-term background of American support and training in Afghanistan and elsewhere during the Cold War); and given the previous attempt to blow up the Twin Towers in 1993. Derrida asks not only why the CIA and FBI did not see it coming, as film-makers uncannily seemed to do (the release of a number of Hollywood blockbusters was halted soon after the attacks, since these movies contained elements which resonated all too uncomfortably with the events in New York and Washington), but also why this event might qualify for 'major' status in contrast to equally large or larger death tolls which, when they happen outside Europe or the United States, seldom cause such intense reaction. Since what is 'major' or distinctive about '9/11' is not, strictly speaking, either the motivation for the attacks, the means and technology used (hijacking aircraft), or the scale of the atrocity, Derrida embarks on a qualitative analysis which examines the events of '9/11' as not only a new phenomenon occurring after the Cold War, but also a distant effect of the Cold War itself (notably alluding to US funding of training camps in Afghanistan during its war with the Soviet Union). Interpreted as an act of terrorist aggression, '9/11' reintroduces the question of so-called state terrorism, including that pursued by the US; and, in the last analysis, as one particularly spectacular incident of quasi-suicidal **autoimmunity**. Autoimmunity is the failure of an organism to recognize its own constituent parts as such, therefore resulting in an immune response against its own 'self'. For Derrida, autoimmunity thus names a process in which, while seeking to protect and defend itself, a thing actually violates itself as the upshot of a violent non-recognition of the '**other**' in the self. The autoimmunitary process is therefore one in which a living being, in quasi-suicidal fashion, itself works to deplete its own sources of protection, and hence to immunize itself against its own immunity to threat. Thus Derrida analyzes the shared quasi-suicidal traits that in fact define the divisible or deconstructible 'identities' of the ostensibly polarized adversaries in the scenography of '9/11'.

Despite the highly complex analysis that this understanding of autoimmunity on a world-wide stage produces, Derrida does not hesitate to express his unconditional condemnation of the attacks. Derrida rejects what is invoked and practised in the name of bin Laden, not just because of its extreme **violence**, cruelty, disrespect for law, women, minorities and others, or indeed since it amounts to the harnessing by religious fanatics of the most terrible instruments of modern technocapitalism. Ultimately, Derrida's condemnation of the actions and discourse of fundamentalist Islamic terrorism stems from the fact that, for him, it can have no possible **future**. While the **European** tradition has fostered international institutions and laws that remain deeply flawed and are frequently ineffectual, these still provide the occasion for a deconstructive **affirmation** of the **democracy to come**, not as a programmable or foreseeable future, but as an opening occasioned in fact by a continuing exposure to the **aporia** of the **demos**.

In examining the 'major' status of '9/11', Derrida insists that any event – precisely in order to be worthy of its name – implies an irreplaceable and unmasterable **singularity** which is so unanticipatable and irruptive as to evade fully effective appropriation by any given language, discourse or **context**. Such an event must therefore dislocate the interpretative horizon on which it is hoped or expected to appear. Yet it is precisely what is unappropriable in the event that in fact charges it with world-opening force. This is one reason why '9/11' leaves the *impression* of a major event. As Derrida points out, if in the aftermath of the attacks the Americans, and indeed the entire world, could have been reassured beyond all doubt that the destruction of the Twin Towers constituted an absolutely unrepeatable violence, an outermost horizon of evil that would never again be crossed, the work of mourning might have been both a smoother and more short-lived process. Yet '9/11' remains an event to the extent that it cannot be consigned to the past, simply memorialized and amortized by its ineradicable archiving in a ritual calendar; but instead continues to inflict upon us the traumatism of the 'to come', always aggravating the wound it has opened both in the course of history and in our sense of what in ordinary experience could be anticipatable and repeatable.

sexual difference   In **'Ulysses Gramophone'**, Derrida's interest in Molly Bloom's memorable phrase, 'Yes I said yes I will yes' acquires particular significance when we recall that, for **Joyce**, 'Yes' is 'the female word'. Thus, although requiring complex thought, the question of sexual difference cannot be excluded from **deconstruction**'s thinking of an 'originary' **affirmation** prior to **linguistic** or ontological determination. In *Spurs*, meanwhile, it is 'woman' that eludes the **metaphysical** question: 'What is . . . ?'. Here, moreover, since the discourse of 'woman' (notably, the contradictory or non-self-identical attributes assigned to 'woman' within the metaphysical tradition) cannot be stably referred to a simple essence, origin or ground, the question of sexual difference comes to be neither reducible nor sustainable in terms of the classical binary opposition between the masculine and the feminine. Instead, 'woman' is inscribed in terms of an inextricable plurality that overflows – and indeed calls upon us to redescribe – the very logic and limits of **phallogocentrism**. In a number of Derrida's writings, then, an apparently (although never 'essentially') female voice pluralizes, complicates or re-directs the exposition under way: see, for instance, 'Restitutions' in *The Truth in Painting* or 'At This Very Moment in This Work Here I Am' in *Psyche*. The question of sexual difference inscribes itself, in other words, upon the very seal or **signature** of such texts, in a way that constantly refuses its reduction in terms of a supposedly transcendent position of neutrality (that of **philosophy**, ontology, etc.) which, as Derrida well understands, in fact allows 'masculine' privilege or domination.

The essay just referred to from *Psyche* suggests that, notwithstanding the primacy of the **other** in **Levinas**'s writings, sexual difference perhaps continues to be relegated by him – indeed, through the very positing of an absolute alterity before sexual differentiation. By contrast, in another text included in the second volume of this collection, Derrida argues that, despite **Heidegger**'s apparent haughty silence on the question of sexuality, which has lead some to imagine that sexual difference may be excluded as inessential to the Heideggerian thinking of Being, *Dasein* does not so much determine itself in terms of a negative resistance to sexual differentiation, but instead disposes itself in more positive terms as the very source of sexuality in general. For Derrida, then, *Dasein* embodies in its disseminal structure the dispersing multiplicity that gives us 'the sexual'. This re-elaboration of *Dasein* on Derrida's part at once resists the movement that secondarizes sexual differentiation, that detaches and relegates it so as to determine a supposedly neutral or undifferentiated 'origin'; while at the same time re-articulating the question of sexual difference in terms of an affirmed 'originarity' or quasi-originarity that outstrips or overflows all binary oppositions (including that which simply opposes the masculine and the feminine). Here, one would also need to consult Derrida's 'Khôra' in ***On the Name***. (Khôra as that which gives place, or which *spaces* as the prior condition of all forms of inscription, may only improperly be named '**mother**' or be feminized as such.) Like the others mentioned here, this text makes it clear that a rethinking of the question of sexual difference remains crucial for Derrida in the deconstruction of the entire metaphysical tradition that determines **being** as **presence**.

See also the interview 'Choreographies' in ***The Ear of the Other***, in which Derrida revisits a number of his own texts so as to put in question this secondarization or neutralization of sexual difference by philosophy, ontology or metaphysics. See, too, **Glas** for Derrida's reading of **Hegel**'s interpretation of *Antigone*, in which the 'feminine' – the mother, but also the sister – is seen to exceed and disrupt the familial relations which it also facilitates or **supplements**, relations which provide the traditional model of cultural, social, religious, economic and political life.

'Shibboleth'   Published in 1986. This essay turns to the poetry and writing of Paul **Celan**, the Jewish Romanian survivor of the Nazi occupation whose parents were killed by the SS, and who went on to receive acclaim as a major poet of the post-war period. For Derrida, Celan's texts constitute extraordinary literary **events**, to the extent that they are at once irreplaceably **singular** acts of writing and testaments to the always repeatable and divisible trait of every singularity. This means that, even in its absolute and untranslatable uniqueness, the poem inscribes itself – here and now, for one time only – in conditions and contexts which nevertheless permit, indeed demand, that the text be read or re-read and repeated. The poem in its most original marking (or its marked originality) is thus, from the outset, given to be **re-marked**, transcribed, translated in some way. That Celan's poetry performs this paradox with such acuity cannot be wholly disentangled from the events of the poet's own life and history, since his poems' intensely singular qualities are both threatened and heightened at every turn by the risk they always run of being, as Derrida puts it, 'exported, deported, expropriated, reappropriated'.

For Derrida, the repeatability that always accompanies the possibility of a singular incision in writing here comes down to a question of the **date**. Like the **signature** and the **proper name**, the date incisively marks that which is irreplaceable or unsubstitutable. Yet the date is also given to be repeated or re-marked as the very condition of its possibility. Thus, dating calls for a certain readability or return at another time and in another place. From the very beginning, then, the date carries away the text that it nevertheless marks as irreplaceably singular, impelling it towards an **other** (other-of-itself) yet to come, rather than simply tying it to a past that may be determined or objectified as such. And for Derrida all texts worthy of their name are in some way signed/dated – as particular and remarkable incisions in language and history – just as all readings and re-markings are in some way dated/signed. Hence, once it is written (dated/signed), the text we are given to read is not simply abandoned to some universal possibility or expansive generality for all time to come, but instead returns to be read *on another date*. Indeed, that every reading comes down to a re-marked date implies that reading is itself an act or event of commemoration, the coming to pass of something like an anniversary (as the date comes round again). Once more, that the reading of his poetry brings out such issues for Derrida cannot be wholly extricated from the fact that Celan writes as survivor. He writes, indeed, as one who not only preserves and commemorates dates (not least, those of a certain twentieth-century **Europe**), but who insists that they exceed both the objectifications of history and the grasp of philosophical mastery. (Here, we should recall that **philosophy** in the classical sense dreams of the possibility of a pure thought not reliant upon signature, date, or proper name, although all the while this project of self-definition remains tied to a 'text' or history that is always, precisely, *dated*.)

To say that the poetic text in its singular repeatability – its *datedness* – crosses from one time (and, inevitably, one place) to another, is to suggest that such traversal of borders is imperative for acts of poetry to take place. Such crossing, in other words, is poetry's very condition. Here, the poem comes to define itself less in terms of a 'content' that might be reproduced intact as the 'object' of a knowledge. Instead, poetry enacts itself **performatively**, in the very experience or event of a crossing which cannot be reduced to such a self-same 'object'. Thus it is that Derrida comes to dwell on a Hebrew word found in one of Celan's poems: 'shibboleth'. Shibboleth is a password that must be given at the border, becoming the very test of passage across. As Derrida observes, the Ephraimites knew the password but could not pronounce it correctly, saying 'sibboleth' instead. It was this that betrayed them – not a lack of knowledge, but of performative ability. And since the shibboleth comes down to more than just an inert repetition of the self-same, Derrida tells us that it multiplies at the borders, cropping up in a host of languages: Phoenician, Judeo-Aramaic, Syriac. In a sense, shibboleth belongs nowhere but at the border. As a password, it is a cipher that does not harbour any essential meaning, and thus gathers within itself only the possibility and commemoration of innumerable migrations. It is itself multiply crossed. Rather than returning to **memory** some elemental and indivisible 'truth' or ground, it re-enacts and re-encrypts that non-signifying difference (***différance***) which traverses the very body of the mark. Thus, the poem as shibboleth speaks beyond knowledge.

'Shibboleth' was first presented as a lecture at an international conference on Celan at the University of Washington, Seattle, in 1984. It subsequently appeared in different versions in French and English translation, but was included in a collection published soon after Derrida's death, ***Sovereignties in Question: the Poetics of Paul Celan***. This volume also includes a text entitled 'Poetics and Politics of Witnessing' which, like 'Shibboleth', dwells on the last words of Celan's poem 'Ash-glory': 'No one bears witness for the witness'. (Let us recall here that Derrida's ***Cinders*** is a writing on ashes.) This line prompts anew Derrida's reflections on the notion of an irreplaceably singular **testimony** which nonetheless always contains the possibility of its re-marking, repetition, or readability 'otherwise'. The collection also contains a text, 'Rams', in which Derrida rereads the encounter of Hans-Georg Gadamer with the writings of Celan in order to ruminate on his own relationship to Gadamer's thought; and a further essay, 'Majesties', which returns to a text discussed in 'Shibboleth', *The Meridian*, Celan's 1960 address on the occasion of the award of the Georg Büchner Prize. There are also two interviews which allow further insights into Derrida's relationship with, and reading of, Celan.

signature   The signature is **singular** and occasional since its authority remains tied to its inscription at a specific time (the signature is customarily accompanied by a **date**) and in a particular place, whether the 'place' of the signature is understood in terms of a document, an institution, a location or an event. If the function of the proper name is not merely to call from a certain distance but also to represent in absence the one to whom it refers, then the signature tries to orchestrate a certain recuperation of **writing** as otherwise essentially a medium of removal or 'loss' by affiliating itself to a vital **presence** in the 'here-now' of a lived time and place.

The highly occasional character of the signature makes it, in one respect, absolutely irreplaceable, a 'once only' occurrence. Yet, on the other hand, the validity of the signature is always and only granted by dint of its comparability to another, previous or future example of itself. Thus it is divided from the outset by a potential repeatability that remains necessary to its function or identity as signature. If one could imagine an original instance of the signature operating as something like a master copy which would then validate all further examples of itself, this self-same **mark** would in fact not yet acquire legitimacy as a signature until another instance (in, necessarily, a *different* time-place) established retroactively the conditions of its authoritative standing. One might say that the copy forges the original.

This situation leads us towards Derrida's thinking of the **countersignature**. The example he gives is of the requirement to countersign traveller's cheques, signed before departure, in order to assure that very same vital presence at a second time of asking precisely through making anew one's reliable individual mark. Given what we have already said, the signature for Derrida is therefore only ever the possibility or promise of its countersignature. (It is in this sense that Derrida tells us that he countersigns the authors, texts and indeed the entire tradition that he gives us to read – a *corpus* without end, indeed, in its own signature. Derrida's 'signature' neither simply replaces nor wholly confirms the identity of the text and the tradition that it countersigns, but aspires more complexly to a certain infidelity that nevertheless remains faithful to the divided principle of the signature which Derrida himself inherits.)

The resemblance of one signature to another, so important in the work of signature and countersignature, must however necessarily remain partial. Of course, each signature must be able to establish a certain measure of repeatability in order to function as valid. Yet an absolutely intact identicality of the kind aspired to by technologically reproduced or scanned copies risks reducing the signature to a mere facsimile, and thus to the dubious standing of a potential forgery. However, for Derrida, as we have already implied, the signature could not exist without the possibility of its forgery, and in a sense the signature is always possibly forged, not least since its validity is granted somewhat fraudulently by what we might call a copy of itself, or indeed by its own claim to a **technical** reproducibility.

Despite its crucial function as a mark of vital presence, the signature nonetheless outlives the one who signs, and thus finally remains 'other' than this presence. Indeed, structurally this is not just the destiny of the signature but its very condition of possibility. For it is precisely in the absence of the signer that the signature puts itself to work in, say, continuing to authorize or validate certain documents. One does not sign or commit to the **promise** that each and every signature inevitably makes for a limited period only. Instead, it is an essential feature of the signature that it has the potential to commit itself to its promise for ever, without remission. One therefore signs not only to confirm one's vital presence, or indeed to leave the impression of an undivided instant that fuses living and writing in order to salvage the latter as otherwise a medium of 'loss'. From the beginning, one also signs for one's own absence and, ultimately, for one's own mortality and demise, after which the signature continues to live on. (The **death**-bound or death-driven character of the signature is found not merely in the last act of signing as nevertheless a privileged example of the signature's testamentary structure.) Thus the signature does not simply function to confirm the uniquely irreplaceable identity of the self or subject who signs, but also works to denominate and depropriate the 'self' by aligning the conditions of possibility of the signature with a death to come that is nevertheless already inscribed in the functioning of the self's 'own' mark.

For Derrida, we should note, the structure and event of the signature opens on to questions of the 'historical' or the 'political' in ways that remain very different from those approaches one might associate with more dominant forms of contextualization or periodization. For instance, in analyzing the American Declaration of Independence, Derrida observes that the document is signed, and thus authorized by, the very same entity that it intends to bring into being as a legal or constitutional body: 'We, the people'. (See **Negotiations**.) This signature thus partakes of the structuring force of the future anterior, whereby what is supposedly prior to the **event** in fact receives its possibility only from a projected **future**, indeed in the very event of this futural projection. Thus, in this example, the historic eventfulness of the Declaration of Independence calls for an analysis which profoundly disrupts a linear, sequential or chronological conception of time of the sort that customarily underpins classical historical interpretation. Instead, by training an acute eye on the question of the future anterior of the signature, Derrida calls attention to the instituting **violence** of the declaration as profoundly irruptive in relation to historical time as normatively understood.

'Signature Event Context'   This essay, which Derrida nicknamed *Sec*, was initially published in the proceedings from a 1971 conference on the topic of 'Communication' held by the Congrès international des Sociétés de philosophie de langue français. The following year, it was included in *Marges de la Philosophy* (**Margins of Philosophy**). The English translation first appeared in 1977, in Volume 1 of *Glyph*, which included in its second issue a response to Derrida's essay by John R. **Searle**. Derrida's reply, 'Limited Inc a b c . . .' can be found, together with *Sec*, in **Limited Inc**, which also contains an afterword by Derrida.

Addressing the theme of the conference for which Derrida's essay was written, *Sec* begins by putting into question the communicability of communication as a concept, and thus its determinate content or meaning. Noting that communication designates not just a **linguistic**, semiotic or semantic value (one can also speak of a movement – a tremor, for example – being wordlessly communicated, and the term can also refer to some transport, opening or displacement between places), Derrida at the same time insists that the linguistic sense of the term cannot be thought of as secondary and derivative in regard to a 'literal' sense referred to the 'physical' world, since this very relation is itself discerned through the work of a **metaphorical** association that would seem to begin in or with language. Communication as a word that remains highly problematic in its essential determination (since it is neither reducible to a linguistic operation nor objectifiable outside it) thus communicates – if it communicates anything at all – a difficulty that one might only arrest by invoking a certain '**context**': for example, that of an academic conference on 'communication', proceeding in a certain language and milieu so as to confer particular linguistic, discursive, technical and cultural values upon the term. Yet Derrida asks whether the conditions of any such context are themselves ever entirely determinable. For Derrida, the thinking of ***différance*** (the double movement of differing and deferral which occasions a certain displacement and transformation of the concept of **writing** beyond its narrow **technical** and linguistic sense) necessarily implies that a context can never be entirely self-same, self-contained, full, present, or, in his terms, 'saturated'. Indeed, for this very same reason, the concept of communication or, for that matter, that of 'context' can never be fully produced as having stable, communicable, or absolutely present meaning.

Through this opening argument, Derrida therefore enacts a certain displacement in the concept of writing by showing that *différance* cannot be reduced to linguistic operations construed in terms of meaning. Indeed, for him the restriction of writing to a narrow interpretation of its operations in the field of language (i.e. its purpose in communicating linguistic 'meaning'), represents something of the history of philosophy itself. Turning to the example of **Condillac**'s *Essay on the Origin of Human Understanding*, Derrida lays out the features of this 'traditional' or 'classical' conception of writing: writing is deemed a technical, artificial and ancillary operation enacted upon some external substrate so as to communicate and conserve in essentially mechanical fashion the inspired thought, the 'ideas', of men. (These 'ideas' arise from reflection upon objects of perception, whose representation communicates 'meaning'.) Writing is no more than a modality of language, derivative in relation to **speech**. Yet in Condillac this very same conception acknowledges writing's function in addressing certain absences: one writes so as to communicate to an absent addressee, while the written **mark** in its persisting legibility drifts free from the sender, and threatens or **promises** to outlive him. Indeed, in its repeatable readability – what Derrida calls its **iterability** – the written mark persists beyond any empirical instance of reading, so that its condition of possibility cannot be reduced to the conceptual determinations of **presence**. While for

Condillac writing extends itself thus in order to extenuate or repair the gap in 'presence' between writer and reader, for Derrida such writing therefore produces itself only on condition of the intractable possibility of a certain *break* in presence. Since it is possible to write to an absent reader, or read an absent writer (and since writing in its repeatable legibility or iterability always continues to call for another reader or reading not currently present), this possibility of absence – or, better still, of a non-present **remainder** – becomes a necessary feature of writing itself. Moreover, the inextricable possibility of absence as a necessary condition or characteristic of writing places its operations ultimately beyond the determining power of a 'present' consciousness or intention, whether that of an empirically given writer or reader.

Circling back to his earlier suggestions, Derrida's next manoeuvre in *Sec* is to insist that this particular trait of an *always* possible – and thus *necessarily* possible – absence, upon which the 'classical' construal of writing unwittingly rests, can in fact be generalized in a transformed conception of writing (that is, in terms of *différance*) that goes beyond its narrow definition: one, indeed, which breaks with its given 'context'. In its very structure rather than just because of its empirical eventuality, therefore, writing re-marks itself beyond its traditional 'context', that of its philosophical-linguistic determination, and thus exceeds the classical filiation of sign and referent.

Here, following what has really been an elaborate preparation, Derrida turns to the operative distinction between 'constative' and '**performative**' found in the **speech act theory** of **Austin**. This distinction can be simplified as follows: constative language states or describes, while performative language enacts. Rather than just saying something, it *does* something. Austin's favoured example is that of the marriage vow, in which utterances make something happen, they transform the existing situation (that of two unmarried individuals) so as to produce a new 'reality'. As should be clear by now, Derrida suspects the very possibility of a purely constative or descriptive language, since the very notion would seem to belong to the restrictive definition of writing that arises within the philosophical tradition which Derrida shows to be deconstructible. For this reason, he admires Austin for placing the accent on the performative utterance as a form of action, if that gesture might be taken to lessen the emphasis on the truth value of language or its inherent meaning. But

Derrida also takes issue with Austin's understanding or presentation of the conditions of performative language. Austin's preferred example of the wedding vow suggests that a successful performative requires a given 'context' or set of conventions – in this case, at once religious, social, linguistic, and so forth – which the speaker as intentional agent must recognize and negotiate effectively in order to make the performative happen as a form of action-taking. However, since Derrida rethinks writing – as the generalized domain in which speech and language take place – in terms of *différance*, the determining power of an intending consciousness in controlling the outcome of linguistic (and extra-linguistic) experience *as a form of action-taking* is not, as in Austin, paramount. As Derrida's preceding discussion hopes to make clear, no context is so fully saturated that we can bet upon it without risk, and no word or concept is so absolutely and transparently communicable that we can wholly depend on the outcome of its usage, even in the most conventionalized of settings. (It should be added that Derrida's subsequent analyses of **invention, hospitality, forgiveness**, the **gift**, the **event**, and so on, extend his questioning of the role of intentionality in making something happen. If I am already capable of inventing something, if I already have it within my means to extend hospitality, if I aim to forgive or to give in terms of my existing understanding of their shareable or exchangeable meanings, then no event will have taken place worthy of the name of invention, forgiveness, hospitality or gift. For example, when forgiving the forgiveable, I operate in a largely programmatic fashion within an existing **ethical** or moral situation, so that no genuine event of forgiveness will have taken place. Thus, far from performing actions, the masterable-possible of intentionality – the **ipseity**, agency or power of the 'I can' – impedes the possibility of the event. Thus, Derrida will have occasion elsewhere to express caution about the idea of **deconstruction** as 'performative' discourse, to the extent that the notion of performativity suggests at bottom the masterable-possible rather than, precisely, 'the experience of the **impossible**' which Derrida tells us is deconstruction.)

In a way that repeats the refusal by Condillac to acknowledge the structural importance of a supposedly negative term (a refusal which is also that of an entire philosophical tradition), Austin considers instances of failure or infelicity where performative utterance is concerned, and seeks to present and exclude these as anomalous, accidental, exceptional or

'Signature Event Context'

extraneous, rather than inherent in the conditions of possibility – or the very **law** – of performativity itself. Here, says Derrida, Austin's tactic is to associate infelicity with non-serious or non-normal language – in other words, theatrical or **fictional** language, the language of metaphor or irony – which he presents as parasitical. This is done, Derrida tells us, so as to protect within an ideal definition of performative utterance the transparency of intentions and the self-evidence of present meaning. But for Derrida the disruption of presence as the structural possibility of the mark puts the necessary possibility of fiction, irony and equivocation (of not meaning what one says or saying what one means) before that of transparent, self-evident 'truth' or 'meaning' conveyed without loss or remainder by an intending subject or consciousness.

In the last part of the essay, this reading of Austin is taken as the occasion to develop Derrida's thought of the **signature**. As Derrida notes, the signature puts itself to work precisely in the absence of the signer. In one respect, the signature attempts to recuperate presence in writing by setting its seal on the literal presence (or having-been-present) of the one who signs. Nevertheless, the signature acquires its validity and identity only to the extent that it is repeatable. This repeatability is manifest not simply in subsequent renditions of the signature which might be compared with the 'original' so as to determine the authenticity of a particular example. Instead, repeatability – and thus divisibility – is inscribed in the very structure of the signature from the outset, since it must *always already* be repeatable (countersignable) if it is indeed to be considered authentic and authoritative. Repeatable and thus divisible at its origin, the signature at once constitutes and deconstitutes or deconstructs these values of authenticity and authority, establishing within its very law the originary parasiticism or **supplement** of the fictional, the false, the counterfeit, or the non-serious (going fundamentally beyond empirical instances of fraudulent signing). It is in this 'context' that Derrida, with some irony, multiply signs the text at its 'end', including an 'actual' facsimile of his supposed signature. (In putting to work or licensing or producing actions, the signature approximates a performative, although as we have seen Derrida demonstrates that the very conditions of possibility of the signature exceed – fundamentally and not just empirically – the operations of a present intention or conscious control.)

Searle's response to Derrida, 'Reiterating the Differences', suggests that Derrida offers us a near unrecognizeable Austin. Searle argues that writing is distinguished from speech not by its iterability but by its permanence, and this more proper distinction unravels Derrida's assimilation of speech to writing. Searle seeks to refute Derrida's argument about absence as a structural feature of the mark by pointing out that writing may well take place in the presence of the reader, or reading in the presence of the author. He insists that an understanding of performative utterances cannot do without recognizing intentions that emerge in the context of certain rules and conventions, and defends as a research strategy Austin's decision not to begin his investigation into performative utterances with a study of the words said by actors on stage. In reply, Derrida's 'Limited Inc a b c . . .' presents us with a lengthy text that answers Searle in meticulous detail. 'Limited Inc a b c . . .' is particularly difficult to summarize in that, as much as reasserting the arguments of Derrida's original essay, it deploys the *Sec* effect so as to **graft** non-serious onto serious discourse, to inhabit an **undecidable** space between truth and fiction, rigour and play, to question mockingly the possible effects of the seal of copyright which Searle publishes above the title of his own text, and to contrast the consequences of the multiple signing of Derrida's own text with that of the triumvirate of names – John R. Searle as author, D. Searle and H. Dreyfus as acknowledged peers – which Searle marshals to lend authority to his published response. Derrida dubs this grouping a Society with Limited Responsibility (Société à responsabilité limitée) since, under the sign of copyright, he detects in the reply an attempt to place limits on the **responsibility** that Austin's insights might impose upon us, albeit perhaps unwittingly, responsibilities which Derrida undoubtedly feels he assumes more responsibly than Searle. (Thus, by way of an acronym deriving from the French, Searle is renamed Sarl.) Indeed, in view of just this understanding of the central gesture of Searle's reply, Derrida notes in his response a recursive *from/to-Sec* effect, whereby arguments are unwittingly borrowed from 'Signature Event Context' only to be turned into objections to the very same essay. (However, Derrida is also at pains to correct Searle on a number of points, for instance concerning Derrida's own argument that it is precisely the *possibility* of absence that enters into the structure of the mark, so that writing in the presence of the reader, or reading in the presence of the author – Searle's examples – are merely empirical possibilities which do not alter the always possible and thus necessary structural trait of a non-present remainder.) Finally, the effects of misreading and misunderstanding which mean, for Searle, that the confrontation of deconstruction with speech act theory never quite takes place are rethought and rewritten by Derrida according to an iterability which allows the latter both to endorse and transform this contention by Searle.

Signsponge   Published in bilingual edition in 1984, this text was first presented, in part, during a colloquium on the French poet Francis **Ponge** held at Cerisy-la-Salle in 1975. The text is written in a highly inventive and **singular** style. In its engagement with Ponge, as well as through its own writing performance, *Signsponge* calls into question traditional forms of literary analysis (whether psychological or biographical, formalist or linguistic, and so on) insofar as they suggest the possibility of a degree of interpretative mastery in relation to their 'object'. In *Signsponge*, the literary **event** makes possible reading in the general sense and, regardless of the specific orientation of such reading, challenges its capacity to dominate the literary text. **Mimetic** or representational models of **literature** and literary discourse are put in question throughout. Instead, the singularity of the literary event proposes itself in terms of a **law** which nevertheless unsettles the law's propensity for generalizing claims or general categories.

The text famously declares that 'Francis Ponge will have been self-remarked'. For Derrida, a text may be 'signed' in three distinctive ways: first, there is the **signature** that would function in a classical or basic sense to assign a work to the **proper name** of its author (typically, at the bottom of the page); second, there is the text's idiomaticity or style, replete with literary or textual 'signatures' which become recognizable as those of the author (for which an explicit signature is not necessarily called); third, there is writing which **remarks**, assigns or designates itself without recourse to a proper name. Derrida suggests that Ponge's text is 'signed' according to each of these modalities simultaneously, so that the very signature of the text – that which makes it proper to him – is also that which conceals his name within its language, and which, in another sense, depropriates him in the work.

singularity   This term arises wherever Derrida is interested in the unanticipatable and unsubstitutable **event**, or the unexchangeable and unreckonable **gift**; or whenever he analyzes the always untimely **violence** of instituting which ruptures, interrupts and makes history; or where he speaks of the **mark** that makes its irreplaceable incision in language; or when he reflects upon the absolutely idiomatic text which at once suspends and powerfully remakes **laws** or norms, including those that render such a text readable. The 'singular', then, is that which remains irreducible to any established concept, code, system or generality. Always more and less than an **example**, its particularity cannot ever be fully apprehended by way of 'universal' categories or criteria. However, Derrida is frequently quick to note the paradox of singularity: namely, that the singular is not absolutely self-contained in its 'once-and-for-all' uniqueness; instead, singularity marks itself, precisely, as the **promise** or possibility of its own **re-marking**, and thus in terms of its own repeatability. Rather than suggesting simple self-identity or self-presence, the trait of singularity is *at its very origin* divisible. It is a condition of the 'singular' that it remain structurally reliant upon the possibility of its own **iterability**, an iterability that is always transformative. Reincorporation into a recognizable context or an already established setting would spell something of an end for singularity, so that the 'singular' is in this sense always *to come*. Singularity is therefore not merely a byword for the 'authentic', but is itself a manifest effect of **différance**, to the extent that each singular text, mark or event doesn't just fall from the sky, but arises (*singularly*) amid a complex force-field of differential play that always exceeds or overruns simple '**presence**'.

Socrates (469BC–399BC)   Ancient Greek philosopher. See **Dissemination**, 'Khôra' in **On the Name**, **The Post Card**. See also entries on **translation**, **writing**.

Sovereignties in Question: the Poetics of Paul Celan   A collection of writings published in 2005. For further comment, see **'Shibboleth'**.

sovereignty   While Derrida is always interested in the highly **singular** and specific operations of power, politics, or **law**, there is a more general sense of the term 'sovereignty' in his writing that goes somewhat beyond its limited common usage, for instance in connection with the historical forms taken by kingship, or the self-determination of a nation-state. (These are, however, of great interest to Derrida, and can never be set aside when one asks about sovereignty.) The question of sovereignty arises wherever an

sovereignty

entity is imagined in terms of its power of mastery (including self-mastery), whenever it is deemed capable of authoritative self-expression, or wherever the ostensible unity, self-identity and self-sufficiency (the supposedly indivisible **presence**) of a being is forcefully imposed at the expense of difference and the **other**. For Derrida, let us recall, **différance** is in fact constitutive or 'originary', yet it is always repressed by the **metaphysical** tradition which holds presence (non-self-difference) to be sovereign. Thus sovereignty is deconstructible – its apparently unquestionable dominion is everywhere traversed by a non-present **remainder**: *différance*, **trace**, **supplement**, **arche-writing**, the other. This may be illustrated through Derrida's reading of the Declaration of Independence (see **Negotiations**). Derrida notes that the Declaration presents the American 'People', rather than a monarch or state figurehead, as the nation's indivisible foundation. Yet since the Declaration is signed and authorized by the very 'People' whom it also *founds* as the basis of the United States, their 'sovereignty' is divided between the *après coup* and the future anterior. Here, we are talking about the internal and irredeemable division of a power whose legitimacy is violently imposed after the fact, and whose otherwise unfounded authority is necessarily projected in terms of what 'will have been'. As Derrida therefore argues in **Rogues**, all states are in some sense rogue states (and this insight must be used to address what Derrida sees as a constant need to review the state form, its politics and law).

Throughout many of Derrida's writings, the question of sovereignty is put alongside discussions of citizenship, statelessness, the historical form of the polis and the modern state, the importance and limitations of international law, and the meaning of biopolitics and **animal** life. In *On Cosmopolitanism and Forgiveness*, for instance, the unlimited or **unconditional** 'welcome' demanded of **hospitality** in its fundamental sense is foregrounded in order to provoke reflection and indeed action regarding the historical forms of right and law associated with sovereignty. By taking this approach, Derrida does not imagine for a moment that it would be practically possible – or even preferable, necessarily – to sweep away sovereignty's borders and powers. Instead, his appeal to the 'unconditional' confronts us with a continual responsibility to think of modifying or transforming them.

Thus in *Rogues* Derrida contrasts the absolute 'unconditional' with the notion of sovereignty. Despite appearances to the contrary, the unconditional is not absolutely sovereign (although it in fact exceeds sovereignty's limits, the limits of 'presence'), in precisely the sense that it does not license or sanction a master or give rise to the 'masterable-possible'. Put differently, the unconditional powerfully resists the very principle of power. The unconditional confronts us with the 'experience of the **impossible**' (welcome of the unwelcomable, forgiveness of the unforgivable, etc.), which nonetheless gives a chance to the **future** or the other as *arrivant*. However, the unconditional must ceaselessly **negotiate** with and elaborate its relation to sovereignty in the interests of the **democracy to come**. (For Derrida, the fact that the ***demos*** is irreparably divided between freedom and equality opens the possibility of a resistance of sovereignty. Far from disempowering democracy, then, this irresolvable division means that democracy remains irreducible to sovereign power and presence.) Derrida's essay, 'The University Without Condition' (in ***Without Alibi***) tasks the **university** with an always pressing and never concludable negotiation with (resistance of) sovereignty.

Specters of Marx: The State of the Debt, the Work of Mourning, and the New International   This work from 1993 responds to the question 'Whither Marxism?' – the title of a conference held in that year at the University of California, Riverside. After the fall of the Berlin Wall, the collapse of the Soviet Union and the protests against the Chinese Communist Party in Tiananmen Square, the sense that free market capitalism and the Western model of liberal democracy were destined to prevail on a worldwide scale led to a declaration of the end of history by Francis **Fukuyama** (in this narrative, the resurgence of ethnocentric nationalisms and the intensifying persistence of so-called religious conflicts were put aside as merely extraneous empirical blips on an irrefutable **global** horizon). Many pronounced **Marxism** dead, sweeping aside questions of the complicated relationship between heterogeneous varieties of Marxist thought and historical examples of communism in its state and party form. The title 'Whither Marxism?' responded to this complex juncture in world politics and history (adding a subtitle, 'Global Crises in International Perspective') by including in its grammatical and rhetorical possibility both the issue of Marxism's demise and the open question of its **future** direction. And, with the decline of Marxism's recognized 'face' in living state or party forms, any possible future 'Marx', appearing on the very threshold of a supposed demise, could only ever return to spook those who had thought he had been stared down. This is the Marx Derrida tells us he inherits, a Marx beyond both hasty renunciation and dogmatic recognition, a Marx precisely of a future still to come – the very **spirit** of Marxism, in other words, for Derrida. Here, then, Derrida acknowledges an incalculable debt to Marx and Marxism, a debt which remains to be decided upon, but which must still be registered all the more urgently in the 'here-now'.

Having long since chosen the title of his lecture, Derrida recalls the near-forgotten curtain-raiser of Marx and Engels's 1848 *Manifesto of the Communist Party*: 'A specter is haunting Europe – the specter of communism'. Derrida reads this assertion in powerfully deciphering style. It suggests to him not merely that communism emerged, on an otherwise fine day, as a terrifying apparition bringing from the outside a threat of night to an essentially shadowless **Europe**, a Europe bathed in the light of Enlightenment. Rather, Derrida advances the proposition that Europe in its very existence may itself be the product of a certain haunting for which communism might be merely one name, a convenient yet also troubling projection. In what ways is Europe always already haunted? In **The Gift of Death** (also from the early 1990s), Derrida reads Jan Patočka's *Heretical Essays on the Philosophy of History* in order to reflect on what he calls the **secret** of European **responsibility** – that is, the secret of Europe's ethics, politics and philosophy – a secret that, for Derrida, remains tied to the deathly remains of a preceding demoniac tradition which cannot be exorcized fully. Meanwhile, in view of the inextricable interplay of Europe with capital and capitalization, a topic he addresses at greater length in **The Other Heading**, Derrida observes in *Specters of Marx* that money is nothing other than a **spectral** conjuration of value, so that when the state prints money, and imprints it with its own image, it itself becomes an apparition. Indeed, for Derrida, the exchange-value of the commodity cannot be neatly opposed to a pure use-value which precedes it. Instead, exchange-value haunts use-value from the very beginning. Use-value is mere apparition – like the **iterability** or divisible repeatability which, for Derrida, always already inhabits the **mark** at its origin, the possibility of exchange is there in use-value from the outset. Thus, use-value is itself a phantasm that is everywhere haunted by the spectre of money. Europe in its economic, moral, political and philosophical formation thus comes from, and remains tied to, the living-dead secret of the spectre.

Acknowledging Marx as an avid reader of Shakespeare, *Specters of Marx* allows itself to become haunted by the ghost of the murdered king in *Hamlet*. Derrida observes that, in the experience of haunting, the spectre always appears, enigmatically, on the very threshold of identity. It is neither pure spirit or soul nor simple reincarnation or living body, neither exactly dead or alive, absent or present. In its incarnated apparition, the ghost as a non-present being-there cannot be unified in its identity, nor will it grant a self-identical knowledge of itself. The spectre is therefore always more and less than one (***plus d'un***: more than one/one no more). Moreover, through what Derrida calls the *visor effect* noticeable in the appearance of Old Hamlet's spirit (an effect that is always constitutive as possibility, even if the visor is up), there is a radically asymmetrical distribution of the gaze in the economy of ghostly looking. Never itself reducible to a self-identical object of perception, it is the ghost that regards us, having us in its (invisible) sights. After a time when Marxism's death has been so confidently announced, the irreducibly plural and heterogeneous remains of Marx's spectres must therefore be recalled. They never were, nor will they remain, a single corpus to be pronounced alive or dead. Instead, beyond any attempt at masterful exorcism of the kind practised in the 'end of history' type of discourse, the spectres of Marx will always return, their gaze preceding our own. The burial of the (supposed) dead is always accompanied by a work of **mourning** – however triumphalist it may be – which hopes to ontologize the remains, to inter them in a knowledge that thinks itself incontrovertibly apposite in relation to its referent or, in other words, which keeps the body in the ground. Yet the spectre (such as that of Marx, which will and could not ever be reduced to a single, lifeless body), is never simply a thing of the past, or of a past past. Rather, as *revenant* it begins – it comes – by coming back. Thus, the question of the spectre and of haunting is one of traumatic apprehension, the unknowing anticipation of a future appearance, indeed of a future still to appear. As returning or troubled **memory**, the ghost is less a figure of a backward-looking orientation than a projection of that which has not yet been exorcized, what remains to come.

Thus, the ghost is always untimely, never reducible simply to an intact and self-contained present. Rather, its time is 'out of joint' (Derrida dwells at some length on this borrowing from *Hamlet*). And Marxism must remain spectral, since this temporal disjointure or disadjustment is a structural feature of Marx's thought, not least in its quasi-**messianic** orientation towards a transformed future, or in its insistence that the *other* of today remains to come as a spectral disruption already inscribed in the very body of the 'here-now'. (For all their historical limitations, Derrida tells us, Marx's writings uncannily presage contemporary debates about global geopolitics and the virtualizing transformation of the state-form, about the constitutive intensity of techno-science and media in the history of capital, and so forth – so that a certain Marx still awaits us in the future.) Any **proper name**, like that of Marx, is bound to outlive its bearer, and thus the name inherits the future; yet inheritance, for example that which we inherit in and from Marx, is never given in self-same or wholly ***present*** form. Since inheritance involves an injunction or demand to respond, we affirm what we inherit only by taking **decisions** which must occur among plural possibilities. Indeed, to decide on the strength of a disadjusted or 'spectral' time, a time which is also the *other* of itself, such as the time of Old Europe which Marx gives us to think, is to risk the possibility of **justice** in radical excess of existing apparatuses of **law**, morality, duty or right. Thus, in its profound **affirmation** of an unprogrammeable justice always remaining possible in the 'here-now', deconstruction inherits a certain spirit of Marx, a certain messianic remains. This is a Marx, after Marxism's declared demise, that cannot be safely reduced to the image of a great philosopher resettled in the tranquil halls of academe. Instead, such a spectre of Marx – like Old Hamlet's ghost – makes demands upon us, tasks us with the future.

In the midst of such ghosts, Derrida turns to Fukuyama's 'end of history' thesis. This rests on the idea that history is itself the product of opposing forces in conflict (such as the ideologies of East and West, socialism and capitalism) which, once they have run their dialectical course, bring to an end the very struggles that *make* history. Fukuyama's pronouncement of the 'end of history' cannot help but draw on what Fukuyama himself identifies as the conceptual apparatus of **Hegel**'s dialectics of **Spirit** and a certain materialist incarnation in Marx, giving rise to the irony that history's 'end' beyond Marxism must remain haunted by some of Marxism's tools and practices of thought. Invoking the names of Hegel, Marx, **Nietzsche**, **Heidegger** and **Blanchot**, Derrida observes that Fukuyama's thesis is itself a ghostly *revenant*, in that discourses of the 'end' had been prevalent some four decades earlier in intellectual debates about the end of philosophy, of history and of man. Indeed, as long ago as 1848 and, subsequently, the time of the First International, Hegelian discourses about the culmination of history in absolute knowledge quickened (otherwise) the Marxist spirit. Thus the spectres of Marx are, in a double sense, *conjured* by discourses of the 'end': conjured away and conjured up, called forth and spirited away according to an undecidable gesture. (Derrida shows how Fukuyama's evangelical rhetoric has its origin in an ongoing **Christianization** of Europe that one might expect to involve such an ambivalent relationship to spirits, evil or otherwise.) Fukuyama's thesis is itself contradictory and incoherent – one might say, it *spooks* itself – to the extent that, while at one moment it wishes to relegate to the status of an empirical anomaly whatever has not yet been fully assimilated to the supposedly victorious models of free market economy and liberal democracy (the conflicts still raging in the Middle East would provide us with ample examples here), at another it rests its arguments precisely on the self-evidence of historical instances and events (the fall of state communism, and so forth). Fukuyama's 'good news' is at one moment empirically embodied or revealed in actuality, while elsewhere apparent realities which might otherwise jeopardize his thesis are renounced as extraneous to the triumph of liberal democracy as a regulating ideal. The ability to have it both ways may have accounted for the popularity in its heyday of Fukuyama's book among liberal democrats and free marketeers. But the incoherence of his thesis inadvertently conjures the spectre anew. In the very workings of Fukuyama's arguments, in other words, Western liberal democracy at the 'end of history' is **undecidably** both present and absent, spirit and flesh. In the disadjusted coincidence of what is manifestly incarnated and what is projected beyond mere incarnations, it is itself *spectral*. The dialectical synthesis implied by the movement of Spirit towards history's end in absolute knowledge here becomes a ghost story. (Once more, as spectre contaminates spirit, communism's apparition is not just an intrusive outsider, but itself uncannily **re-marks** the divisible traits of European liberalism and democracy. This spectre is spirit's **other** side or self, which nonetheless awaits another future.) Meanwhile, it is Marxism that offers the better resources for thinking this non-coincident simultaneity of the actual and the ideal in the disadjusted time of the present.

Marx himself, of course, tried to conjure way the ghosts of Old Europe. What Derrida wishes to endorse in Marx is the affirmation of a certain messianism without metaphysico-religious determination, a messianicity without the messiah. Marx wishes to chase away the phantasmic or ideological appearance of the Emperor, State, Fatherland, Nation, People, God, Religion, Humanity, Man – the arche-spectres of European capital – in order to analyze the actual **remains**. Yet Derrida's account of the spectral persistence of exchange-value in use-value questions the possibility of such a shadowless return to the exorcized body of capital. As the thinker of *différance*, the **trace**, or the non-present **remainder**, Derrida suggests that Marx was perhaps too hasty in seeking to chase away ghosts. The spectral may give us ways to think everything which today connects religion, **technicity**, media and the 'virtualization' of politics, space and time on the worldwide stage. The spectral, too, may remain the only way of doing justice to Marx and, indeed, of orienting Marxism non-dogmatically towards the *arrivant*, turning its no longer recognizable 'face' towards justice.

In *Spectres of Marx,* Derrida lists ten plagues of the 'new world order' (a reconjuration of the same number of arche-spectres that constitute Marx's inventory in *The German Ideology*): unemployment; homelessness, migrancy and asylum; economic warfare among nation states; the contradictions inherent in the free market; the foreign debt; the arms industry and trade; nuclear proliferation outside state control; inter-ethnic wars; the rise of phantom states linked to organized crime; the present condition of international law and institutions. He calls for a **New International** – as yet without name, title or status – which would share a secret affinity with the First International. This would be devoted to a transformation of international law, politics and economics beyond the limitations imposed by state forms, at once adjusting actualities to the ideal and rethinking the ideal in terms of the realities before us. Such a double logic is also that of the (untimely) spectre, the spirit which calls us.

spectre   See especially ***Specters of Marx***. More generally, the spectre in Derrida is to be thought in terms of **deconstruction**'s thinking of a non-present **remainder** at work in every text, entity, being or '**presence**'. A remainder, we should add, that is neither spiritually transcendent nor fully embodied, but which is instead, like the ghost, a sort of non-present being-there. There are a number of nicknames for such ghostly 'remains': ***différance***, trace, cinder, supplement, etc. Spectrality is also in the machine, in every programme, and is to be thought, too, in terms of the actuvirtual, the tele-effect, and so on.

speech For Derrida, the **metaphysical** tradition gives priority to speech over **writing**, in the sense that speech is held to express living **presence**. Speech confirms and communicates the self-identity of the subject, marrying the 'word' with the 'soul' or **'spirit'** so as to refer language to an essentially undivided, **onto-theological** foundation. Writing, in contrast, is considered the lifeless instrument of a representation that remains derivative, auxiliary and extrinsic in relation to the spoken word. Writing, indeed, threatens to supplant presence with absence, to subject the living to the dead, to substitute difference and detachment for fullness and identity, and to replace the harmonious immediacy of 'nature' with the **violence**, artificiality and **technicality** of culture. In texts such as ***Of Grammatology*** and **'*Différance*'**, however, Derrida **deconstructs** the metaphysical priority of speech, and analyzes its role in the determination of **being** as presence. In several major texts, particularly from the mid- to late-1960s and soon afterwards, Derrida shows that speech is in fact dependent on writing in the more general sense that he wants to elaborate (this is not to be confused with a simple reversal of the hierarchy that traditionally subordinates writing to speech).

See also ***Dissemination***, **logocentrism**, ***Margins of Philosophy***, **phonocentrism**, ***Positions***, **'Signature Event Context'**, ***Speech and Phenomena***.

speech act theory From **'Signature Event Context'** onwards, several of Derrida's arguments and ideas draw upon an evaluation and critique of the speech act theory of J. L. **Austin** and his follower John **Searle**. In particular, Derrida is exercized by the distinction that speech act theory wishes to make between constative and **performative** language (language which describes or states, versus language which enacts or does). 'Signature Event Context' puts in question the mastery which speech act theory accords to performative acts of language. It furthermore analyzes the limits of speech act theory's concept of '**context**' as that which anchors the possibility of such performative control. For Derrida, no 'context' is so fully unified and conclusively established (or, in his terms, 'saturated') as to ensure the total effectiveness of the language performances that take place 'within' it. 'Signature Event Context' also puts in question the distinction made by speech act theory between felicitious and infelicitous or serious and non-serious language. This analysis proceeds against the backdrop of Derrida's broader **deconstruction** of **logocentrism** and **phonocentrism** as key features of a **metaphysical** tradition that determines **being** as **presence**.

Derrida also develops or reworks the distinction that speech act theory makes between mention and use. See for instance 'The Law of Genre' in *Acts of Literature*. (In several places, 'Envois' in *The Post Card* also plays on this terminology.)

Speech and Phenomena   First appearing in French in 1967, this text starts out from **Husserl**'s *Logical Investigations* in order to examine the basic structures underlying his philosophical project, and indeed that of **phenomenology** more generally. Published in the same year as *Writing and Difference* and *Of Grammatology*, Speech and Phenomena is often seen as crucial to the basis of Derrida's thought, insofar as this entails rigorous **deconstruction** of the determination of **being** as **presence** in the tradition of Western **metaphysics**.

Derrida's engagement with Husserl goes back to some of his earliest writings. In his Introduction to Husserl's *Origin of Geometry*, first published in 1962, Derrida traces the attempt by Husserlian phenomenology to reconcile the transcendental nature of an ideal object – a geometrical shape, for instance – with questions of the historical emergence of such objects as phenomena. In Husserl's work, Derrida suggests, the ideal or objective status of geometry – that is to say, the standing of its knowledge as universal truth – cannot but depend upon material (and repeatable) inscription in and across space and time. Put differently, the possibility of the transcendental in Husserl's phenomenology emerges only by dint of that which the transcendental supposedly transcends: namely, **writing**. Earlier still, **The Problem of Genesis in Husserl's Philosophy** (Derrida's first work of major length, originally written as a dissertation for his *diplôme d'études supérieures* in 1953–54) had identified a similar, irreconcilable tension inherent in Husserl's approach to the problem of genesis. Here, meaning and temporality are the products of a prior transcendental subject, yet transcendental subjectivity must itself be produced by an act of genesis that is not in itself transcendent.

Speech and Phenomena extends Derrida's deconstruction of Husserl. In the *Logical Investigations* Husserl distinguishes between two concepts of the 'sign'. Where the word 'sign' carries the sense of 'expression', we are given to understand the sign's meaningfulness precisely in terms of an *intention* to say or to mean. Expression is thus always animated by a voluntary or purposeful consciousness. Indicative signs, meanwhile, signify without conveying an intended meaning. The canals of Mars provide Derrida with an example here, in that they indicate the possibility of intelligent life but cannot be reduced to a definite meaning secured by a meaning-giving intention. Put differently, non-expressive signs may *mean* only to the extent that a non-intended meaning can be derived from them.

In its intrinsic relationship to intention, expression is therefore closely tied to verbal discourse and to the **linguistic** field, whereas indicative signs, although not entirely excluded from spoken language as Derrida points out, do not enjoy a purely linguistic status. By way of this separation, which due to the indicative or non-expressive residue attached to any discursive sign Derrida insists cannot hold entirely, Husserl wants to understand the expressive and logical purity of meaning in terms of **logos**. This, for Derrida, goes to the heart of the phenomenological project. By stressing the production of sense and value through signs, phenomenology in one regard seems to distance itself from ontological naïveté, and yet in wanting to discern from linguistic expression the possibility of truth, a truth that is necessarily prior to the sign, it remains anchored to a classical metaphysics of presence.

Husserl attempts to show that expression is more than a mere species or subset of the indicative field in which it is always caught up, by seeking to locate a pure form of expression uncontaminated by the facticity or empiricity of the indicative system. This purity is sought by Husserl in a form of expression beyond worldly communication, in **speech** as (inner) monologue or in the silent voice of 'solitary mental life' purely present to itself in its transcendent 'ownness'. Even after indication is ostensibly excluded or transcended by the terms of the Husserlian distinction between two concepts of the sign, expression understood in terms of meaning-intending signification continues to imply a certain exteriorization found in the passage to the **other** as addressee. All expressive speech, insofar as it intends communication or the imparting of meaning, cannot help but pass through the indicative field construed as a worldly domain or medium irreducible in its entirety to any expressive intention. If this is so, pure expression would, paradoxically, fail at precisely the point of achieving its ends. Its spirit or breath would be corrupted by the very body of language.

Thus, for Husserl, pure expression must be distinguished from communication in its contingent function as a vessel or carrier of meaning. It must be located, beyond communication and thus outside the very concept of sign, in the pure consciousness of a self that is immediately and instantaneously present to itself, which as it were speaks to itself without signifying. In such 'inward speech', Husserl argues, nothing can indeed be communicated by the self to itself, precisely since there would be no need or basis for such communication. A self could not inwardly communicate to itself a meaning it already intended or 'had'. This could only be a pretence, a useless, redundant or imaginary gesture. Pure consciousness outside the worldly domain of signs, for Husserl, thus enjoys an immediate expressive relation to itself beyond communication. As Derrida argues in a number of texts from this period, such a relegation of the sign as merely an extrinsic and privative **technical** instrument in relation to the **spirit** or consciousness which animates living speech is the very basis of a classical metaphysics of presence that defines the history and **philosophy** of the West.

However, since the purity of a self-present consciousness derives from its transcendence over the contingent or empirical domain of all signification (whether indicative or not), its pure expression or presence-to-itself would necessarily outlive the finitude and facticity of the individual as intentional agent. Put differently, this construal of the essence of truth as presence – truth without loss or **remainder**, finding itself capable of absolutely intact expression and thus pure repeatability beyond the contingent realm of signs – displays a certain indifference to the very mortal subject that would otherwise seem to provide the conditions of possibility for intention, expression, meaning, and thus truth, in the first place. The relationship to **death** therefore haunts the same system which determines being as presence.

Moreover, Husserl's notion of a purely expressive self-consciousness, immediately present-to-itself, suggests an instantaneous experience given in the undivided present. Yet if such a 'now' is imagined as scrupulously timely or punctual, as **Heidegger** points out there is no purely punctual moment that does not imply reference to an extended sequence in which it acquires its value as, precisely, punctual. Punctuality can never 'be for itself' without the supposition of that which it is not, i.e. the unpunctual or other-timely. For Derrida, not only is this privileging of an undivided present, a simple 'now', part of the long-standing history of metaphysics. More than this, the unavoidable reliance of this metaphysical construal of simple immediacy upon a conceptual matrix which necessarily includes the other-timely or the 'not-now' inscribes alterity at the origin of the 'instant'. For that matter, it is what makes the 'instant' possible. Furthermore, the very 'identity' of the instant can emerge only through the **iterability** of its concept. Iterability, as Derrida tells us, is the always altering repetition that permits a concept to signify or, as it were, allows its sign to **countersign** itself at another time or in another place. Thus, as the very identity of the 'instant' is spaced or distributed within both a differential conceptual matrix and the spatio-temporal field of (its own) repeatability or iterability, the differing-deferring movement of ***différance*** comes to be seen as more original than this 'instant' itself, more original than its supposed presence, immediacy or originality. The apparently uninterrupted purity and presence of monadic self-consciousness is thus powerfully dislocated by its own origin, with differentiality playing irreducibly at the source of its **auto-affective** self-constitution. The entire project of metaphysics in which phenomenological discourse plays its part – that of construing difference as merely derivative – is thus deconstructible at its very origin.

spirit   See ***Glas***, ***Margins of Philosophy***, phonocentrism, ***Psyche***, ***Specters of Marx***, speech, ***Speech and Phenomena***, ***The Other Heading***, ***The Work of Mourning***, writing, ***Writing and Difference***.

Spurs: Nietzsche's Styles   In this 1978 text it is 'the woman question' that orients Derrida's reading of **Nietzsche**, whose multiple and frequently conflicting 'styles' preclude a discourse of 'woman' from stably referring to some essence or ground which might otherwise secure **sexual difference** within a classical binary structure. In *Twilight of the Idols*, it is at a certain point in the history of Platonic and **Christian** notions of an ideal 'real', beyond the earthly realm of mere appearances, that the idea of the 'real world' comes to be identified by Nietzsche with 'woman'. Derrida argues that it is the figure of castration (the absence of **presence**) that unstably affects this identification. At one turn, woman is construed in terms of absence, lack, and thus privation and menace. At another moment – at once different, more rare and yet in effect inseparable – woman is affirmed as 'dionysiac', perhaps primordially wild or elusive, something like a fabulous or ecstatic origin. Derrida reads the Nietzschean 'styles' of such

supplement

plural figuration with extreme vigilance, yet it is this inextricable plurality that itself opens up the possibility of a **writing** of 'woman' that cannot be fully contained within the logic of **phallogocentrism**. In the myriad styles of the feminine 'text', in other words, 'woman' cannot be reduced to a stable meaning, or subjected to a phenomenological reduction that would re-anchor 'truth', '**logos**', essence or Being. Not only could Nietzsche not have foreseen the full consequences of this plurality of inscription, but the very self-difference of his writing enfolds it within the same problematic of the 'feminine' that it styles, beyond the stable moorings of a masculine **signature**.

structuralism   For Derrida's relationship to structuralism, see **deconstruction, linguistics/linguisticism,** *Of Grammatology, Points, Positions,* 'Letter to a Japanese Friend' in *Psyche, Writing and Difference.*

supplement   This term crops up throughout Derrida's writing, but is worked out most extensively in *Of Grammatology.* In the second part of the book, Derrida examines **Rousseau**'s notion that **writing** forms a 'dangerous supplement' to **speech**. For Rousseau – and, indeed, the entire metaphysical tradition before and after him, from **Plato** to **Saussure** to **Husserl** and beyond – speech constitutes itself as the immediate expression of living **presence**. Writing, in contrast, is viewed as merely a **technical**, auxiliary and extrinsic form of representation. The 'supplement' of writing is 'dangerous' to the extent that it threatens to usurp speech, corrupt the living word, and divide and deaden language. Derrida, however, reinhabits the 'text' of Rousseau in order to show how writing augments speech not just as a mere 'extra' laid on top of an already fully present and self-sufficient 'thing', but as a crucial addition which compensates for a certain shortfall in speech itself. Writing, then, is not merely an inessential appendage, but becomes instead the indispensable supplement without which speech could not constitute itself in the first place. Thus, for instance, it is writing that – for Rousseau himself – facilitates **autobiographical** self-expression. As *Of Grammatology* also demonstrates, via a reading of the structural anthropology of Claude **Levi-Strauss**, it is writing (the advent of the **proper name** as a form of **violent** inscription) that in fact comes to define Nambikwara tribal culture; a culture heralded by Levi-Strauss as purely 'oral', pre-literate and, therefore, immediate, organic, living, ideal and uncorrupted.

Derrida's reading of Rousseau in *Of Grammatology* identifies a series of dangerous yet irreducible supplements: education as the supplement of maternal 'nature'; masturbation as the supplement of 'natural' sexual relations; 'harmony' as the supplement of 'melody'; linguistic 'articulation' as the supplement of voiced 'accent', 'need' as the supplement of 'passion', and so forth. In each case, the supplement adds itself to an ostensibly ideal or original presence in the form of exposing the lack and self-difference at its very origin. For Derrida, in other words, supplementarity is at the always divided 'origin' of presence. It is, precisely, that without which the **metaphysical** tradition could not constitute itself. But the supplement is also that which metaphysics projects as an inessential and privative attribute, something it could well do without. (In **Dissemination**, Derrida treats **Hegel**'s attitude to philosophical prefaces precisely in terms of this logic of the supplement.)

For the supplementarity of writing, see also 'Plato's Pharmacy' in *Dissemination*. See also *Margins of Philosophy* (especially 'The Supplement of Copula').

— T —

technicity (also technical/technology) For Derrida, the **metaphysical** tradition prioritizes **speech** over **writing** by construing the spoken word as a living expression issuing from a vital source of meaning. In contrast, writing is depicted as the merely *technical* instrument of potentially detachable representations. Within this tradition, then, writing is considered at once derivative and dispensable in relation to the spoken word, yet also a constant source of menace in that it imperils **presence** with the possibility of absence. Writing threatens to substitute **death** or the deathly for the living. It risks corrupting the purity and immediacy of nature by introducing the artifices and devices of culture. Where speech expresses unity and identity, writing suggests **violence** and difference. For Derrida, however, the **supplement** of writing is in fact irreducible and constitutive for the tradition of metaphysics. Nevertheless, the metaphysical construal

technicity

of being in terms of presence and self-sufficiency means that this 'dangerous supplement', as **Rousseau** puts it, must be downgraded, excluded and repressed. And writing is subordinated *precisely as* a technology or technical tool. Yet Derrida's thinking of an irreducible supplement at the 'origin' leads him to rethink *techné* in terms of a making, fabrication, or fabulation that is in fact originary – even for 'truth' itself. (One needs to be careful here – throughout all his arguments, Derrida is not concerned to dismiss or devalue 'truth', but to rethink what it may come to mean for us.) Thus, for instance, Derrida's neologism '**artifactuality**' acknowledges that actuality (as artefact) is made rather than given. However, this does not amount to a crude denial of actuality, the sense of which remains irreducibly marked in the neologism itself. Instead, Derrida wants to show that our sense of 'reality' – its coherence and consistency – cannot simply be detached from synthetic operations and media productions; and yet that our very experience of the 'present' depends on *différantial* traces it cannot contain. For Derrida, moreover, certain **singular events** – in a sense, the most 'actual' of all, although always marked by their own **iterability** – harbour the potential to resist and indeed change the very forms that 'artifactuality' takes.

A thinking of technology is therefore indispensable to **deconstruction** and informs many of Derrida's writings (in interviews and audio-visual recordings, too, Derrida typically begins by noting the technological conditions surrounding the event, and by meticulously examining their implications). In **Archive Fever**, certain technologies of archivization are seen to be inextricably linked to the history and thinking of **psychoanalysis** (that is, to the psychoanalytic 'archive' as that which itself contains the nevertheless uncontainable idea of the psyche as 'archive'). These technologies produce as much as record the psychoanalytic 'text'. The latter would have been determined very differently, Derrida speculates, had psychoanalysis been born in the era of email, fax and computer. (For Derrida's work on the changing culture and technology of print, see also **Paper Machine** and **Geneses, Genealogies, Genres and Genius**.) Similarly, in **Echographies of Television** Derrida explores the constitutive impact of technology on modern life (including the notion that life today is 'modern'). Here, however, Derrida speculates that the origin of technology cannot itself be considered 'technical', any more than the founding of law might be thought of as 'lawful'. (Up to a certain point, Derrida is here following

Heidegger. However, his concern is not to herald some pre-technical moment, state, condition or possibility.) To the extent that the 'technological' is therefore called up by the '**other**' of itself, it cannot be thought of in terms of an 'essence'; nor, for that matter, can it be determined merely as an 'object' – and thus, a technical instrument – of knowledge. One must therefore think 'technology' from a perspective which hesitates to proclaim technological innovation and development as, on its own terms, simply the bottom line or the last word. Instead, as with the relation of **différance** to writing in the more narrow sense, *techné* is neither merely reducible to technological forms nor simply transcendent in regard to them.

In **'Faith and Knowledge'**, meanwhile, Derrida deconstructs the distinctions which ostensibly divide the realms of **religion** and technology; while, in 'Telepathy' (included in **Psyche**), Derrida explores the relationship of telepathy to tele-technology in Freud and beyond. These are just some examples of texts in which questions of *techné*, technicity and technology are at stake for Derrida.

See also **Dissemination**, **Of Grammatology**, **Without Alibi**, **Writing and Difference**.

telepathy   See 'Telepathy' in **Psyche**.

testimony   In **'Demeure: Fiction and Testimony'**, Derrida explains how testimony can only justify its name on the strength of its radical difference from an informational or knowledge-based conception of truth. Put differently, testimony is not evidence. In **Echographies of Television**, Derrida more amply illustrates this point by referring to the Rodney King trial in Los Angeles in 1991, during which the videotape of police brutality against King was submitted as an important exhibit amid a body of evidence for the prosecution, although it was not considered as the testimony of the individual who held the video camera, who himself had to testify quite separately, swearing that he saw what the camera filmed.

Interestingly, Derrida's understanding of testimony resonates throughout his remarks about profession in 'The University Without Condition' (see **Without Alibi**), where instrumental, 'content-bound' knowledge – disciplinary or technical competence, expert training or archivable know-how – is distinguished from the act of profession understood in the rigorous sense. In its **performative** imperative, the discourse of profession is for

Derrida always in excess of (although never entirely divorced from) the constative utterances that frequently serve the techno-scientific concept of positive knowledge. Profession principally entails a **promise**, an act of recommitted faith or a pledge of **responsibility** opening on to an unanticipatable **future**. Thus, profession cannot easily be assimilated, mastered or exhausted by knowledge-based academic discourse, or by informational concepts of truth-content or value.

Following **Augustine**, in 'Demeure' Derrida identifies testimony with a promise to make truth on the part of an irreplaceably **singular** witness. The very condition of possibility of testimony as an irreplaceable making of truth is therefore also that of **fiction**, perjury and **lying**. Despite intricate historical connections operating within the sphere of **law**, testimony must always remain irreducible to evidence or proof, and if this irreducibility were to be eliminated – if testimony were to be appropriated as evidence without **remainder** –then it would deserve its name no longer. Should testimony be judged 'true' in the sense of being considered factual verification, it would lose its character as testimony in the strictest sense. Giving testimony or professing therefore entails attestation, but also powerfully implies the **secret**, since testimony holds in reserve what can never ultimately be subjected or exposed to a demonstration of proof. Indeed, as 'Demeure' unfolds, Derrida sets himself the extraordinarily difficult task of thinking the paradoxical power of that which is irrecoverable to knowledge – of that which remains 'secret' – in the attestation of a testimony. The divisibility of testimony between truth and fiction, and between telling or making the truth and keeping a certain secret, is also allied to a certain divisibility in relation to **presence**: on the one hand, to testify legitimately is always and necessarily to do it in the first person and thus in an indivisible present, without mediation by any **technical** apparatus or contrivance; on the other hand, however, there must always be a temporal dimension to testimony, implied for instance by a sequence of testimonial sentences which must promise their own repetition and, indeed, technical reproducibility if only according to Derrida's notion of **iterability**. Thus, testimony might itself be thought as that which carries or projects the present outside of itself, dividing it inextricably from itself. The very conditions of possibility of testimony are those of its own **impossibility**, meaning that – at the very moment of attestation, apparently so vital to testimony itself – testimony simply cannot be made to speak fully, in or by right of its own name.

Testimony attests to this irreplaceable 'secret' precisely as it speaks – a provocation and resistance indeed to positive, informational or instrumentalist conceptions of truth as knowledge.

For Derrida, we should add, testimony is always haunted or parasitized by the possibility of what he calls 'literature' as something that, in other ways, it might wish to exclude. While testimony remains inassimilable to **archivable** knowledge or information, the testimonial remains complexly tied to the inextricable possibility of its own impurity: if it endures as testimony on the strength of its profoundly non-symmetrical relation to forms of proof, information, knowledge or evidence, nevertheless it 'itself' does not consist of a pure essence, an authentic property or uncontaminated self-identity, since, as Derrida himself tells us, testimony entails parasitism, the radical impurity of an **undecidable** co-possibility of truth and lies, testimony and fiction. Moreover, it consists not only of this inseparable admixture found in the hybrid potentiality of literality and literarity; testimony must also give itself (while, in its very pledge, withholding what it simply cannot give for the purposes of exchange) in a language or discourse produced by a basic grammatical or rhetorical technicality, by an iterability that the oath itself implies and, by extension, via a certain field of technical (re-)production which would otherwise seem somewhat in tension with profession or testimony. Testimony is therefore linked to the discourse of **literature**, in that the definition of the latter resides not in an authentic literary essence but in literature's always precarious standing (tied to the **unconditional** right to say everything), which Derrida tells takes shape in regard to a complicated set of historical conditions informed by juridical institutions, acquired rights, the history of the nation-state and classical and modern models of citizenship, freedom, democracy and the social body.

The Animal That Therefore I Am Published posthumously, this volume includes Derrida's ten-hour address to the 1997 Cérisy conference on 'The Autobiographical Animal'. Derrida himself chose this title for the event, the third of four such colloquia devoted to his work. As Derrida noted during the lecture, the question of the '**animal**' recurs throughout his writings, and in a sense it therefore remained inextricable in regard to the possibilities of his own '**autobiography**'. Thus, the Cérisy address provided an opportunity for him to reflect upon and draw together some of

The Animal That Therefore I Am

the guiding threads which maintained his interest in animals and animality over many years.

For Derrida, the 'animal' question has a structuring importance throughout the entire text of **philosophy**. In particular, the term 'animal' has been used right across philosophical history to found and maintain a classical opposition through which the concept of the 'human' may be proposed in binary terms. Thus, what might be presumed to be 'proper' to the human – including, as Derrida puts it, 'speech, reason, experience of death, mourning, culture, institutions, technics, clothing, lying, pretense of pretense, covering of tracks, gift, laughing, tears, respect, etc.' – is brought to the fore through the negative determination of the 'animal' as binary opposite. From Aristotle to Heidegger, Descartes to Kant, Levinas and Lacan, the animal has been denied the *logos*. (In one sense, we might say, the *logos* and thus philosophy in its classical sense is founded upon the 'animal' as oppositional 'other' – that is, at once the object of appropriation and yet also a projection of philosophy's or indeed humanity's own limitations.) Furthermore, the homogenizing concept and category of the 'animal' offers **violence** both to the sheer diversity of animal life and to the irreducibly complex and always deconstructible relation of the 'animal' to the 'human'. Derrida therefore challenges the grounds of this opposition between the 'human' and the 'animal'. In the last part of the book, for instance, during an improvised speech on Heidegger and the animal, he points up the contradictions which run through Heideggerian thought on this very subject. (Derrida ruminates on the 'animal' in **Heidegger** throughout a number of earlier texts including 'The Ends of Man', 'Heidegger's Hand' and 'Heidegger's Ear' in the **Geschlecht** series of essays, as well as in *Of Spirit* and *Aporias*.) For at one moment, in comparison to *Dasein*, the animal is excluded from 'being-towards-death', and as such does not properly die. And yet, at another time, the animal is accorded the character of a living being, in contrast to the inanimate or 'worldless' stone, suggesting the very possibility of dying which is common to 'man'. Derrida thereby suggests at once the limits and exemplarity of the Heideggerian 'text' on the animal. For, here, the animal both *does* and *does not* have the 'as such' which founds the possibility of the *logos*, and indeed this difference-beyond-opposition calls for new forms of thinking – **ethical** as much as philosophical – which cannot be based simply on the 'as such' and its absence or deprivation. Thus, Derrida suggests the need for a rigorous and transforming reinvestigation, rather than a simple defence, of 'human rights' and 'animal rights' – something which calls for a more fundamental questioning of what is meant by 'life', both within and beyond philosophical thought.

The Ear of the Other   This volume is linked to a colloquium held at the University of Montreal in 1979. It includes an essay, 'Otobiographies: The Teaching of Nietzsche and the Politics of the Proper Name', in which Derrida investigates two texts by Friedrich **Nietzsche**: his **autobiographical** work *Ecce Homo* and an earlier series of lectures, *On the Future of Our Educational Institutions*. The English translation appears with two subsequent roundtable discussions on autobiography and translation, and includes an interview from 1981, 'Choreographies'. It is worth noting that Derrida's 'Declarations of Independence', presented as a public lecture at the University of Virginia in Charlottesville in 1976, was published in the 1984 French edition of *Otobiographies* (although it is not to be found in *L'oreille de l'auture* from 1982), since it immediately preceded Derrida's presentation of 'Otobiographies' in Charlottesville.

In 'Otobiographies' Derrida disputes the traditional separation of biographical material from legitimate philosophical thought. This classical division construes biography as the amalgam of chance empirical data extraneous to the immanence of the philosophical system. Derrida wishes instead to analyze the dynamic and divisible border between the system and the biographical subject of the system in **philosophy** – and thus to question the conventional understanding of both – by tracing the extent to which the **proper name** forms part of the structure not only of Nietzsche's autobiographical writing, but also his philosophical orientation (which is also the philosophical orientation of Nietzsche towards a future coming after Nietzsche). In Nietzsche's texts – as well as in those by **Freud** and **Kierkegaard**, as Derrida points out – philosophy and life, or for that matter writing and life, cannot be neatly distinguished by a single, consistent and thus undividable line separating the two. For in these kinds of texts, albeit in very different ways, the living subject is intimately implicated as an interested party in precisely a writing and a philosophy, one that comes indeed to be associated with the author's very name.

For Derrida, to put one's name to a text by signing it in the 'here-now' is implicitly to acknowledge the text's persistence in one's absence and, for that matter, after one's death. In other words, only the proper name will inherit a legacy, of which the mortal bearer will be deprived. Thus the living autobiographer assigns his name to a text in order to speculate on a presently incalculable credit to be countersigned in or by a future in which the proper name will return nothing to him as a dead man. By way of a secret contract with a future time, then, the autobiographer tells himself a life in his own name, yet the supposed present-presence of this autobiographical 'life' always comes down to a prejudicial anticipation of what is yet to come, what is lived on credit, as it were.

In 'Otobiographies' Derrida moves around within the question of (a) teaching in the proper name: of Nietzsche. However, the legacy of Nietzsche as a proper name implies and underscores not just *a* teaching to be received and understood, but a surplus or plurality of teachings to come. Derrida therefore indicates that we might examine, in a complexly divided field, the relationship of the Nietzschean inheritance to the cultural and educational institutions of **Nazism**, and yet also to institutions still to be invented, which may yet still countersign differently (in) Nietzsche's name. For Derrida, such an investigation also entails tackling wider problems concerning the relationship between scholarly and pedagogical mastery, the authority and legacy of the **signature** and the proper name, and the possibility or necessity of receiving or hearing 'teaching' otherwise, with the ear of the **other**. In this essay, then, Derrida confronts the doubleness of teaching as, on the one hand, the supposed manifestation of an authoritative, self-crediting self-presentness where the pedagogue or *magister* is concerned; but also, on the other, of teaching as an inextricably **différant**, untimely address to an other, and indeed a response called forth and countersigned by an other to come, which – here, in Derrida's attention to Nietzsche's writing – inevitably occurs as **supplement** of the supposed manifestation of self-presence or self-identity on the part of the magisterial teacher. Since the question of the effects of an authoritative, self-crediting pedagogy and the complex problem of teaching's legacy and return here supplement one another, Derrida shows that we are called upon to witness, in both of Nietzsche's texts under discussion, the complicated interplay between the living and the dead. As we have said, the proper name alone inherits the credit opened up by autobiography (a 'life of'), and this proper name is a name of **death**. More widely, it might be suggested that this interplay between the living and the dead, and between the legacy and the proper name, in fact structures the histories and relations of the teaching institution itself. Certainly, as Derrida goes on to show, it is this interplay between the living and the dead (between so-called living and dead languages and living and dead cultures, as well as living and dead masters) which imposes itself precisely on academic institutions of the sort described and critiqued by Nietzsche. This raises in turn the question of how to think about a state-sponsored age of pedagogy after the Enlightenment, since in the case of Nietzsche's understanding of his contemporary educational institutions as vehicles of the state, what is evident to him is a disfigurement of the **mother** tongue accompanying a return to a dead, paternal language.

For Derrida, as he begins his reading of or teaching on Nietzsche, the question of a living-dead pedagogy is primary. It is neither that academic convention and orthodoxy can simply be ignored, surpassed or abandoned; nor that they permit themselves to be unquestioningly defended and thereby unproblematically reproduced. Rather, any teaching necessarily partaking of pedagogical tradition that tries nonetheless to remain wholeheartedly devoted to the unsupplemented conservation of its enabling method or system will surely dwindle into circularly self-justifying practices that actually inhibit and eventually preclude everything to do with the **event** of (a) teaching. One can therefore neither simply take nor leave classical pedagogy, and in fact one must simultaneously partake of and depart from it in order for teaching to take place at all.

Such insights have their bearing on Derrida's reading of Nietzsche's 'On the Future of Our Educational Institutions'. Here, Derrida observes that Nietzsche's recommendation of the very strictest linguistic discipline as a counter to academic freedom is not merely a reactionary or proto-fascistic gesture, but that instead it aims to resist an ideological ruse in which state-driven goals are achieved through the very discourse of academic freedom or laissez-faire. In 'The University without Condition' (see **Without Alibi**), Derrida similarly notes how the humanities' prized ideal of autonomy frequently permits other university departments to benefit from higher funding given to end-oriented research in the service of state-backed economic, industrial, technical and military interests. (For Derrida on the academic institution, see also **Right to Philosophy**, **university**.)

In the interview 'Choreographies', Derrida answers questions about feminism, femininity and **sexual difference**. Revisiting a number of his own texts, including **Spurs**, **Glas**, **The Post Card**, 'The Double Session' in **Dissemination** and **'Living On: Borderlines'**, as well as returning to his various readings of Hegel, Nietzsche, Heidegger and Levinas, Derrida puts – or rather confounds – the question of 'woman's place' in order to resist the appropriation of sexual difference to binarized oppositions or dialectical structures in which the role of the feminine is subordinated. While the question of the 'feminine' as fetish is raised, Derrida also interrogates the apparent neutralization of sexual difference in ontological thought or, indeed, philosophy more generally, the effect of which is classically to reinscribe masculine priority by various degrees of stealth. Part of Derrida's response in this section of the interview also recalls the first essay in the '**Geschlecht**' series, where, for Derrida, **Heidegger**'s thinking of *Dasein*'s essential 'neutrality' must be accounted for in terms of a disseminal structure that nevertheless gives us the very possibility of sexual difference or sexuality itself. Derrida ends the discussion by reflecting on his choreographing of a number of texts that are, in effect, signed 'polysexually', for instance 'Restitutions' in **The Truth in Painting** and 'At This Very Moment in This Work Here I Am', found in **Psyche**. This technique is adopted, Derrida tells us, precisely in order to disrupt a supposed sexual neutrality in 'philosophical' discourse, which typically veils various reimpositions of **phallogocentric** domination over the topic or field.

The Gift of Death   French publication, 1992. The four essays included here start out from Derrida's engagement with Jan Patočka's *Heretical Essays on the Philosophy of History*. This encounter occasions a series of reflections upon the relationship between **responsibility** and the **secret** within the **European** tradition. Patočka wants to distinguish the possibility of responsibility from the mystery of the sacred experienced as a form of demonic rapture. However, for him, **Christianity** is exemplary among the **religion**s of the Book in providing the basis for the responsible subject in the history of Europe. Christianity effects a certain mutation of the ethico-political 'self' found in the Platonic tradition – a mutation that, Patočka admits, Christianity itself barely understands – and yet, as Derrida shows, this 'self' itself rises on the very back of the orgiastic mystery from which Plato sought to extricate **philosophy**. For Derrida, then, the Platonic and Christian inheritance must be understood in terms of a series of conversions, incorporations and repressions that not only depart from what they seek to replace or overcome, but which reactivate – albeit in unacknowledged ways – certain aspects of a demonic or orgiastic tradition of the **secret**. This is another way of thinking the history of European responsibility as one that remains tied to an irreducible secrecy. (For Patočka, as Derrida notes, Platonism is to be distinguished from Christianity in that it utterly denounces mystery in its idea both of philosophy and politics. To the extent that Europe inherits such Platonism, its traditions of democracy and freedom are therefore bound to be accompanied by a near totalitarian desire for disclosure and mastery – a desire, however, that Europe wishes in other respects to deny or repress.)

Derrida shows that, for Patočka, it is **death** that provides the basis for the very possibility of the responsive and responsible subject. The interpretation or representation of death which can be made by, of or for the subject, as much as any real death he or she might experience, is what *gives* the subject (even if, in **Heidegger**, to whom Patočka draws close on many occasions, 'death' as the condition of possibility of the authentic existence of *Dasein* is also a condition of **impossibility**, inasmuch as death itself remains ungiven to philosophical thought). Patočka here follows a tradition that goes back to the *Phaedo*, in which philosophy itself is defined as precisely a vigilant meditation on the death given *as its very concern* to the 'self', the 'subject' or the 'soul', a concern which calls the 'self' to gather itself, apprehend itself, identify with itself, become conscious of and responsive to itself. Such a vigil, however, animates the life of the 'soul' only in the form of an as yet unfulfilled **mourning**, so that Platonic and Christian responsibility remain haunted by a returning, defining secret of which full knowledge cannot be possessed in the conscious life which death gives to the subject. Death cannot be looked at in the face or faced up to (the very dream of philosophy in a tradition that runs from Plato all the way to Heidegger) since the orgiastic secret remains deeply enveloped, enslaved and unrecognized within the Platonic and Christian conceptions of responsible freedom and responsive consciousness that hope to find authentic existence in the relation to death.

During this reading of Patočka, Derrida is quick to point out that the capacity for responsibility or **decision** cannot itself be derived from a history (let's say, of responsibility), so that, far from establishing the conditions of responsibility through historical recounting, responsibility must be thought of as that which profoundly interrupts or disturbs the contextuality or conditionality demanded by historical thinking and writing. However, to the extent that this very same history – if it is a history of European responsibility tied in its **religious** formation to faith, the **gift** and secrecy – cannot be reduced to a self-same object of knowledge, the problem of responsibility's historicity reopens itself as precisely a problem of the secret, of what is secret *to* and *in* it. To know what responsibility *is*, to thematize or represent it adequately, suggests a programmatic conceptualization which risks becoming *irresponsible*, or which lessens the chances of a responsibility that can occur only where decision is not blunted by established codes, protocols, morals, doctrines or rules. Which amounts to saying, when one rethinks responsibility as the hyper-responsibility of the responsible-irresponsible type, that such responsibility falls on the side of heresy as much as paradox and secrecy. And that the secret of European responsibility is that it provokes apostasy and therefore conversion from the beginning.

Death is always **singular** and irreplaceable – one can only die one's own death, one cannot die in place of another or deliver another from the inevitability of their own inimitable demise. If such thinking draws close to a certain Heideggerianism, Derrida reminds us that **Levinas** reprimands Heidegger for arguing *Dasein* from the perspective of its own (relation to) death. For Levinas, the foremost death is that of the **other** – it is from the other's mortality that our responsibility is derived. While Patočka cannot be sided neatly with one or the other of these thinkers in considering the secrets of European responsibility, Derrida's next move is to rethink the relation to death and responsibility of self and other by revisiting **Kierkegaard**'s *Fear and Trembling*. The title itself cites Saint Paul's letter to the Philippians: in profound solitude, we fear and tremble before a God who makes us responsible for our own salvation from a standpoint that itself remains inaccessibly secret. Thus we receive this responsibility from God as *wholly other* (*tout autre*). In Kierkegaard's *Fear and Trembling*, Abraham is asked to sacrifice his only son Isaac, and thus to step for ever outside the **ethical** domain which, in **Hegel**'s philosophy, ties responsibility to answerability or accountability within the public, social or non-secret domains. (Here, Hegel is as intolerant of secrecy in the ethical realm as **Plato** is in politics and philosophy.) As Kierkegaard insists, Abraham's willingness to sacrifice Isaac can have no ethical explanation. Indeed, since it is Isaac who was promised to found the very nation or people that make possible ethical exchange, such an act risks putting an end to the ethical itself. And since the meaning or essence of this sacrificial act is profoundly un- or rather a-ethical, any account or explanation Abraham might hope to venture – since it could only manifest itself in public and linguistic terms as an expression of the ethical demand or impulse – would be bound to tell us nothing about its origin *outside* ethics. And yet, however irresponsible Abraham must be in declining ethical explanation or in failing to observe his commonsense duty to family and community, he is at the same time hyper-responsible in refusing the irresponsibility of a merely ethical recounting. Put another way, rather than acting on the basis of ethics or duty, Abraham must be *irresponsible* in order to be absolutely responsible before God as the wholly other. Bereft of the consolations of a tragic hero who can openly lament his situation, Abraham must madly violate all ethics by waging hate against that which is least hateful of all, by remaining in unintelligible silence before the community, and by enduring the ethical censure which does not properly apply and yet still rightly applies to him. Yet, as Derrida points out, the **aporetic** horror of Abraham's circumstance is to be found not only in the far-distant drama of Mount Moriah. On the contrary, it holds everywhere, every day, in a way that presses to the limit the unacknowledged implications of Kierkegaard's reading. If responsibility is, absolutely, nothing else than responsibility to the other as wholly other, then an uncountable number of singular or irreplaceable others place us in Abraham's situation at every turn and at all times. For every other (one) is every (bit) other: **tout autre est tout autre**. Through entering into a (responsible) relation with an other, at a stroke we sacrifice the 'same' responsibility to all other others (others that, in each and every case, cannot be reduced to merely a tautological self-reflection of, let's say, God as the absolute). This is perhaps the secret truth that ethical thought has been incapable of acknowledging: certainly, the sacrifice of all others to the other to whom I *do* relate or respond cannot be justified, cannot acquire ethical justification through a reasoned account. By making this argument, it is not that Derrida wishes simply to paralyze ethical thinking, far from it. Instead, he wishes to transform the legacy of thinking found among or between the religions of the book and the traditions of ethical, political and philosophical thought, in the interests of acknowledging the constitutive limits and paradoxes – the secrets – of European responsibility, within and against which we must somehow go on operating.

The Other Heading: Reflections on Today's Europe This volume contains two texts written in 1989 and 1990: 'The Other Heading: Memories, Responses, and Responsibilities' and 'Call It a Day for Democracy'. (French publication 1991.) While the latter is a short interview of interest principally for its reflections upon media politics and, indeed, public opinion as a powerful yet ultimately un-present-able or **spectral** force within the institutional fields of an electoral and representative politics (making public opinion a somewhat ghostly European phenomena), the lengthier essay is more explicit in situating this volume as a whole at a time when Eastern and Central **Europe** felt the shock waves of perestroika and democratization, the decline of Soviet power, German reunification, the seeming victory of a liberal market economy, and the resurgence of nationalisms and religious and ethnic conflicts in and on the borders of Europe. Eurocentric and anti-Eurocentric discourses abounded in the political and media spheres. In this context, while rereading Valéry, **Husserl** and **Heidegger** on the very notion of a European **spirit** and indeed its *crisis*, Derrida re-asks the question of Europe itself. (Derrida acknowledges himself both an old European, nearly saturated by its culture and language, and yet in his **Algerian** beginnings a partial outsider, a hybrid figure on the cusp of Europe's borders.) Europe seems both old and young, at once a long-since exhausted theme and a still youthful **promise** of what is yet to come. Europe has always been a heading (*cap*), a cape or peninsula but also the (capital) launching point for adventure, discovery, colonization, **invention**, indeed the very promontory for the 'historical' in its trajectory as a concept, the headland for an exemplary idea or image of human civilization as advancement itself. However, at a juncture in which something is very obviously afoot in Europe, Europe must recollect its cultural and philosophical resources anew, in order to embark on another heading – the ***other*** of its heading(s) – in the interests of a Europe yet to exist, one which preserves difference in its own identity, resisting totalizing unification of the kind foreseen by **Hegel** in the movement of Spirit through ever-increasing dialectical synthesis. Yet this Europe must also remain tirelessly vigilant in its suspicion of a discourse of the 'new'. If a 'new Europe' implies a 'new order' of sorts, then the double bind is that Europe must open itself to a **future** unprogrammed by its past, a future that could never be homogenized as fully **present** in its absolute identity, while at the same time keeping watch over the possible monstrosity of a pure, obliterating invention with which, indeed, one might associate a certain **memory** and discourse of totalitarianism. Beyond the crude choices presented by Eurocentricism and its opponents, and indeed by ethnicist-nationalistic or fanatical-religious resistance to the self-congratulatory 'end-of-history' discourse of liberal economics (choices which in fact misrepresent the complexity of the *other* heading of Europe that remains possible 'today'), the turn of the 1990s sees the emergence of fresh possibilities for international **law**, organizations and politics in deciding inventively and responsibly amid the complex forces of transnational capital, federalist ambition, human migrations, and backward- and inward-looking nationalistic chauvinism, sometimes calling up the state-form as a bulwark against powerful 'non-state' forces, while at other times limiting or adjusting its claims. For Derrida, it is this characteristically European responsibility to and for another heading – the *other* of the European heading – which responds to the **aporetic** question of Europe 'today'. This is politics itself, taking itself beyond a mere **technology**, knowledge or programme, in the interests of the **democracy to come** here and now.

The Post Card: From Socrates to Freud and Beyond This volume from 1980 brings together three texts, each well known in their own right, which nevertheless may also be seen to address themselves to each other in far from simple ways (suggesting indeed the **postal principle** at stake throughout *The Post Card*): 'Envois', 'To Speculate – on "Freud"' and 'Le Facteur de la vérité'.

Derrida's interest in and indebtedness to **psychoanalysis** can be traced across countless pages of his writing. Resemblances between **deconstruction** and psychoanalysis were suggested to Derrida on several occasions throughout his career. For instance, in one interview in **Positions**, Derrida's approach to 'differences' is likened to the concept of the 'symbolic' in **Lacan**. Such purported similarities between psychoanalysis and deconstruction can be accounted for in a number of ways. A deconstructive thinking of **différance**, **supplement**, **trace**, or in general the logic of a non-present **remainder** at work in the **deconstruction** of **presence**, appears to share affinities with the psychoanalytic conception of repression as that which leaves an unresolved residue destined to return in the form of the symptom. Derrida's thinking of identity or presence as divided from the outset by the necessary possibility of repeatability seems to recall the splitting

The Post Card: From Socrates to Freud and Beyond

of the subject and the primacy of the signifier in the symbolic as key themes in Lacanian psychoanalysis. In some prefatory remarks to 'Freud and the Scene of Writing', found in **Writing and Difference**, Derrida acknowledges certain of these resemblances between psychoanalysis and deconstruction, but nevertheless wants to distinguish his project from that of psychoanalysis on the grounds that the latter's concepts and practices still remain tied to the **metaphysical** tradition. In 'Le Facteur de la vérité' Derrida shows how, despite appearances to the contrary, Lacan's seminar on Poe's 'The Purloined Letter' remains in thrall of a traditional hermeneutics of disclosure and truth. For Lacan, the purloined letter in Poe's story acquires its significance without discernible reference to an available 'content' (what is 'inside' the letter is never revealed to the reader and, as the plot thickens, this is increasingly besides the point), thus exemplifying the primacy of the letter over the subject, the signifier over signified. Yet since this insight serves to illustrate the profundity of Lacanian psychoanalytic theory, the letter is in a sense restored, redirected or, one might say, 're-posted' to the truth. The double, undecidable or supplementary operations which might otherwise seem to circulate in the vicinity of this enigmatic letter (as it itself circulates within the textual space of Poe's tale, and for that matter within that of Lacan's own seminar) are reduced as its psychoanalytic 'message' is so forcefully deciphered. For Derrida, this returning or re-posting of the signifier to the signified reinscribes the letter's 'lack' within what is – for psychoanalysis – its proper place: the truth of the phallus, or in other words the thinking of an original presence upon which lack supervenes as castration (for Derrida, this notion of castrated presence echoes the classical, pejorative sense of **writing** as the fallen exteriority of living **speech** in its self-presence). Thus the metaphysics of truth, **logos** and presence are shown to underpin Lacan's notion of the 'symbolic' as the place of castration ('le manqué à sa place': missing-from-its-place, lack-in-place-of). Once 'lack' is restored or returned to its proper place – that of the phallus as signified – Lacan's theory of the 'symbolic' remains inassimilable to a deconstructive thinking of disseminating *différance*.

In 'Envois' another postal principle is at work. In his earlier discussion of **Condillac**'s *Essay on the Origin of Human Understanding* found in **'Signature Event Context'**, Derrida had shown how Condillac figures writing as the site of potential recuperation or repair where a gap in 'presence' between the author and addressee is concerned. For Derrida, however, Condillac unwittingly acknowledges as the very condition of writing a certain 'break' in presence. Derrida shows how the repeatability or **iterability** which structures (and divides) the written **mark** at its origin always renders possible another reading beyond the empirical fact of any individual engagement with a 'text'. Thus, inscribed at the very origin of the written mark is a *non-present* remainder that cannot be resolved or reduced either in terms of a masterful intention or the anticipated destination implied by a particular addressee. In other words, the very condition of writing is not only that of a certain depropriation of the author, but the irreducible possibility of non-arrival. Thus, on the basis of a deconstructive rethinking of its classical or metaphysical construal, Derrida is able to generalize a transformed conception writing which remains, as it were, in the post.

In contrast to Derrida's image of Lacan as a veritable postman of truth, restituting presence to the signified, we therefore find in 'Envois' a postal system exemplified only by the incomplete remains of a correspondence which may not (yet) have arrived. 'Envois' records a series of textual fragments written in the form of letters and post cards directed to an undesignated addressee (or addressees) and emanating from an implied correspondent that it would be too hasty to reduce to the **proper name** – still less the person – of Jacques Derrida. (In 'To Speculate – on "Freud"', Derrida notes that, while psychoanalysis aspires to scientific and original knowledge, with **Freud** imagining himself unencumbered by any philosophical inheritance, unlike other sciences it is founded on or in the proper name, precisely that of Freud. For Derrida, this name therefore speculates on itself, bequeaths to itself, inherits from itself, less as a scene of triumphant auto-foundation or self-completion than one of an interminable repetition compulsion akin to the fort/da.) According to the postal principle which provides the medium as much as the analytic focus of the correspondence in 'Envois', identity is principally the effect of a self-address that must necessarily *space* (itself). Any attempt to restitute this correspondence to a name, to *the* name, therefore always risks getting lost in the post. The intimate address of many of the entries in 'Envois' ('you, my love') seems to turn, in apostrophe, to a singular recipient, yet this address is always divided or turned from itself by the possibility of non-arrival and, for that matter, non-return to the sender.

Part of the correspondence concentrates on the discovery, staged for the principal letter-writer by others, of a post card depicting the thirteenth-century illustration of **Socrates** and **Plato** by Matthew Paris. This portrays Socrates writing at a table, while Plato stands at his back, seeming to indicate and indeed direct the writing process. The illustration contrives a certain reversal that would be shocking for the entire philosophical tradition which holds that Socrates did not write (indeed that Socratic wisdom was essentially unwritten at its origin) and that Plato was, for want of a better word, his scribe. Such longstanding conceptions of the Socrates–Plato relationship resound with a metaphysics of presence that privileges living speech (in its supposedly essential connection with inspiration, divinity, thought, concept, meaning) over the traditional construal of writing as secondary, extrinsic and derivative – in other words, merely a support for that which it relays. Thus in redrawing or rewriting 'Socrates–Plato' so strikingly, with the supposed writer behind the back of the one who purportedly just speaks, the illustration fascinates in recalling deconstruction's transformed notion of writing as the generalized domain in which speech and language take place. (See, for example, *Of Grammatology* and *Sec.*) And in 'Envois' Paris's image of Socrates–Plato – one that is turned around and can be turned over on a card – gets put in the post countless times. With, written on its back, the **undecidable** remains of an unprivatizable correspondence that nonetheless keeps its **secrets** out in the open.

The Problem of Genesis in Husserl's Philosophy   Derrida's first work of major length, originally written as a dissertation for his *diplôme d'études supérieures* in 1953–54. For a comment on this text, see the entry on **Speech and Phenomena**.

The Truth in Painting   This 1978 volume, which includes texts on the plastic arts of Valerio Adami and Titus Carmel as well as the subject of pictorial painting, takes its cue from Paul Cézanne's remark: 'I owe you the truth in painting and I will tell it to you'. Such a phrase gives rise to multiple interpretations, none of which can dominate the phrase itself, none of which it is entirely bound or framed by. Is it the truth *about* painting which is owed, a truth to be restituted for instance in the written letter to Damisch in which this phrase itself appears? Or must the truth rather be told by way of a speech act still to be performed? Or, instead, is truth to be discerned only *in* painting? Is the 'truth' of painting (itself rendered ambiguous by the double genitive here) necessarily to be *painted*, rather than written or accounted for by way of a certain type of linguistic telling? In view of this last interpretation, we cannot help but wonder whether Cézanne should be taken as being literal or merely metaphorical about truth's 'paintability'. To the extent that this question of the 'literal' and the 'metaphorical' is bound to return, we must therefore ask whether painting might ever truly present its truth without recourse to representation, without going via an irreducible detour of language or discourse. (After all, the 'truth in painting' or 'the truth of painting' remain phrases of always double and **undecidable** rhetorical force.) Thus, the multiply complex relations and responsibilities between writing, speech and painting at once provoke and derail the **performative** possibilities of this promised restitution of 'truth'.

In the collection, Derrida confronts the Kantian problem of aesthetic judgement. To establish the properly philosophical investigation of art above and beyond merely individual or subjective judgements is, as **Kant** recognizes, a difficult matter. Art cannot be subjected to determinate judgements whereby particular examples can be evaluated by reference to general laws, rules, categories or concepts that are already given. In the absence of such universal criteria, the reflective judgement of art instead treats aesthetic phenomena as if their unity were given by another 'understanding' than our own. The name Kant assigns to this other understanding is 'form'. If this notion of form establishes the conceptual ground of aesthetic judgement, its characteristic trait for Kant is that of the contour, silhouette or outline which in fact delineates art in a basic way. Yet the defining impact of the outline or contour worryingly suggests the decisive nature of the frame as in effect the enabling limit of the art work itself. While the frame should stand as mere trapping or finery in relation to the higher grandeur and essential integrity of the art work, its irreducible participation in the very determination of form renders the unity or coherence of art divisible at its origin. Art is in essence always contaminated by the **'other'** found at its supposed limits. Furthermore, this thinking of aesthetic judgement only re-poses the question: What exactly demarcates the art work as such? For if the frame remains so indispensable in the constitution of form as to participate in the work itself, what then frames the art object? If another frame is called for, the very same delineating function would guarantee its non-extraneous involvement in the work, of which it would then be an irreducible part. Which would call for another frame . . . In *The Truth in Painting*, the figure of the passe-partout (the cardboard piece

The Truth in Painting

inserted in the frame with a rectangular cut-out at its centre to house the art work) provokes a thinking of these multiple framings and, indeed, figures the irresolvable play between the outer and inner edge of the 'edge' itself, as that which at once (and impossibly) constitutes and limits, originates and ends. The deconstructibility of the frame and framing function therefore imposes itself on the work of art as much as upon Cézanne's ambiguous saying.

'Restitutions', the last part of the book, revisits a debate involving Meyer Schapiro on the subject of Van Gogh's painting of shoes. Schapiro had strongly disputed the interpretation of these paintings found in **Heidegger**'s essay, 'The Origin of the Work of Art'.

In 'The Still Life as a Personal Object' (1968), dedicated to Kurt Goldstein, Schapiro disputes Heidegger's attribution of Van Gogh's shoes to a peasant, and by extension takes issue with the supposed authenticity of the rural landscape, the pathos rooted in the call of the earth and the labour of the field, and in fact the entire folk world which Heidegger seems to present as the truth of the painting. At the time of the lectures by Heidegger that produced 'The Origin of the Work of Art' (1935–36) such representations were of course not unconnected with the rise of those forces which saw **Jews** such as Goldstein leave **Europe** for America, as 'Restitutions' points out. Against Heidegger, then, Schapiro insists that the shoes in the painting belong not to the peasant's feet rooted in the soil, but to Van Gogh himself as, by the time the paintings were undertaken, an uprooted city dweller. By wresting the shoes from the earthy world of the peasant portrayed so eloquently by Heidegger and restoring them as property to the dispossessed emigrant, Schapiro's essay dedicates itself not only to Goldstein, but more fundamentally to the multitude of victims of techno-industrial modernity, mass warfare and migration, totalitarianism and the death camps.

While Derrida is keenly aware of the political stakes involved in Schapiro's critique of Heidegger, he nevertheless detects in this dispute between the two not only an oppositional struggle, but a certain correspondence and, indeed, a common interest. As one of the voices in this polylogue suggests, the disputed question of attribution thinly veils a desire for appropriation on the part of both these noted intellectuals. By investing in the act of attributing the painting 'properly', a certain return is doubtless to be had. Truth is therefore restituted as much to the critic as to the painter or the painting itself. Yet Derrida's point is not merely that Schapiro and Heidegger are somehow disingenuous or egotistical in falling upon these shoes only to assert their own academic credentials. More than this, attribution and restitution are seen to occur only via a series of detours or slippages, by way of mediating interventions and investments of energy which trouble the very idea of intact return, unstinting reparation and indeed undisputed property. Yet upon such an idea of absolute restitution, it would appear, rests the truth in painting – of either the 'city' or the 'fields', the industrial or rural world – that both Heidegger and Schapiro wish to restitute.

Furthermore, while by way of this imputed connection with the shifting and transient world of the modern metropolis, Schapiro wishes to uproot Van Gogh's shoes, and thereby to dislodge the specious groundedness he feels Heidegger attributes to them, Schapiro's act of restitution in fact regrounds the link between representation and reference in that it assumes an unstinting identification between the subject and object of the canvas, sealed by painting's signatory: Van Gogh's shoes are the shoes of Van Gogh. This tautological situation means that, far from roaming the itinerant pathways of the exile or emigre, the shoes can go nowhere. They get rooted, self-referentially, to the spot. Schapiro therefore restitutes the shoes to the eternally dispossessed through a procedure of repossession that means they cannot travel any road of return. The way in which Schapiro claims the shoes' proper ownership in fact destines them to remain disputed property.

Schapiro reproaches Heidegger both for being too referential (for Schapiro, Heidegger restitutes truth to the shoes by grounding them in an authentic folk world with all its dubious politico-ideological connotations), and for being insufficiently referential (Heidegger neglects to delimit the pictorial specificity of the shoes within a defined period and place of origin). Leaving aside this apparent contradiction, Derrida shows that Heidegger's own procedure for establishing or 'presenting' truth is in any case not as 'grounded' as Schapiro supposes, and certainly less so than Schapiro's problematic recourse to a sort of crude empiricism or literalism as a way of uprooting the shoes. For Heidegger the question of the origin, essence or 'truth' of truth resists simple attribution or direct explication. Art, as that which puts truth to work, is not merely a matter of mimetic reproduction or of the representation of nature. For Heidegger, the shoes belong in no particular place in that they equip us to recall the constituting rift (*Riss*)

The Truth in Painting

between 'earth' and 'world' which resides at the very heart of belonging or design. In Heidegger's interpretation, then, far from grounding themselves in the peasant world, the shoes 'belong' only by dint of a basic rift that displaces their literal ground. Meanwhile, far from being restituted to the exiled and anonymous victims of modernity, the shoes claimed by Schapiro for the city-dwelling Van Gogh are placed firmly on the side of what is sedentary and rooted.

The proofs submitted therefore prove nothing, so that restitution founders on its own intention. The disagreement between Schapiro and Heidegger takes the form neither of dialecticalizable conflict nor of a regulated play of differences because the positions adopted or ascribed on either side of the dispute in fact correspond with one another, owing to the fact that both function in a self-contradictory or non-self-identical way.

The non-self-identicality throughout the dispute of this pair of professors in fact corresponds to a problem that is nowhere visible in the debate itself. As Derrida shows, both professors assume too hastily that the shoes in the painting form a pair. This much does not constitute a point of disagreement between them. Indeed, it has to be agreed upon for the dispute to take place. For Derrida, Heidegger and Schapiro need to assume that the shoes in question form a pair so that they can go about the business of attribution or appropriation. But what makes them so sure the shoes are a pair? Looking at the shoes, one could never be so sure. Yet on the basis of this assumption of a pair of shoes, this 'pair' of professors (always more and less than a pair) restitute not undisputable truth but the 'truth in painting' as always disputable supplement. In the play of attachment/detachment or the interlacing of **différance**, of laces tied neither too tightly nor loosened to the extent that they unbind, this truth is never simply tied up nor totally undone.

See also **Memoirs of the Blind: The Self-Portrait and Other Ruins**, in which Derrida reflects upon a range of images selected from the prints and drawings department of the Louvre, all of which portray blindness in some form or other. In this work, Derrida combines detailed readings of pictures that draw upon classical and biblical traditions with a powerful philosophical engagement that takes in a whole series of texts (by Diderot, Baudelaire, Merleau-Ponty and others) where drawing, painting and art are in question. For Derrida, drawing is itself blind, since one must turn one's gaze from what one sees in order to produce the image as a condition of both recollection and anticipation. (One does not, therefore, simply produce an 'image' or 'vision' of the blind person from the perspective of full 'sight'.) Thus, **presence** and immediacy are dislocated in the very drawing which reconstitutes 'vision' by means of the hand as much as the eye. The image itself is also not a self-identical 'whole' but is instead composed of a multitude of marks and re-marks which are neither the product nor the basis of a purely immediate 'vision'. The irreducible **supplementarity** of the **mark**, then, calls up all the detours (not least, between word and image) that Derrida detects in Paul Cézanne's remark about 'the truth in painting'.

The Work of Mourning This 2001 volume brings together a series of texts drawing upon the several genres of **mourning** writing (eulogy, funeral oration, letter of condolence, memorial essay). The pieces, fourteen in all produced over numerous years, are each devoted to a noted figure in the worlds of literature, poetry, philosophy and the humanities whom Derrida also thought of as a friend, sometimes despite intellectual or personal differences. Several confront **death** as a theme in the work of these figures themselves, and frequently Derrida is minded to cite from and even give the last word to his subject, rather than appropriate their thought in the name of a memorial address. Included here are texts on Roland Barthes, Paul de Man, Michel Foucault, Max Loureau, Jean-Marie Benoist, Louis Althusser, Edmond Jabès, Joseph N. Riddell, Michel Servière, Louis Marin, Sarah Kofman, Gilles Deleuze, Emmanuel Levinas and Jean-François Lyotard.

Across the body of Derrida's writings, death is never far away. For Derrida, one might say, it is not simply that we are always in the presence of death, but rather that death in its numerous guises everywhere haunts the **metaphysical** determination of '**presence**'. This could be demonstrated by reference to a greater number of Derrida texts than is possible here. In **'Signature Event Context'**, the possibility of absence and thus of death enters in as an irreducible condition of **writing**. As Derrida suggests in *Of Grammatology* and **'Différance'**, writing – no less than **speech** – requires the production of differences via a structuring movement or play that cannot itself be reduced to a concept, a name, a 'presence' or category of **being**. Furthermore, towards the end of 'Sec', the signature's function as repeatable **mark** implies a divisibility at the origin in which a non-present

The Work of Mourning

remainder always haunts this supposed sign(ing) of presence. In many texts, of course, Derrida reminds us that the **proper name** is destined to outlive its bearer, so that death is encrypted in the name which gives us identity from birth; a name which, in anticipating the departure of its bearer, depropriates in itself the very 'self' it would seem to announce. Mourning thus begins with the name. In **Speech and Phenomena**, meanwhile, **Husserl**'s need to elaborate a pure form of expression beyond the contingent world of signs entails the predication of an uninterrupted self-consciousness that transcends the facticity of any existent individual. Thus, for Derrida, an irreducible relationship to death loiters in the very system which determines being as presence. In **The Gift of Death**, the relationship to death which would seem to give possibility to the subject in its '**European**' form is tied at its origin to a demonic tradition of the **secret** which returns aporetically in the suspension of the **ethical** for Abraham (a suspension which unravels the very entity of the 'self' as responsible being); while in **Specters of Marx** the Hegelian movement of **spirit** towards absolute knowledge at the 'end of history' is so spooked by the conjuration of **spectres** as to become something like a ghost story. In **Glas**, the writings of Jean **Genet** sound the death knell for the totalizing aspirations of Hegelian dialectics which, by figuring synthesis in terms of filiation, seem fated to encounter their own deconstructible limits.

In *The Work of Mourning*, therefore, Derrida is enjoined to testify to the **law** of mourning which is found at the very origin of our conception of (what is) 'living' or 'present'. Throughout these texts, a certain law of mourning permeates **friendship**'s very conditions of possibility, since there is no friendship without the chance of one friend dying before the other. Friendship is thus forged amid this structurally irreducible possibility, in which survival and mourning enter into the relationship right from the start, long before death. Mourning therefore *begins* with the friend rather than at friendship's end in death. However, the 'theoretical' resources of Derrida's work on death, non-present remains, mourning or ghosts cannot be taken to provide adequate reserves for dealing with the irreplaceable **singularity** of the other's death. For all their obvious worth, they do not give us the ability to mourn or to undergo mourning worthy of the name. Indeed, the preservation of a 'know-how' about mourning or, for that matter, assured 'knowledge' of the departed risks a domesticating reappropriation of the other's death. This is, for Derrida, poorly calculated in that it encourages unresponsiveness, and indeed irresponsibility, in regard to that death. (In **Adieu**, Derrida reminds us that for **Levinas** the death of the **other** is the first death in that it is this *other* death, rather than my own, which individuates me in my **responsibility**.) Without enduring this **aporia** whereby every deliberate act of mourning founds itself on a certain **impossibility**, one risks the worst in mourning: narcissism, self-regard, self-pity, good conscience, denial, overstated intimacy, veiled score-settling. At the same time, however, one cannot simply forgo a certain interiorization of the other in death. (It is the death of the other, indeed, which calls for the 'interiority' in me, or of me.) Since death implies the irreversible disappearance of the other, the dead are no longer anything 'outside' us, and if we are to remember or mourn at all we cannot but interiorize them. (Once more, 'living' is nothing other than living on, surviving *in* or *as* the experience of mourning the other, as if from start to finish.) Yet what we endure in the experience of mourning is the resistance of the other in us, the inassimilable alterity of the departed friend, that which – as Barthes puts it – remains undialectical. Similarly, one cannot easily forgo all the genres, rhetorics, rites or institutions of mourning which tend to domesticate death, and yet through enduring them one hazards exposure to *whatever* resists the work of appropriation that they inevitably encourage. Each death is in a sense absolutely unique, demanding a singular response each time of asking; yet between the asymmetrical difference of the other and the irrepressible tendency towards interiorization, mourning remains far from indivisible. This divisibility repeats itself in the experience or representation of each death (even at its most intense, mourning is never simply 'present', once and for all), which it is the task of each mourning rite to **negotiate** anew.

It is worth noting that such issues arise in '**Fors**: The Anglish Words of Nicolas Abraham and Maria Torok'. Derrida poses the question of mourning by reconsidering, as he does in **Memoires for Paul de Man**, the difference between introjection, which is love for the other in me (the other is introjected into the subject's person), and incorporation, where the other is retained as a discrete foreign body (the other is incorporated as nonetheless distinct). For post-Freudian psychology, effective mourning generally works to introject the other. In this perspective, the retention of a separated other within the self through incorporation is seen to risk the onset of pathology. As Derrida points out, however, incorporation – by resisting an interiorizing

trace

assimilation of the other in the mourning process – may involve a certain respect for the other's difference and heterogeneity. Since incorporation may therefore entail a greater fidelity to the otherness of the other, we should not be too quick to suppose that introjection is wholly unproblematic as a type of mourning. While Derrida resists the established interpretation of the work of mourning, he nonetheless recognizes that incorporation can serve to externalize and deaden the other that now lives nowhere but in me. By seeking to preserve, contain or encrypt the other as a sort of hermetic pocket, incorporation fails to acknowledge the non-excludable or non-separable nature of this foreign body, and may amount to an impossible sort of narcissism. In mourning, then, the alterity of the other offers resistance to both these processes of incorporation and introjection, and it is precisely these resistances which one must respect, recognize and negotiate in assuming one's responsibilities to and for the other.

touch   See **on touching**.

Tout autre est tout autre   See especially ***The Gift of Death***.

trace   In ***Of Grammatology*** Derrida examines **Saussure**'s theory of language as a signifying system. (See also ***Margins of Philosophy***, ***Positions*** and ***Speech and Phenomena*** for Derrida's reading of the concept of the sign within the Western tradition.) For Saussure, the connection between the signifier and the signified is purely relational and arbitrary. Language is therefore construed by him as a system of differential relations. For Derrida, however, if every sign acquires its value only on the strength of its difference from other signs, nevertheless other signs leave their trace in the sense that they are constitutive of the difference that maintains the sign's identity. Every sign bears the traces of the others from which it differs, but to which it also defers in order to receive its value as a (differential) sign. The trace is thus not reducible to the sign, nor can it be turned into a sign. Instead, the trace calls to be thought in terms of the non-signifying difference that is 'originarily' at play in all signification. However, since for Derrida the trace is always the trace of another trace, it does not give itself as simple origin. (For Derrida, trace is not a master word but an always replaceable term in an unmasterable series including *différance*, **supplement**, **writing**, **cinder**, and so on.) Nor can the trace be thought in terms of the logic of **presence**. Since every sign in its manifestation or apparent 'presence' always includes traces of others which are supposedly 'absent', the trace can be reduced to neither side of the presence-absence opposition so prized by the **metaphysical** tradition. The trace thus redescribes the entire field which the metaphysics of presence seeks to dominate throughout history. The trace names that non-systematizable reserve which is at once constitutive and unrepresentable within such a field.

See also, for instance, **Cinders**, '*Ousia* and *Grammē*' in ***Margins of Philosophy***, ***Positions***.

translation For **Derrida**, philosophy in the classical sense generally prizes thought above **writing**. For philosophy, the concept in all its purity and rigour transcends linguistic inscription. **Socrates**, as the philosopher who supposedly does not write, provides a model for the entire tradition here, although in ***The Post Card*** Derrida gets much mileage from Matthew Paris's thirteenth-century illustration which depicts Socrates writing with **Plato**, his philosophical scribe, seeming to direct the process from behind his back. (The apparent reversal that is suggested here powerfully recalls the redescription of writing's relationship to **speech** which characterizes Derrida's **deconstruction** of the **metaphysical** tradition.)

However, to the extent that **philosophy** generally believes in the transcendence of the idea over writing and language, the problem of translation is rarely accorded much philosophical significance. For Derrida, however, since philosophy cannot transcend or surpass its own inscription, translation is a condition of philosophy itself. Translation, however, is at once always necessary and **impossible** in absolute rigour. The **proper name**, for instance, appears utterly resistant to translation since, while it remains a basic element or inscription of language, it seems in its irreplaceability to stand outside the linguistic system of differential-exchangeable values. In 'Des tours de Babel' (in ***Psyche***), however, Derrida argues that Babel as untranslatable proper name is also precisely the name that, in the Biblical story, inscribes itself in language in order to usher in translation's necessity. To the extent that the proper name (or the title – in this case, of Derrida's own essay) enjoys a legibility which nevertheless remains somewhat **undecidable** or unreckonable as an object of linguistic exchange, it calls for precisely the translation it resists. Derrida's essay provides a long commentary on Walter **Benjamin**'s 'The Task of the Translator', in which the relationship of the original to the translation is in question. Here, the translation is indebted to the original from which it receives its very task (although let us be wary here – Derrida's own writing puts in question the idea of an 'original' before translation, and indeed 'Des tours de Babel' reads Maurice de Gandillac's translation of Benjamin's essay, being itself originally written for translation). Yet the original is also beholden to translation for its very survival (and translation might be another name, here, for the irreducible yet always **singular** advent of 'reading'). Translation, then, would appear to throw up an economy of unreckonable debt in which balancing the books is the impossible and unremitting task of the translator. And no amount of general, 'theoretical' elaboration of the problem of translation will lessen this task in its always singular calling.

See also **'Living On: Borderlines'**.

— U —

'Ulysses Gramophone: Hear Say Yes in Joyce' First published in French in 1987, and subsequently included in **Acts of Literature**. For some comments on this essay, see the entry on **Psyche**. See also **sexual difference, yes, yes**.

unconditional The unconditional is that which remains without limit or condition. Derrida frequently appeals to the unconditional. He speaks of a **hospitality** which cannot truly earn its name within the limited or conditional forms of the conventional welcome extended to the expected guest. He reminds us that the only forgiving genuinely worthy of the name goes beyond **forgiveness** of that which is already deemed forgivable. His thinking of the **decision** makes of it a **singular event** called up by profound **undecidability** rather than by an established set of conditions (rules, laws, norms, etc.) which equip us with the resources to decide. For Derrida the **gift**, if there is any, must exceed all exchangeable values or calculable relations; the **invention**, if there is any, must go (impossibly) beyond what is presently inventable. In contrast to an always constructed and constructable **law**, **justice** is unconditional in that it is beyond such construction. Thus justice is undeconstructible and indeed indestructible.

Hospitality, giving, forgiving, invention, decision, justice – Derrida reminds us that the unconditional abides at the very origin of the seminal concepts which give the West its history, politics and culture. However, Derrida does not insist upon the unconditional simply in order to deride or delegitimize the conditional forms which, for instance, hospitality must take, forgiveness must take, or decision must take. Rather, since the unconditional remains indestructibly at the origin of such concepts in their conditional or historical forms, it must be recalled wherever they are at stake in order to continually rethink and indeed actively transform the 'conditional', notably in the fields of law, state-craft, international relations, and so on.

In *Rogues*, Derrida contrasts the unconditional with the notion of **sovereignty**. For him, the unconditional is not sovereign (and, indeed, extends beyond sovereignty's limits), to the extent that it does not license or empower a master, or arise *on condition of* the 'masterable-possible'. The unconditional, in other words, powerfully resists the principle of power, or is powerful precisely in its powerlessness. The unconditional leads instead to the 'experience of the **impossible**' (forgiveness of the unforgivable, invention of the uninventable, etc.), yet opens up the very possibility of the **future** and the **other**. Nonetheless, the unconditional must continually transact with and articulate its relation to sovereignty in the interests of the **democracy to come**. Derrida's essay, 'The University Without Condition', included in *Without Alibi*, tasks the **university** itself with this always pressing and never fully reconcilable **negotiation**.

See also *Geneses, Genealogies, Genres and Genius*, *Learning to Live Finally*, *Negotiations*, *On Cosmopolitanism and Forgiveness*, *Rogues*, *Without Alibi*.

undecidability   See **decision**.

university   Despite the classical origins of the university in the medieval world and ancient academies, the emergence of the modern institution, characterized by the foundation of Humboldt's University of Berlin in

university

1810, might be viewed more broadly as a reflection of the philosophical project of German Idealism. If the founding of the modern university takes place on the strength of this philosophical movement, however, it simultaneously raises questions for **philosophy** itself. For what exactly *is* it that founds the university? Just as the founding of the **law** cannot be considered exactly 'legal' (nor, for that matter, can the lawfulness be decided of *whatever* founds the law), since it must by definition precede the distinction between the lawful and unlawful that can only take place within the field of law itself once instituted, so the instituting of the university cannot be considered merely a university event, an auto-foundational moment in which we witness the university's inauguration by itself. (Elsewhere, Derrida makes a similar point about the American Declaration of Independence, which is signed and thus given authority by the very same "People" that it in fact establishes and projects as the founding concept of the nation – see **Negotiations**.) Since, in the German model, the modern university is granted authority and legitimacy by dint of the principle of **reason**, the question of the grounding of this principle as the source of the modern university's rationale is one that Derrida is quick to take up. For what is the rational basis of the Enlightenment's appeal to reason? If the answer resides in reason itself, then this implies a worrying degree of question-begging, giving rise to a tautological situation that hardly squares with the very precepts of rational thought. If not, however, then the university's origins remain suspended, beyond commonplace reason, over something of an abyss. Just as the question of the legality of the law cannot be answered definitively by or within the law, so the university as both an instrument and expression of reason cannot articulate its own rationality or grounding without entering into an **aporia**, albeit one that Derrida tells us we must confront in the interests of a more faithful response to reason's call.

Kant seeks to recast and reduce this intractable crisis surrounding the university's foundations and legitimacy, by reimagining the modern university's organization in terms of a parliamentary model in which the higher faculties (theology, law, medicine) occupy the right bench and defend the statutes of government. The philosophy faculty, meanwhile, occupies the left bench in order to defend and promote truth and thus to arbitrate within the university in the interests of a free system of government. (See 'Mochlos in **Right to Philosophy**.) Philosophy supplies secure foundations for the positive knowledge produced by the other disciplines which largely serve the interests of the state. Philosophy's 'freedom' to tell the truth in and to the university is in a sense unfettered by the law or by the responsibility for law-making, although of course this 'freedom' is also given or instituted by the law or the state itself. Such a 'freedom' constitutes both philosophy's strength and its weakness (or, we might say, its strength-as-weakness or its weakness-as-strength). The division of the university according to this parliamentary model seeks to resolve an insoluble legitimation crisis, then, by recasting the aporia that besets the institution's institution in terms of a 'conflict' that ultimately gives the university its organizational structure and overarching unity. However, as Derrida points out, borrowing from Kant himself, the distinction between 'left' and 'right' which gives the university this orientation cannot be thought to arise from a purely logical determination that transcends the always subjective standpoint of a body. 'Left' and 'right' thus belong to a sensory topology which hardly grants access to a fixed and reliable concept or a universal or objective ground for the university.

In the German university model, not only is philosophy an integral part of the institution in its indispensable function as the very discipline which poses rigorous questions to the other faculties in the name and pursuit of truth; it is also, of course, that which itself institutes the institution. This leaves philosophy in a strange position, if indeed it is a 'position' at all. The classical desire of philosophy to attain a meta-institutional or extra-territorial standpoint, to become pure thought thinking itself, is continually confounded by the fact that philosophy remains an indispensable part of the institutional body it institutes. Philosophy cannot hope to transcend the field that it itself partitions. Neither, however, can it wholly belong to the university of which it is inextricably a part, as one discipline among others. Since the university could not have been founded without it, philosophy is never just found on the university's 'inside' as an entirely interior element participating in and contributing straightforwardly to the 'whole', the *universitas*. The part thus remains larger than the whole of which it is a part: in **Glas**, Derrida names this type of effect one of transcendental excrescence, close to the logic of the **supplement**. This produces a situation which Derrida refers to in terms of an asymmetrical contract between philosophy and the institution, one that makes an angle between the university and itself. Such an 'angle' might be taken to mark out the deconstructibility of

violence 235

the university's concept and space, opening the institution to the uncontainably **other** and, indeed, to an unpredictable **future**.

Thus, when confronted in the 1970s with government plans for aggressive reform of the French educational system, plans which threatened to undermine the place of philosophy in the curriculum, Derrida took up an activist stance of clear opposition to the proposals, yet called less for a straightforward defence of philosophy in its established institutional guise, than for a transformative rethinking of the 'philosophical' which was itself tied to a rethinking of the question of the institution. This was to happen alongside the setting up of counter-institutions such as the **Greph** and the International College of Philosophy (**Ciph**). Far from dictating the anarchic abandonment of institutions, something Derrida considered at once impracticable, undesirable and impossibly 'purist', **deconstruction** (of the kind found in Derrida's eventful **re-marking** of the Enlightenment tradition of the university, let us say) called for counter-institutional initiatives that would on each occasion partake of some form of structural impermanence or continual transformation and therefore profound instability. Each, in other words, hoped to assume rather than deny their own deconstructibility, **negotiating** in their own singular fashion those interminable struggles, at once internecine and heteronomous, that beset the institution as a species of its **auto-immune** disorder.

Veils   A volume published in French in 1998 and in English in 2001, which includes 'Savoir' by **Cixous** and Derrida's '**A Silkworm of One's Own**'.

violence   On ethics, politics, violence and the state, see **Adieu**.

On Europe, the state, etc. and violence see also **On Cosmopolitanism and Forgiveness**, **Rogues**.

On the violence of foundation, see **'Faith and Knowledge'**, **'Force of Law'**. See the latter, too, for violence and the law, mystical and divine violence. See also 'Declarations of Independence' in **Negotiations** for the violence of foundation.

On violence, metaphysics and the other see 'Violence and Metaphysics' in **Writing and Difference**.

On violence and the animal, see **The Animal That Therefore I Am**.

For violence, writing and the proper name, see **Of Grammatology**. On writing and violence, see also **phonocentrism, speech, technicity**.

— **W** —

Without Alibi   This 2002 collection includes five essays in English translation, dating from 1993 to 2000, mostly written as lectures to be given for specific occasions. The project for the volume which brings them together arose at the suggestion of Peggy Kamuf, one of Derrida's foremost translators. It includes an invaluable introduction by her.

To think the alibi is, in a sense, to think our ethical, political, legal and juridical history, since it is difficult to imagine how the concepts and practices licensed by these historical categories could be founded without some recourse to a notion of the alibi. This is also true of the **lie**, as Derrida observes in the first essay included in this volume. Without the lie and without the alibi (remembering, as Kamuf suggests, that an alibi may also be another name which we give to all the figures and processes of resemblance which permit particular instances to be subsumed under general categories), one would not only struggle to think **ethics** and **law** in the classical sense, but 'truth' in its Western guise more generally. Derrida, however, wants not simply to resist the alibi, but to trace out its internal resistances. Thus, he attempts to think the 'without alibi' beyond the classical discourse of the autonomous and intentional subject, as one who is able to declare presence freely at a place and time construed as indivisibly present or 'here-and-now'. Seeming to take himself as example, Derrida acknowledges that his entire life has been lived by way of the alibi, and in terms of all the displacements or removals it implies, not least since the very language – **French** – that in a certain way defines the cultural, intellectual, political and geographical movements and upheavals through which he has lived is at once singularly irreplaceable for him, and yet the persistent site of an inextricable non-belonging. Put more simply, in **Monolingualism of the Other**, Derrida writes: 'I have only one language; it is not mine', a formulation which inscribes upon any ensuing testimonial utterance an irreducible displacement or dislocation of the subject in language. Indeed, it is only *as if* Derrida proposes this statement for himself – *by definition*, in fact, since such a linguistic utterance declares and, for that matter, re-enacts a certain non-belonging or non-appropriability which structures the very relation of language to the subject. Put another way, the claim, plea or 'excuse' that one was *elsewhere* cannot be eliminated from the very speech act we might make of Derrida's supposed declaration at the beginning of Monolingualism of the Other, one that we nonetheless take irresistibly as a certain **confession**, profession or **testimony**. This is another way of saying that what is inventive or fictive cannot be excluded from the structural conditions of possibility that impose themselves on a telling of the 'truth'. The task Derrida therefore sets himself in these essays is to put in question the notion (indeed, the **fiction**) of an indivisible unity, **presence**, non-self-difference, or masterful **sovereignty** – of subject, law, language, truth, and so on – while acknowledging the impossibility of acquitting oneself (for instance, in this very task) entirely without alibi.

In 'History of the Lie: Prologomena', Derrida reminds us that the dominant conception of the lie rests upon the assumption of an intentional act on the part of the liar. Thus one can utter a false statement by way of an error or mistake, and yet not lie. To lie is therefore to intentionally mislead or deceive the other, which of course one can do while still telling a certain 'truth'. But is it possible to lie to oneself? On the strength of this classical determination of the lie, to tell oneself lies would appear to involve deliberately concealing from oneself a truth which one already knows, or at any rate believes one knows. This seems illogical and undoable. Yet, as we have just observed, when Derrida writes 'I have only one language; it is not mine', we cannot assume that he is telling (himself) the truth in a simple sense. The phrase itself implies that the subject is not wholly or 'truly' present in (its) language (even if a subject finds it possible to declare as much). But is Derrida therefore lying to others or indeed to himself, by way of this remark? If the subject is somehow other than fully or 'truly' present in this statement – which would seem an essential feature of the lie in its prevalent sense – then the phrase nevertheless openly declares this very 'truth'. In precisely the sense that it admits or declares certain structural features of the lie (the disjuncture of subject and language), Derrida's remark – if it can indeed ever be 'his' – conveys and contains a particular truth; yet at the same time the phrase itself stages the very impossibility of Derrida telling himself the truth, or 'his' truth, without possible remainder or (self) difference. And Derrida – at any rate in the form of this particular remark – knows this; that is, he doesn't exactly deceive himself, but nor is he able to reclaim his own language or utterance in order to reflect or restitute to himself his 'own' truth. To put it differently, Derrida cannot but testify to the truth of a statement which he knows must *enact* as much as declare a certain dislocation of language and the subject. It is as if he must perjure himself, if one may allow the legal reference. Such 'perjury' is therefore always possible, in fact it is a condition of possibility, there where truth is told. The lie promises truth (in the sense that its dominant conception presupposes an underlying 'truth'), but truth cannot promise itself (to itself) without the possibility of the lie. Thus, once the traditional conception is questioned of the sovereign subject (that is, of a wholly unified, masterful, non-self-different figure endowed with the intentional or performative possibility of an 'I will' or 'I can'), indeed once it is rethought as phantasm or fable, dominant conceptions begin to unravel of the lie and of the alibi (or, for that matter, of testimony and confession), conceptions that are so critical to ethical, legal, juridical, political and philosophical sovereignty. The aporia of the 'lie to oneself', in other words, deconstructs the indivisibility of sovereignty in a variety of forms.

Derrida examines the question of the lie via Socrates, Plato, Aristotle, Augustine, Rousseau, Kant, Nietzsche and Arendt (among others), but asks whether it would be possible to tell (to ourselves) the history of the lie in a truthful sense, not only where 'truth' equates to knowledge but also perhaps where it constitutes a certain 'belief' (we can believe what we tell ourselves to be true, and yet remain unreconciled with the truthful utterance, which may indeed demonstrate its very truthfulness through precisely this irreconcilability, as Derrida's remark in *Monolingualism of the Other* implies). Nor should we presume too hastily to relate (to ourselves) the history of the *concept* of the lie, as if this concept could attain a unified, self-identical or absolutely 'truthful' form.

Nevertheless, we must also recognize that, since the lie in its classical determination cannot maintain itself in the purity and rigour of a self-identical and ahistorical concept, it does have an historical determinacy (consonant with the classical conception of the subject and of sovereignty) whose conditions may not extend infinitely. Derrida's work in exploring not only the heterogeneity of truth/lying, on the one hand, and the fabulous or phantasmic, on the other, but also the deconstructibility of the former in relation to the latter, may be seen as part of a larger set of interests in **(actu)virtuality, spectrality,** modern mediatization, **technology, mondialization,** and the '**democracy to come**'. The analysis of such phenomena is, for Derrida, not well served by a **metaphysics** of truth as revelation or unveiling.

In the latter stages of this lecture, Derrida turns to the question of **France**'s reluctance, after the Second World War, to acknowledge or admit its culpability in the events of the Holocaust. (This is raised by Derrida in the context of what he sees as an intensifying worldwideization of scenes of public repentance.) For Mitterand, the French president from 1981 to 1995, the post-war French Republic had nothing to confess, since during the period in question it had been effectively suspended by the advent of the *État Français* (as the French state was renamed by the Vichy government). While Derrida was among those who urged Mitterand to adopt a different position (one which President Chirac subsequently reversed), he also observes in the lecture that other French politicians of the time saw the danger of effectively legitimating the *État Français* through the process of a post-war acknowledgement of guilt. For such a move might imply there was some continuity between the *État Français* and the French Republic itself. While Derrida does not affiliate himself with such views, they do open the question of whether the post-war hesitation over an official declaration of the historical 'truth' of the French state should be understood simply in terms of lying, or by way of a history of lying. For that matter, does the official acknowledgement of culpability on the part of the post-war French state during the 1990s in fact inhibit further **memory** work as a work of 'truth'? While such declarations are perhaps a sign of 'progress' towards the Enlightenment goal of perfectibility, is the cause of truth less than perfectly served by the ideological function doubtlessly imagined for such 'confession'?

Without Alibi contains a series of texts, then, with a number of discernible connections around such issues. 'Typewriter Ribbon: Limited Ink (2)' looks once more to the work of **Paul de Man**, alongside a reading of the confessions of **Rousseau** and **St Augustine**, in which truth-telling is everywhere **supplemented** by the irreducible possibility of fiction. (Derrida is particularly interested in a lie recounted by Rousseau in his *Confessions*, whereby Rousseau perjures himself by blaming another for his own crime.) The essay sees Derrida tackle de Man's thinking of a certain resistance offered by the materiality of the letter. More widely, Derrida endeavours to think the **singularity** of the **event** and the technical reproducibility implied by the 'machine' or the machine-like, in terms of a heterogeneous yet inseparable conjunction. As Derrida observes in a number of texts, the possibility of repeatability remains at the origin of the singular instance, which far from attaining some indivisibly self-contained and thus static self-presence, always **remarks** itself in terms of the **promise** of the 'to come'. In *Without Alibi* the notion of the *oeuvre* provides a means to think this relation of 'event' and 'machine'. '"Le Parjure," *Perhaps*: Storytelling and Lying' takes its title from a novel by Henri Thomas which fictionalizes a 'real' event, namely the charge of perjury brought against de Man in America in the 1950s. Here again, this accusation exposes the legal subject in precisely its fictionality to the force of a certain **deconstruction**. In a highly resonant phrase, perjury is therefore thought of as a 'fatal experience'. In 'Psychoanalysis Searches the States of Its Soul', Derrida suggests that the key psychoanalytic insight concerns psychic cruelty. At a time when, as Derrida observes in *Resistances of Psychoanalysis*, psychoanalysis has widely fallen from favour, it may yet provide the resources to resist the cruelty of sovereignty, as that which exemplifies itself in the death penalty. In 'The University Without Condition', it is the 'unconditional **university**' which offers resistance to the fiction or phantasm of sovereignty. The very task of the university is thus to **counter** and deconstruct sovereignty, whether in its state form, its legal or institutional form, or in the form of a subject construed in its broadest sense: namely, as that which reimposes the 'masterable-possible' as a resistant limit to the singular possibility of the event or the 'to come'. Here, then, the '**unconditional**' as the very principle of the university is distinguished from the form that sovereignty itself takes, precisely by way of the resistance that unconditionality offers to (the fiction of) sovereignty's mastery or authority. (The university's unconditionality is in this respect similar to literature's 'right to say everything'.) In contrast to the vested power of sovereignty, that is, the 'unconditional' is powerful only in its powerlessness, or in other words, through its resistance to the very principle of power. Derrida asserts the 'university without condition' not as a description of what in fact exists, but rather in terms of a declarative commitment or appeal, a profession of faith in the university 'to come', a profession which – as a public pledge – gives the university its specificity and potentiality in the 'here-now'. By way of what he sees as a particular mutation in the university's classical form, Derrida associates the task of profession with the production of singular *oeuvres* by the professor of today and tomorrow. For Derrida, the principle of unconditionality is promised most of all by the Humanities, as the scene of a certain resistance and questioning in the name of 'truth'. Derrida proposes several tasks for the Humanities 'to come': research into the histories of man, humanity, and the discourse of rights (here, once more, questions of **animality** and **sexual difference** cannot be excluded from consideration in determining the nature and direction of such inquiry); the study and analysis of democracy, sovereignty, the nation-state, the subject and citizen, and international **law**; the history and future of 'profession', in all its senses, in view of these sorts of projects; and, similarly, the history and possibility of **literature**, fiction, the **performative** and the 'as if'. For Derrida, such tasks would not just be 'academic' or 'theoretical' in nature, but as would give rise to practical interventions and transformations in and beyond the terrain upon which they operate. In other words, they would commit themselves to the possibility of the event, beyond the horizon of an already possible possibility.

The university today is also the scene of a certain virtualization occurring in a variety of senses (computerization, electronic communication, digitization, delocalized **archivization, global** migrancy and 'internationalization', and so on). While Derrida asserts that the idea of the university space must be protected, through an always vulnerable type of immunity, from absolute and disintigrative disruption, nevertheless through precisely the disruption of its topology or 'place' the university is well positioned to offer analyses and interventions in relation to a host of contemporary forces and trends. Derrida's lecture asks searching questions about the history of 'work' (presumed, by some, to be undergoing profound transformation as **globalization** intensifies), and also poses the question of its relation to profession and professionalization. Indeed, the Humanities might be the very place to ask such questions since, as Derrida speculates, the figure of the humanist may have emerged in response to the question of work – from the question of work's duration in the middle ages, to that of worker's rights and the right to work more recently, which Derrida sees as historically linked to the question of *human* rights.

writing Within the **metaphysical** tradition that determines **being** as **presence**, **speech** as an expression of living immediacy is typically given priority over writing as merely a lifeless copy, a worldly instrument of detachable representations, and thus a harbinger of absence and **death**. Writing in the classical sense is, then, viewed as auxiliary, extrinsic, privative and indeed **violent** in relation to the spoken word as the source of the subject's self-expression. In speech, the 'word' gives access to the 'soul' or '**spirit**', and thus appeals ultimately to an **onto-theological** foundation or transcendental signified that rescues language from the forms of difference which writing then comes to embody.

In 'Plato's Pharmacy' (see **Dissemination**), Derrida examines the following scene from the *Phaedrus*: Phaedrus keeps under his cloak the written manuscript of a speech which he has not learnt by heart, hoping as he does to convince **Socrates** of his ability to bring it back to life without recourse to mechanical memorization. Here, the potentially 'good' sense of writing as an aid to living **memory** nevertheless always risks the 'bad' possibility of a return to mechanical reference, inanimate and unthinking recitation, lifeless **supplementation** of the living word (the script under the cloak). Writing is therefore a drug (***pharmakon***), the remedial properties of which cannot be reliably distilled from its potentially poisonous effects. For Derrida, then, the metaphysical tradition (from Plato to Rousseau to Saussure to Husserl and beyond) thinks of writing as, in Rousseau's own terms, a 'dangerous supplement'. Supplementation is that which the metaphysics of presence projects as inessential, impure, perverse, violent, or, at bottom, different in an oppositional sense. Deprived of the supplement, however, the metaphysical tradition could not constitute itself, as Derrida painstakingly argues. **Différance, supplement, trace, cinder** – for Derrida, these substitutable terms improperly name the non-signifying difference that traverses every **mark**, at once producing and overflowing each mark's very possibility. Such terms, moreover, allow us to redescribe the entire field that the metaphysics of presence has sought to dominate through the exclusion or repression of writing. For they all imply that the forms of presence prized by metaphysics rely on an unpresentable and unsystematizable remainder, an 'originary' play of difference that remains irreducible to oppositional thought – and, for that matter, to the classical determination of a pure 'origin'. This play of difference or *différance* is given a number of nicknames by Derrida: originary or **arche-writing**, the general 'text', and so on. While this enlarged and transformed sense of writing is clearly different from that which the metaphysical tradition attributes to writing in its narrow or classical guise, nevertheless for Derrida it is the deconstructibility of the metaphysical opposition between speech and writing – that is to say, it is his insight that the supposedly 'negative' features of writing in fact irreducibly supplement speech, presence, and so forth – which leads to deconstruction's thinking of arche-writing more broadly.

See also **'Différance'**, **Dissemination**, **'I Have a Taste for the Secret'**, **Margins of Philosophy**, **Of Grammatology**, **'Signature Event Context'**, **Speech and Phenomena, Writing and Difference**.

Writing and Difference   This volume, one of Derrida's three major publications in 1967 (**Of Grammatology** and **Speech and Phenomena** were the other two), includes a series of essays which elaborate many of the themes and arguments central to his work during this period.

The collection opens with 'Force and Signification', which is largely devoted to a reading of Jean Rousset's *Forme et Signification*. In this essay, Derrida analyzes the **structuralist** phenomenon or attitude, which for him far predates the advent of Structuralism in the mid-twentieth century. One key feature of a structuralist approach is the fascination with **form** rather than **force**. (Here, Derrida asserts that literary criticism therefore tends fundamentally to be structuralist.) All structuralisms look for structural totalities in which they see a coherent and determined system of relations – a unified 'whole' – dominating over and ultimately neutralizing the living energies or forces that one might otherwise think produced them. For such forces are ultimately to be understood, by structuralist thought at least, as a condition of a system rather than constitutive of it.

In Rousset's book, a concern to avoid historicism, biographism or psychologism in discerning the internal 'truth' or underlying structure of the work leads to a certain inattentiveness to the question of historicity (which is not the same as history in the ordinary sense). Putting this question differently, the structuralist viewpoint considers its 'object' to be fully *presentable*, without rigorously confronting the issue of the play of forces that produce and maintain structures. (Derrida's larger aim here is to align key features of structuralist thinking with the metaphysical determination of **presence**, in order to dispute the suggestion that Structuralism breaks with **metaphysics**.) Force, as **Nietzsche** teaches us, is never simply present as a unitary, static, self-same phenomenon; rather, it only arises amid a struggle of forces. Force always receives its possibility from counter-force. Thus, force is never simply in one place at one time, but happens between things (thus spacing itself, we might say) in a movement that is also irreducibly temporal. From such a perspective, we might even say that forms do not so much exert force as receive their very possibility from forces in struggle, forces which exert themselves according to a process which we cannot think simply in terms of the activity of a being, object or presence (not least since force, as spatio-temporal play, cannot be referred to as a simple or single form). If, here, Derrida strategically reverses the priority of form over force, this reversal is just one feature of his deconstructive technique. For to differentiate form and force according to a simple opposition would be to reinstate just the kind of metaphysical duality that **deconstruction** is concerned to put in question. (It would also be, in a sense, to beg the very question of form and force rather than resolve it, since such an opposition in merely its restated or reasserted form would leave unanswered the question of what it is that forms or forces the opposition itself.) To portray force, in total contrast to form, as an accident which befalls structure *from the outside* is to miss certain difficulties that are in fact inherent in the very question of form. For instance, a structure is nothing if not organized. Yet what organizes it? As Derrida observes, the sense of coherence of a structure is typically maintained by the assumption that it is motivated and has purpose. In other words, structures determine themselves as non-anarchic only by reference to a telos (an 'end' or goal that implies an 'origin' or motivating intention, even if not a subjective one). This recognition brings out, once again, the reliance of structuralism on metaphysical assumptions. But it also implies that, precisely in order to maintain itself *as* form, form must in a certain way be forced or enforced. Force is, therefore, precisely a feature or condition of form, a condition which form seeks to stifle but cannot exclude.

In 'Cogito and the History of Madness', the second piece in the collection, Derrida weighs **Foucault**'s attempt to write a history of madness while necessarily repeating forms of discourse that find their origin or context in the precepts and language of **reason**. Such a project therefore risks the re-internment or reappropriation of madness – or rather the madness/reason opposition – as an 'object' of knowledge or inquiry. A key question here, however, concerns the manner in which such an 'object' is produced in analytical terms by way of its empirical determination in a critical discourse which cannot but pretend to transcend the empiricity it wants to analyze. Furthermore, Derrida finds in Foucault's historicism the same effect that in **Of Grammatology** he discerns in **Levi-Strauss**: a particular event assigned a certain historical significance comes to rely on conditions of possibility that the analysis itself renders universal. Derrida therefore argues that Foucault makes of the violent partition and objectification of madness at once an historical occurrence taking place in seventeenth-century France, and yet also effectively a condition of the very possibility of history in general. If history itself is the history of reason (a reason which, Foucault argues, constitutes itself at bottom by a decisive separation from madness), then the seventeenth-century discourse of madness is but an instance in this history, a determinate form that reason takes in a particular setting. As such, it cannot provide the basis to account for what Derrida calls 'the historicity of reason in general', and can therefore be granted neither 'absolute privilege' nor 'archetypal exemplarity' in the way Foucault seems to attempt.

Derrida, however, does not highlight apparent contradictions in Foucault's project simply to castigate his work as a fall from reason, logic, rigour or sense. Instead, he puts in question the very distinction between madness and reason that establishes the grounds of Foucault's argument and, indeed, of its limitations. Turning to **Descartes** (for Foucault, the exemplary thinker of the 'classical age' which itself becomes responsible for the partition of the mad), Derrida shows that madness is not for him the most serious threat to the quest for rational certainty that takes place through a general process of doubting. Indeed, madness is not just a condition of possibility of reason in the sense that it facilitates one phase in the process of doubting on its way towards certitude. Madness is, as Derrida shows, more radically a possibility of reason, in the sense that Descartes's argument has to acknowledge the possibility of 'thought' being all the while *mad* as it proclaims the Cogito. For *Cogito, sum* must hold true whether one is awake or in dreams, mad or sane, enlightened or deceived. At its most 'proper' or 'inaugural' moment (which is also its most 'hyperbolical' or excessive moment), nothing is therefore less certain than the 'good sense' of the Cogito, since for Descartes's thesis to work, sanity is precisely *not* constitutive of its certitude. Rather than seeking to decide between the empirical and the universal as the origin of reason's historicity and madness's partition, then, Derrida shows how, when one turns to the Cartesian heritage, 'thought' can propose or grapple with the determinate, conceptual or historical form of all except the hyperbolic moment that grants its possibility. This, perhaps, is the very condition of **philosophy** itself, its interminable crisis, which is also its historicity. Foucault's reply to Derrida's essay, 'My Body, this Paper, this Fire' was published several years later. While Derrida had begun his essay by declaring gratitude and admiration for his erstwhile teacher, the exchange damaged their relationship for a long time, perhaps irreversibly.

'Edward Jabès and the Question of the Book' reads the writings of Jabès in terms of the always fraught and risky confrontation with the metaphysical tradition and, by extension, the concept of the **book** to which it may be linked. Derrida's reading leads him to aver that what gives the book its very possibility does not belong to the book itself, and that the book's 'origin' therefore remains illegible to and within it. Here, Derrida is most decidedly *not* identifying such an 'origin' with an author figure construed as stably external to the text. Instead, he is making the suggestion (as he does in the essay **'Différance'**) that what structures the identity of terms, or produces their legibility in general, cannot be included by them. Thus, the significations that seek to find meaning or sense in the supposedly stable and settled form of the book are produced by that which can never be limited to the space or work of the book itself. In other words, the book writes itself only on the strength of the *différance* that it may never simply appropriate or contain, a *différance* which refigures the unitary structure of the origin in terms of play, non-presence, and the original possibility of repetition. Such arguments are reprised in 'Ellipsis', the last text included in *Writing and Difference*.

'Violence and Metaphysics' sees Derrida embark on an extended reading of the work of Emmanuel **Levinas**, to whose thought he returned in several later texts. Levinas is read against the backdrop of the question of the **Greek** and the non-Greek (as both limit and possibility) in the philosophical heritage, and in relation to the 'great voices' of post-Hegelian thought: **Husserl** and **Heidegger**. In this essay, Derrida explores the problem of otherness occasioned by Levinas's claim that, if the **other** could be known as such, it would not be other. For Levinas, the **ethical** relation to the other must conceive of itself in terms of a nonviolence based on respect for the other's absolute alterity. Such thinking, says Derrida, looks to a possible liberation from metaphysics. However, the philosophy, language, concept or phenomenon of the other always risks a certain **violence** to the other – and indeed to itself, inflicting its own limits upon itself, negating itself in its own affirmation. This relates to a complicated play of 'egoity' in the discourse of the other, which Derrida pursues in the relation of Husserlian to Levinasian thought. (Rather than simply dismiss the alter egoity of the other as a violent appropriation, Derrida suggests that to think of the 'I' as itself always the other's other grants the very possibility of respect.) Derrida explores ways in which Levinas – for all the complexity of his thought – nonetheless tries to salvage living **speech**, over and above **writing**, as the source of a more immediate relation to the other in its fundamental alterity. Yet if the possibility of an end to violence can only be stated through discourse, this is nevertheless violent to the other at its very origin, Derrida suggests. Such an **aporia** cannot be overlooked if a lesser violence is to be practised within an economy (which is also that of philosophy) that can never be wholly purified from violence.

Next in *Writing and Difference* is an essay first dating from 1959, '"Genesis and Structure" and Phenomenology'. Since Husserl's philosophy bears a complex relation to the analysis of structures, this essay may usefully be read against the backdrop of Derrida's various critical readings of the structuralist phenomenon. However, it also points towards Derrida's treatment of Husserlian thought in his own introduction to the **Origin of Geometry** and also relates to the 1953–54 dissertation by him, later published as **The Problem of Genesis in Husserl's Philosophy**. Derrida's review of the Husserlian attempt to reconcile structure and genesis links to the readings found in these other works; and in such writings more generally Derrida seeks to put in question the metaphysical residue that comes with **phenomenology**'s attempt to go beyond metaphysics.

In 'La parole soufflée', Derrida sees in the theatre and writings of Antonin Artaud a concerted attempt to overturn the metaphysical dualities of mind and body, thought and life, being and becoming, living word and dead letter, theatre and commentary, author and actor, force and form, madness and the work of reason. As Artaud knew, these oppositions determine the Western tradition in terms of its civilization and philosophy and by way of its theatre as a privileged mode of representation. For Artaud, such classical oppositions entail dissociation and dispossession of what is 'proper' to him in the totality of existence. Thus, Artaud dreams of a theatrical 'text' in which speech is not simply conserved by way of writing as transcription, nor abandoned to a chaotic spontaneity that would in fact preserve the notion of the spoken word's immediacy; but which instead produces and maintains a system of physical signs (including, but not limited to, words) that remain irreducible to the metaphysical priority of voice. Yet, as Derrida observes, in seeking to obliterate the structured differences which underpin the history and theatre of the West, erecting in their stead inalienable 'life' as transcendent possibility, Artaud's project continually runs the risk of re-elevating notions of self-presence, self-identity, unity and propriety which themselves dominate the metaphysical tradition (and which, indeed, have always served to represent difference as derivative and recuperable rather than primary or constitutive). Here, then, Derrida recognizes that each and every destructive discourse confronts metaphysics only by risking its repetition. This gives rise to the suggestion that we find picked up in 'The Ends of Man' (see **Margins of Philosophy**): namely, that deconstruction in its most rigorous form must continually negotiate between a destructive breaching that always ventures itself somewhat naïvely, and a thoroughgoing exposure of the existing field which must nevertheless continually struggle not to sink back into its grounds of possibility.

In 'The Theater of Cruelty and the Closure of Representation', Derrida once more characterizes Artaud's theatre as that which seeks to move outside the **mimetic** or imitative conception of art, one that bases itself on deeply structured distinctions and inter-relationships between reality and representation, original and copy, presence and absence, and so forth. More than any other art form, for Artaud it is theatre that emerges as the site of a possible departure from mimeticism. Yet, first of all, the theatre must free itself from the domination of speech in its classical metaphysical or **ontotheological** sense. Stage play must not restrict itself to the transmission of a 'word' or discourse which refers to an original truth, reality or presence, one that the theatre simply mimes or dramatizes. Theatre must not limit itself to a spectacle mounted in order to deliver the 'message' of the master (author/God). Instead, it should aspire to a more original representation or auto-presentation of itself. It must constitute itself, in Artaud's

Writing and Difference

terms, not as reflection but as pure force. Here, again, spoken language is neither to be discarded nor given over to pure improvization (the latter risking a sudden fall back into the metaphysics of **logos** and presence). Instead, the spoken word (as something like a material husk or even a near **spectral** remnant left over once the animating origin of '**spirit**' or 'psyche' is radically disputed or displaced) takes its place in reconfigured form as an element in a wider or indeed total play of *gesture*, of movement and clamour not yet reduced to speech as notation or dictation from on high. Derrida likens this rethinking of the word as gesture in Artaud to **Freud**'s understanding of the function of speech in dreams. Here, words do not give pure expression to thought, but operate instead as elements in something like a 'pictographic script', as Freud puts it. Thus, far from conveying an essential or self-same meaning which establishes the very origin, the word more complexly acquires its force according to the role its image plays in the dream's composition, a role which is mutable and thus potentially unstable. However, to the extent that **psychoanalysis** aspires to offer creditable theories or commentaries at a certain masterful distance from its subject matter, thus interpreting its objects through a movement of critical dissociation, Derrida acknowledges that Artaud's theatre – one of inalienable 'life' – calls to be distinguished from the scenography of psychoanalysis. Indeed, since psychoanalysis thinks of dreams as having what Artaud calls 'a substitute function', its analytic orientation remains towards a divided understanding of existence which Artaud wishes to dispute or overcome.

Artaud's theatre is ultimately to be understood as the scene of a radical festivity which cannot be co-opted by ideological programmes or interests, but also as irreducibly political in that it remains public, indeed resolutely questioning the distinction between 'private' and 'public' itself. (Of course, dominant forms of theatre, for instance those of a naturalistic type, tend to reduce stage play to the expression in 'public' of the basically 'private' thoughts, emotions or intentions of the author or characters.) Nonetheless, Derrida once more positions Artaud at the limit of – rather than 'beyond' – metaphysics, in that his destructive impulse towards the metaphysical tradition continues to harbour the dream of a pure presence undivided by representation or repetition.

'From Restricted to General Economy: A Hegelianism without Reserve' sees Derrida turn to the work of Georges **Bataille**, and to the question of its possible connection with Hegelianism. Since they appear to have a certain conceptual similarity, Derrida compares Bataille's notion of **sovereignty** with **Hegel**'s conception of lordship. For Hegel, since servility may be understood in terms of a life which does not put itself at stake, lordship as a type of freedom is attained at the point where life itself is ventured. This may happen through direct confrontation with **death**. Yet as Bataille himself saw, the passage towards lordship entails a repression of the 'slave' – the 'slave' *within* – in the identity-formation of the 'master', and thus a certain thraldom in the very movement of transcendence. Moreover, for Hegel, lordship – as putting life at stake – is maintained only by retaining the life one has risked. Life, that is, is not absolutely ventured in lordship, and as such the freedom it entails is equally limited. For Derrida, then, the partial or compromised freedom which one might ultimately associate with Hegelian lordship occasions a burst of laughter from Bataille's point of view. Lordship frees itself by enslaving itself. This is the result of its dialectical formation, through which the play of negativity is restricted and reappropriated in the movement towards conservation or self-reproduction. In contrast, sovereignty for Bataille emerges beyond the work of dialectics, risking absolute and profitless expenditure of life, consciousness, seriousness, presence and meaning in the interests of a more radical or unreserved freedom which may be reduced neither to the subordination of the slave nor the retention of a ventured existence. Derrida explores sovereignty's relation to an ecstatic, poetic or sacred form of speech which not merely opposes or sacrifices 'significative discourse' (such discourse puts sovereignty at risk since it implies seriousness and servility), but which opens itself perhaps as a more original economy within which dialectics – as a type of restriction, compromise or 'economizing' – finds its resources. Thus, sovereignty may be understood as that which transgresses the thinking of difference as always recuperable according to a more original presence. Sovereignty, we might say, is another name for a more radical difference no longer in the service of presence or signification.

As the essay develops, Derrida discusses the relation of sovereignty to writing. On the one hand, sovereignty objects to the servility of writing. It does so, not in the sense of the Platonic tradition's disdain of writing as extrinsic, auxiliary and inanimately technical in relation to living speech. Rather, sovereignty mistrusts writing (in, let us say, its significative or dialectical forms) as that which in fact *serves* the life which wishes to retain itself as presence. On the other hand, however, the more original or general economy opened up by Bataille's thinking of (an always non-present) sovereignty relates to Derrida's own conception of the **trace** structure of writing (writing in the enlarged sense) that forms the interest of much of his work from this period.

Between the two essays dealing with Artaud we find 'Freud and the Scene of Writing'. This opens with some prefatory comments acknowledging certain resemblances between psychoanalysis and Derrida's own project, while also noting that psychoanalytic concepts and practices retain vestiges of the metaphysical heritage. Nonetheless, Derrida argues that the originality of the Freudian 'text' (to the extent that this can be marked) has less of a connection than one may think with the structural linguistics which became such a prominent feature of the intellectual climate of the post-war period. For, as Derrida argues in a host of other writings, structuralism in its twentieth-century guise – for all its supposed radicality – tends to reinscribe the priority of the spoken word and the model of phonetic writing (in other words, **logocentrism**). In contrast, Freud shows his recurrent fascination with signs that cannot be thought simply to transmit an essential meaning of the sort which metaphysics holds to be more fully expressed by living speech. Instead, the signs which tend to interest Freud function in the context of hieratic and pictographic types of script (as Derrida notes in his essay on Artaud). At key moments in his work, then, Freud finds he must resort to a rethinking of **metaphor** that sits uneasily with **phonocentric** discourse. Indeed, as his thinking develops, Freud comes to characterize the psychic apparatus as a writing machine – one which cannot be thought to operate by dictation of a master's 'voice' or 'word' (that is to say, on the strength of a simple 'origin' or presence that wields full power and control). Psychic life is, thus, not reduced to the transparency of meaning by Freud, but is understood instead in terms of a complex topography of traces, an original *spacing* which operates according to a radical principle of difference. For Derrida, then, the psychic 'text' that one may elaborate in Freud draws close to the notion of a general writing developed by deconstruction, a writing that remains irreducible to speech insofar as it is determined by the metaphysics of presence. (Here, again, the spoken word is not simply excluded from the psychic 'text' but reconfigured as an inscribed **mark** within the larger field of scenic or gestural play.) Such a conception of psychic 'writing' as a non-finalizable system without simple origin or possibility of pure expression calls upon us to rethink many of the notions we tend to reduce or simplify within logocentric discourse (among these, Derrida notes metaphor and **translation** in particular).

In the last part of the essay, Derrida observes that Freud initially thinks of writing as a technical aid to **memory**. In this respect, he appears to belong to a Platonic tradition that Derrida analyzes in 'Plato's Pharmacy' (in ***Dissemination***). In contrast to **Plato**, however, Freud comes to regard the psyche as thoroughly caught up in a text-machine, rather than constituting itself as a being or presence that precedes and transcends the advent of writing.

Freud turns his thinking to the question of how memory inscribes itself in psychic life. Metaphors drawn from the conventional idea of writing are unsatisfactory here. For a sheet of paper retains marks more or less indefinitely but is quickly filled or saturated, whereas an infinite number of marks may be made upon a slate but each new set are recorded only at the expense of the last. In order to capture the effects of psychical memory, Freud must therefore find a different model of mnemonic inscription that goes beyond classical writing. This occurs with his discovery of the *Wunderblock* or mystic writing pad. Here, a double sheet is secured over a slab of wax or resin, the upper layer being made of transparent celluloid, and the lower of translucent waxed paper. When the pad is laid out, a stylus is used to scratch marks upon the surface, with the top sheet acting as a medium that can be lifted away more or less unscathed to reveal the sheet underneath. Having been pressed into the wax or resin by the writing utensil, this retains the marks that were made, which can themselves be cleared simply by raising the translucent paper and thus ending its contact with the slab. (For Freud, the irreversibility of this erasure marks the limit of the analogy with psychical memory.)

Derrida notes that the apparent depth granted by the layers of the mystic pad is nevertheless bottomless, since the apparatus functions through specific contacts or relations between its various levels (none of which may be considered absolutely primary or determining) rather than by dint of a constitutive 'ground'. These relations are everywhere constituted, too, by movements in time and space, rather than issuing from a stable or timeless foundation. Nor are the inscribed or perceptual marks of the mystic pad (able to tell) the whole story of the machine. The *Wunderblock* therefore fashions such marks as somewhat akin to the products of an 'unconscious' which itself remains un-presented or un-presentable. In setting aside a simple origin, a founding presence or presentable ground, and in giving itself over to complex movements of differing and deferring (*différance*) that cannot be thought outside of an originary **technicity**, the mystic writing pad therefore seems to presage the trace structure of writing or the general 'text' which Derrida is so concerned to elaborate during this period of his career. For Derrida, then, the future of psychoanalysis is not with a **linguistics** still ruled by an age-old phonocentrism, but with a 'graphematics' to come.

In 'Structure, Sign, and Play in the Discourse of the Human Sciences', a paper given at the Johns Hopkins conference in 1966 which significantly advanced Derrida's name and reputation outside France, we are once more confronted with a deconstruction of the structuralist paradigm, which Derrida again asserts as having deep roots in the Western tradition of metaphysics. The argument that begins this essay is as follows: in order to regulate and delimit the play of differences which constitute structural relations, what might be thought of as the structure's centre (that which gives it structural order) must simultaneously be located outside, over or above the structure of which it is the centre, in order to escape destabilizing exposure to this very same play, something which might otherwise occur if the centre were to be positioned simply and solely *within* the structure's own space. Here, then, the inconsistency and deconstructibility of the centre as a concept – one which supposedly grants coherence to the structure – implies in turn the non-self-identical conceptuality of 'structure' itself, thus calling into question the assumption that structures may be characterized by their unity, integrity, or total systematicity. Instead, the play that goes to the very heart of 'structure' reinscribes force within form.

Derrida observes, however, that modern forms of thought have sought to displace or dispense with the centre as a concept. Here, he evokes Nietzsche's critique of metaphysics, Freud's critique of self-presence, and Heidegger's destruction of metaphysics. Nonetheless, Derrida reasserts once more that in order to oppose metaphysics, destructive discourses invariably draw on the resources of the metaphysical tradition. Structuralism in its twentieth-century guise, for Derrida, therefore remains up to its neck in metaphysics. Thus, the conception of the sign within structural linguistics and, for that matter, the ethnology of structural anthropology, are shown to rely on a long-standing fund of Western concepts (as such, this text contains several echoes of Derrida's treatment of Saussure and Levi-Strauss in **Of Grammatology**). Derrida's essay concludes by contrasting the idea of play as the risk of loss and thus a threat to the metaphysics of logos and presence, with the Nietzschean affirmation of play as joyous becoming no longer commanded by the sign in its classical sense. While the former attitude to play remains wedded to the project of unveiling a 'truth' or 'origin' that precedes, transcends and ultimately dominates all difference, the latter seeks passage beyond all the centrisms that derive from the metaphysical tradition (including ethnocentrism and, indeed, humanism). Yet Derrida is quick to point out that, while these two 'interpretations' of structure, sign and play are entirely incompatible, nevertheless we are not confronted with a simple choice between them. Rather, in a way that echoes 'La parole soufflée' and 'The Ends of Man', Derrida insists that deconstruction must venture itself at the very limits of these two interpretations, which encounter one another within what he here calls an 'obscure economy'.

Yale School   Colloquial name for a group of literary scholars more or less affiliated to Yale University, including Derrida, Harold Bloom, **Paul de Man**, Geoffrey Hartman and J. Hillis Miller. In 1979, *Deconstruction and Criticism* was published, with the so-called Yale School members each writing a text on Shelley's *The Triumph of Life*. Included in this collection is Derrida's **'Living On: Borderlines'**.

yes, yes   In 'A Number of Yes', included in **Psyche**, Derrida focuses on the work of Michel de Certeau in order to explore the idea of a 'yes' to language which precedes each and every **linguistic** utterance, including those which aspire to the most radical type of questioning or critique. From this point of view, all discourse includes an essentially **affirmative** dimension: a first 'yes'. However, for Derrida, this first 'yes' is itself continually fabulated, always re-made by each and every linguistic act or inscription which, even if its discourse is deeply critical or negative, cannot help but serve as a type of 'yes' to the 'yes'. In **'Ulysses Gramophone'**, Derrida therefore dwells on Molly Bloom's memorable phrase, 'yes I said yes I will Yes' (interestingly, Joyce described 'yes' as 'the female word', so that the question of **sexual difference** cannot be left out of the thinking which takes place here); and, indeed, Derrida's thinking of this 'yes' to the 'yes' – or of the 'yes, yes' – powerfully answers all those opponents of **deconstruction** who want to dismiss it as purely negative, nihilistic, and so forth.

The first 'yes' is, then, the condition and effect as much as the origin of the innumerable 'yesses' ('yes, yes') that repeatedly re-affirm it. In this sense, the second 'yes' each time presupposes and thus calls up the first. Since for Derrida this situation of an unreckonable 'number of yes' repeats itself across the general space of **writing** according to the interminable play of ***différance***, the 'yes, yes' is the very condition of language; and yet it cannot be determined as the stable 'object' of a linguistic theory. Nor, for that matter, can it be fully apprehended by any science, **phenomenology**, ontology or empiricism. The 'yes, yes' cannot be predicated *as such*, in terms of an objectivity that is presentable to an extrinsic standpoint or subject-position. For Derrida, the *near* originarity of the 'yes' makes of it a fable which goes before the logos and, indeed, which defines **philosophy**'s limits.

See also 'A Number of Yes' in ***Psyche***, **'Ulysses Gramophone'** and, for instance, ***Cinders***, **gift**, **promise**, 'Khôra' in ***On the Name***, **'Shibboleth'**.

Bibliography

Works by Jacques Derrida

This is a selective bibliography primarily designed to support readers who wish to go as straightforwardly as possible to the writings by Derrida in English translation covered in this book. Dates are of original publication in English. Many of the texts included in edited collections and other volumes by Derrida were first published elsewhere as individual essays or interviews. Sometimes the history of publication and translation of these pieces is detailed and complex. I have therefore largely refrained from listing such texts separately, except where it may assist the reader in tracking down source materials. However, each entry on the works by Derrida tries to give a good sense of the various pieces contained in each. I have also included here some other publications by Derrida that are of interest, but which do not substantially feature in this book.

For other Derrida bibliographies, see *A Derrida Reader: Between the Blinds*, ed. Peggy Kamuf (New York: Columbia University Press, 1991), *Jacques Derrida* (with Geoffrey Bennington), trans. Geoffrey Bennington (Chicago: Chicago University Press, 1992) – I would like especially to record my indebtedness to these two books – and *The Derrida Reader: Writing Performances*, ed. Julian Wolfreys (Edinburgh: Edinburgh University Press, 1998).

'A Certain Impossible Possibility of Saying the Event', *Critical Inquiry* 33:2 (2007): 441–61 (included in a special issue of the journal devoted to the memory of Jacques Derrida).

A Derrida Reader: Between the Blinds, ed. Peggy Kamuf (New York: Columbia University Press, 1991).

'A Silkworm of One's Own (Points of View Stitched on the Other Veil)', trans. Geoffrey Bennington, *The Oxford Literary Review* 18:1–2 (1996): 3–65. Also in *Veils* (with Hélène Cixous), trans. Geoffrey Bennington (Stanford: Stanford University Press, 2001).

Acts of Literature, ed. Derek Attridge (London and New York: Routledge, 1992).
Acts of Religion, ed. Gil Anidjar (London and New York: Routledge, 2002).
Adieu to Emmanuel Levinas, trans. Pascale-Anne Brault and Michael Naas (Stanford: Stanford University Press, 1999).
Aporias, trans. Thomas Dutoit (Stanford: Stanford University Press, 1993).
Archive Fever: A Freudian Impression, trans. Eric Prenowitz (Chicago: University of Chicago Press, 1996).
'Biodegradables: Seven Diary Fragments', trans. Peggy Kamuf, *Critical Inquiry* 15:4 (1989).
Choral Works (with Peter Eisenman), eds. Jeffrey Kipnis and Thomas Leeser (New York: The Monacelli Press, 1997).
Cinders, trans. Ned Lukacher (bilingual edition), (Lincoln: University of Nebraska Press, 1991).
Counterpath: Traveling with Jacques Derrida (with Catherine Malabou), trans. David Wills (Stanford: Stanford University Press, 2004).
'Countersignature', trans. Mairéad Hanrahan, *Paragraph* 27:2 (2004): 7–42.
'Deconstruction and the Other', in *States of Mind: Dialogues with Contemporary Thinkers*, ed. Richard Kearney (New York: New York University Press, 1995), pp. 107–26.
Deconstruction in a Nutshell: A Conversation with Jacques Derrida, ed. John D. Caputo (New York: Fordham University Press, 1997).
'Demeure: Fiction and Testimony', in *The Instant of My Death/Demeure: Fiction and Testimony*, Maurice Blanchot/Jacques Derrida, trans. Elizabeth Rottenberg (Stanford: Stanford University Press, 2000).
Dissemination, trans. Barbara Johnson (Chicago: University of Chicago Press, 1981).
Echographies of Television: Filmed Interviews (with Bernard Stiegler), trans. Jennifer Bajorek (Cambridge: Polity Press, 2002).
'Economimesis', trans. Richard Klein, *Diacritics* 11:2 (1981): 3–25.
Edmund Husserl's Origin of Geometry: An Introduction, trans. John P. Leavey, Jr. (New York: Harvester Press, 1978).
Eyes of the University: Right to Philosophy II, trans. Jan Plug and others (Stanford: Stanford University Press, 2004).
For What Tomorrow . . . A Dialogue (with Elisabeth Roudinesco), trans. Jeff Fort (Stanford: Stanford University Press, 2004).
'Force of Law', in *Deconstruction and the Possibility of Justice*, eds Drucilla Cornell et al. (New York and London: Routledge, 1992), pp. 3–63. Also in *Acts of Religion*, pp. 228–98.

'Fors', trans. Barbara Johnson, *The Georgia Review* 31 (1977): 64–116.
Geneses, Genealogies, Genres and Genius: The Secrets of the Archive, trans. Beverley Bie Brahic (Edinburgh: Edinburgh University Press, 2006).
Given Time: 1. Counterfeit Money, trans. Peggy Kamuf (Chicago: University of Chicago Press, 1994).
Glas, trans. John P. Leavey, Jr. and Richard Rand (Lincoln: University of Nebraska Press, 1986).
H.C. for Life, That Is to Say . . . , trans. Laurent Milesi and Stefan Herbrechter (Stanford: Stanford University Press, 2006).
'I Have a Taste for the Secret', in *A Taste for the Secret* (with Maurizo Ferraris), eds Giacomo Donis and David Webb, trans. Giacomo Donis (Cambridge: Polity Press, 2001), pp. 1–92.
Jacques Derrida (with Geoffrey Bennington), trans. Geoffrey Bennington (Chicago: Chicago University Press, 1992) (includes Derrida's 'Circumfession').
Learning to Live Finally: An Interview with Jean Birnbaum, trans. Pascale-Anne Brault and Michael Naas (Hoboken, New Jersey: Melville House Publishing, 2007).
Limited Inc., ed. Gerald Graff, trans. Samuel Weber and Jeffrey Melman (Evanston: Northwestern University Press, 1988).
'Living On: Borderlines', trans. James Hulbert, in Harold Bloom et al., *Deconstruction and Criticism* (New York: Seabury, 1979), pp. 75–176.
Margins of Philosophy, trans. Alan Bass (Chicago: University of Chicago Press, 1982).
Memoires for Paul de Man, trans. Cecile Lindsay, Jonathan Culler and Eduardo Cadava (New York: Coumbia University Press, 1986; 2nd enlarged edition published by Columbia University Press, 1989).
Memoirs of the Blind: The Self-Portrait and Other Ruins, trans. Pascale-Anne Brault and Michael Naas (Chicago: Chicago University Press, 1993).
Monolingualism of the Other; or, The Prosthesis of Origin, trans. Patrick Mensah (Stanford: Stanford University Press, 1998).
Negotiations: Interventions and Interviews 1971–2001, ed. and trans. Elizabeth Rottenberg (Stanford: Stanford University Press, 2002).
'Of an Apocalyptic Tone Recently Adopted in Philosophy', trans. John P. Leavey, Jr., *The Oxford Literary Review* 6:2 (1984): 3–37.
Of Grammatology, trans. Gayatri Chakravorty Spivak (Baltimore: The Johns Hopkins University Press, 1976).
Of Hospitality (with Anne Dufourmantelle), trans. Rachel Bowlby (Stanford: Stanford University Press, 2000).

Of Spirit: Heidegger and the Question, trans. Geoffrey Bennington and Rachel Bowlby (Chicago: University of Chicago Press, 1989).

'On a Newly Arisen Apocalyptic Tone In Philosophy', trans. John P. Leavey, Jr., in *Raising the Tone of Philosophy: Late Essays by Immanuel Kant, Transformative Critique by Jacques Derrida*, ed. Peter Fenves (Baltimore: The Johns Hopkins University Press, 1993), pp. 117–73.

On Cosmopolitanism and Forgiveness, trans. Mark Dooley and Michael Hughes (London and New York: Routledge, 2001).

On the Name, ed. Thomas Dutoit, trans. David Wood, John P. Leavey, Jr. and Ian McLeod (Stanford: Stanford University Press, 1995).

On Touching – Jean-Luc Nancy, trans. Christine Irizarry (Stanford: Stanford University Press, 2005).

Paper Machine, trans. Rachel Bowlby (Stanford: Stanford University Press, 2005).

Philosophy in a Time of Terror: Dialogues with Jürgen Habermas and Jacques Derrida (with Jürgen Habermas and Giovanna Borradori) (Chicago: Chicago University Press, 2003).

Points . . . Interviews 1974–1994, trans. Peggy Kamuf and others (Stanford: Stanford University Press, 1995).

Politics of Friendship, trans. George Collins (London: Verso, 1997).

Positions, trans. Alan Bass (Chicago: University of Chicago Press, 1981).

Psyche: Inventions of the Other, Volume I, eds Peggy Kamuf and Elizabeth Rottenberg (Stanford: Stanford University Press, 2007).

Psyche: Inventions of the Other, Volume II, eds Peggy Kamuf and Elizabeth Rottenberg (Stanford: Stanford University Press, 2008).

Religion, eds Jacques Derrida and Gianni Vattimo, trans. David Webb and others (Stanford: Stanford University Press, 1998) (includes Derrida's 'Faith and Knowledge: the Two Sources of "Religion" at the Limits of Reason Alone', pp. 1–78).

Resistances of Psychoanalysis, trans. Peggy Kamuf, Pascale-Anne Brault and Michael Naas (Stanford: Stanford University Press, 1998).

Rogues: Two Essays on Reason, trans. Pascale-Anne Brault and Michael Naas (Stanford: Stanford University Press, 2005).

'Scribble (writing-power)', trans. Cary Plotkin, *Yale French Studies* 58 (1979): 116–47.

Signeponge/Signsponge, trans. Richard Rand (New York: Columbia University Press, 1984).

'Some Statements and Truisms about Neologisms, Newisms, Postisms, Parasitisms, and other small Seismisms', trans. Anne Tomiche in *The States of Theory*, ed. David Carroll (New York: Columbia University Press,

1989), pp. 63–94.

Sovereignties in Question: The Poetics of Paul Celan, eds Thomas Dutoit and Outi Pasanen (New York: Fordham University Press, 2005).

Specters of Marx: The State of the Debt, The Work of Mourning and the New International, trans. Peggy Kamuf (London and New York: Routledge, 1994).

Speech and Phenomena and Other Essays on Husserl's Theory of Signs, trans. David B. Allison (Evanston: Northwestern University Press, 1973).

Spurs: Nietzsche's Styles, trans. Barbara Harlow (bilingual edition) (Chicago: University of Chicago Press, 1979).

The Animal That Therefore I Am, ed. Marie-Louise Mallet, trans. David Wills (New York: Fordham University Press, 2008).

The Archeology of the Frivolous: Reading Condillac, trans. John P. Leavey, Jr. (Pittsburgh: Duquesne University Press, 1980).

The Ear of the Other: Otobiography, Transference, Translation: Texts and Discussions with Jacques Derrida, ed. Christie MacDonald, trans. Peggy Kamuf and Avital Ronell (Lincoln: University of Nebraska Press, 1988).

The Gift of Death, trans. David Wills (Chicago: University of Chicago Press, 1995).

The Other Heading: Reflections on Today's Europe, trans. Pascale-Anne Brault and Michael B. Naas (Bloomington: Indiana University Press, 1992).

The Post Card: From Socrates to Freud and Beyond, trans. Alan Bass (Chicago: University of Chicago Press, 1987).

The Truth in Painting, trans. Geoffrey Bennington and Ian McLeod (Chicago: University of Chicago Press, 1987).

The Work of Mourning, eds Pascale-Anne Brault and Michael Naas (Chicago: University of Chicago Press, 2001).

'Two Words for Joyce', trans. Geoffrey Bennington, in *Post-Structuralist Joyce: Essays from the French*, eds Derek Attridge and Daniel Ferrer (Cambridge: Cambridge University Press, 1984), pp. 145–61.

'Ulysses Gramophone: Hear Say Yes in Joyce', trans. Tina Kendall and Shari Benstock, in *James Joyce: The Augmented Ninth*, ed. Bernard Benstock (Syracuse: Syracuse University Press, 1988), pp. 27–75.

Who's Afraid of Philosophy?: Right to Philosophy I, trans. Jan Plug (Stanford: Stanford University Press, 2002).

Without Alibi, ed. and trans. Peggy Kamuf (Stanford: Stanford University Press, 2002).

Writing and Difference, trans. Alan Bass (London: Routledge and Kegan Paul, 1978).

Selected Works about Jacques Derrida

Beardsworth, Richard, *Derrida and the Political* (London: Routledge, 1996).

Bennington, Geoffrey, *Legislations: The Politics of Deconstruction* (London: Verso, 1994).

Bennington, Geoffrey, *Interrupting Derrida* (London: Routledge, 2000).

Bennington, Geoffrey, *Not Half No End: Militantly Melancholic Essays of Jacques Derrida* (Edinburgh: Edinburgh University Press, 2010).

Bradley, Arthur, *Derrida's Of Grammatology* (Edinburgh: Edinburgh University Press, 2008).

Caputo, John D., *The Prayers and Tears of Jacques Derrida: Religion without Religion* (Bloomington: Indiana University Press, 1997).

Cixous, Hélène, *Portrait of Jacques Derrida as a Young Jewish Saint* (New York: Columbia University Press, 2004).

Clark, Timothy, *Derrida, Heidegger, Blanchot: Sources of Derrida's Notion and Practice of Literature* (Cambridge, Cambridge University Press, 1992).

Clark, Timothy, *The Poetics of Singularity: The Counter-Culturalist Turn in Heidegger, Derrida, Blanchot and the Later Gadamer* (Edinburgh: Edinburgh University Press, 2005).

Clark, Timothy and Royle, Nicholas, eds, 'Derridas', special issue of *The Oxford Literary Review* 18 (1996).

Cohen, Tom, ed., *Jacques Derrida and the Humanities: A Critical Reader* (Cambridge: Cambridge University Press, 2001).

Cornell, Drucilla, *Beyond Accommodation: Ethical Feminism, Deconstruction, and the Law* (New York: Routledge, 1991).

Critchley, Simon, *The Ethics of Deconstruction: Derrida and Levinas* (London: Blackwell, 1992).

Culler, Jonathan, *On Deconstruction: Theory and Criticism after Structuralism* (London: RKP, 1982).

Elam, Diane, *Feminism and Deconstruction: Ms. en Abyme* (London: Routledge, 1994).

Gasché, Rodolphe, *The Tain of the Mirror: Derrida and the Philosophy of Reflection* (Cambridge: Harvard University Press, 1986).

Gasché, Rodolphe, *Inventions of Difference: On Jacques Derrida* (Cambridge: Harvard University Press, 1994).

Gaston, Sean, *Derrida and Disinterest* (London and New York: Continuum, 2006).

Bibliography

Gaston, Sean, *Derrida, Literature and War: Absence and the Chance of Meeting* (London and New York: Continuum, 2009).

Glendinning, Simon and Eaglestone, Robert, eds, *Derrida's Legacies: Literature and Philosophy* (London and New York: Routledge, 2008).

Hart, Kevin, *The Trespass of the Sign: Deconstruction, Theology and Philosophy* (Cambridge: Cambridge University Press, 1989).

Hartman, Geoffrey, *Saving the Text: Literature/Derrida/Philosophy* (Baltimore: The Johns Hopkins University Press, 1981).

Harvey, Irene E., *Derrida and the Economy of Difference* (Bloomington: Indiana University Press, 1986).

Haverkamp, Anselm, ed., *Deconstruction is/in America: A New Sense of the Political* (New York: New York University Press, 1995).

Hobson, Marian, *Jacques Derrida: Opening Lines* (London and New York: Routledge, 1998).

Hodge, Joanna, *Derrida on Time* (London and New York: Routledge, 2007).

Howells, Christina, *Derrida: Deconstruction from Phenomenology to Ethics* (Cambridge: Polity Press, 1998).

Kerrigan, William and Smith, Joseph H., eds, *Taking Chances: Derrida, Psychoanalysis and Literature* (Baltimore: The Johns Hopkins University Press, 1984).

Leavey, John P. Jr., *Glassary* (Lincoln: University of Nebraska Press, 1986).

Leitch, Vincent B., *Deconstructive Criticism: An Advanced Introduction* (New York: Columbia University Press, 1983).

Llewelyn, John, *Derrida on the Threshold of Sense* (London: Macmillan, 1986).

McQuillan, Martin, ed., *The Politics of Deconstruction: Jacques Derrida and the Other of Philosophy* (London: Pluto Press, 2007).

McQuillan, Martin, *Deconstruction after 9/11* (London and New York: Routledge, 2008).

McQuillan, Martin, ed., *Deconstruction Reading Politics* (London: Macmillan, 2008).

Melville, Stephen W., *Philosophy Beside Itself: On Deconstruction and Modernism* (Minneapolis: University of Minnesota Press, 1986).

Miller, J. Hillis, *For Derrida* (New York: Fordham University Press, 2009).

Morgan Wortham, Simon, *Counter-Institutions: Jacques Derrida and the Question of the University* (New York: Fordham University, 2006).

Morgan Wortham, Simon, *Derrida: Writing Events* (London and New York: Continuum, 2008).

Naas, Michael, *Taking on the Tradition: Jacques Derrida and the Legacies of Deconstruction* (Stanford: Stanford University Press, 2002).
Norris, Christopher, *Deconstruction: Theory and Practice* (London: Methuen, 1982).
Rand, Richard, ed., *Futures of Jacques Derrida* (Stanford: Stanford University Press, 2001).
Rapaport, Herman, *Heidegger and Derrida: Reflections on Time and Language* (Lincoln: University of Nebraska Press, 1989).
Rapaport, Herman, *Later Derrida: Reading the Recent Work* (London and New York: Routledge, 2003).
Royle, Nicholas, *After Derrida* (Manchester: Manchester University Press, 1995).
Royle, Nicholas, ed., *Deconstructions: A User's Guide* (Basingstoke: Palgrave, 2000).
Royle, Nicholas, *Jacques Derrida* (London and New York: Routledge, 2003).
Royle, Nicholas, *In Memory of Jacques Derrida* (Edinburgh: Edinburgh University Press, 2009).
Silverman, Hugh J., ed., *Derrida and Deconstruction* (New York: Routledge, 1989).
Ulmer, Gregory L., *Applied Grammatology: Post(e)-pedagogy from Jacques Derrida to Joseph Beuys* (Baltimore: The Johns Hopkins University Press, 1985).
Weber, Samuel, *Institution and Interpretation* (revised 2nd ed.) (Stanford: Stanford University Press, 2001).
Weiner, Allison and Morgan Wortham, Simon, eds, *Encountering Derrida: Legacies and Futures of Deconstruction* (London and New York: Continuum, 2007).
Wolfreys, Julian, *Deconstruction – Derrida* (Basingstoke: Palgrave, 1998).
Wood, David, ed., *Derrida: A Critical Reader* (London: Blackwell, 1992).
Wood, David and Bernasconi, Robert, eds, *Derrida and Différance* (Evanston: Northwestern University Press, 1988).
Wood, Sarah, *Derrida's Writing and Difference: A Reader's Guide* (London and New York: Continuum, 2009).

www.ingramcontent.com/pod-product-compliance
Lightning Source LLC
Chambersburg PA
CBHW062124300426
44115CB00012BA/1799